The American Roman Noir

WILLIAM MARLING

The American Roman Noir

Hammett, Cain, and Chandler

The University of Georgia Press   Athens and London

© 1995 by the University of Georgia Press
Athens, Georgia 30602
All rights reserved

Designed by Sandra Strother Hudson
Set in 10.5 on 14 Electra by Tseng Information Systems
Printed and bound by Maple-Vail
The paper in this book meets the guidelines
for permanence and durability of the Committee on
Production Guidelines for Book Longevity
of the Council on Library Resources.

Printed in the United States of America
99 98 97 96 95 C 5 4 3 2 1

Library of Congress Cataloging in Publication Data

Marling, William, 1951–
   The American roman noir : Hammett, Cain, and Chandler /
William Marling.
      p.   cm.
   Includes bibliographical references and index.
   ISBN 0-8203-1658-X (alk. paper)
   1. Detective and mystery stories, American—History and criticism.
   2. American fiction—20th century—History and criticism.
   3. Detective and mystery films—United States—History and criticism.
   4. Hammett, Dashiell, 1894–1959—Criticism and interpretation.
   5. Cain, James M. (James Mallahan), 1892–1977—Criticism and
interpretation.   6. Chandler, Raymond, 1888–1959—Criticism and
interpretation.   7. Literature and society—United States—History—
20th century.   8. Popular culture—United States—History—20th
century.   9. Capitalism and literature—United States.   I. Title.
PS374.D4M33   1995
813'.08720905—dc20   94-25550

British Library Cataloging in Publication Data available

FOR DANIEL,

in memory of Kenneth Eble

Contents

Preface

Only when I finished this study did I realize I had written about the American roman noir. While exploring the relations between the detective novel, art nouveau, economic history, film, and advertising, I had sensed common ground, but it wasn't until I wrote about film noir, in a coda, that I realized this logical end recast the subject. I had been writing myopically: I had labored with genres, wherein Dashiell Hammett was a "detective novelist" but James M. Cain was not. Literary scholarship lacks a term for the complex of values that began in the mid-1920s and led to film noir. Appropriating the French term *roman noir* estranged the novels for me when I rewrote, allowing me to see them in relation to the technology, the economy, the design, and the new media of the period. But if the term is borrowed, the noir novel and its creators have simply been repatriated.

In the 1920s and 1930s in the United States, this dark style of narrative emerged from the American imagination. It is present not only in Hammett, Cain, and Raymond Chandler but also in F. Scott Fitzgerald, John O'Hara, William Faulkner, and Dorothy Parker, among others. It glimmers in the Jazz Age illustrations of John Held and Ralph Barton and blooms in the Depression satires of Al Hirschfeld and George Grosz. It contributes to our understanding of the first talking movie (*The Jazz Singer*, 1927) and our received wisdom about the trial of Sacco and Vanzetti the same year. If it culminates in the film noir of such directors as William Wellman, John Huston, and Billy Wilder, that is because the emerging techno-economic form of society found it the perfect vehicle for a master narrative about consumerism.

The American Roman Noir, then, details how American narrative explained and reacted to unprecedented technological and economic change. It integrates economic history and biography, design values and narrative analysis, film scholarship and a theory of technological momentum. At the center of these approaches is the subject of prodigality: how does narrative represent having, and having had, too much? Never in the United

States did wealth impinge on the national conscience as in the 1920s, and never was such conscience so sharply rebuked as in the 1930s. What was the popular understanding of wealth after it vanished? What were the paradigms that explained accumulation and windfall, waste and failure?

My introduction examines the events of 1927 and the changes that unprecedented wealth introduced to the United States. Without some sense of the contemporary milieu, we cannot understand the reaction to it in the 1930s. Stories about prodigality, I argue in my first chapter, are the most common answer, usually versions of a narrative we know as the parable of the prodigal son. The basic plot, or fabula, is marvelously flexible, offering three points of view; it can be narrated to highlight spending (the younger son), giving (the father), or saving (the elder brother), which makes it a wonderful economic as well as theological tool. Another of its attractions, evident ever since Jesus' use, is its ability to put hearers or readers in the conflicted position of the father, the giver who must arbitrate between the forces of spending and saving—a role that film noir later appropriates. Chapter 1 explains how economic forces are represented in this fabula and how the parable has been used historically by authors to introduce emergent techno-economic systems. I have approached "The Prodigal's Tale" from the vantage of narrative theory and cultural materialism, because of their flexibility in following the permutations of such an investment and in "reading" it in novels, films, illustrations, and artifacts.

The tale of prodigality has not only theological and economic value systems but axes of inner/outer, near/far, soul/self, and desire/discipline as well. The prodigal son journeys outward to a far country, for example. Often these axes are misaligned, and the narrative works to restore harmony. The prodigal's demand for his inheritance, his spending on whores and "riotous living," are at odds with familial discipline. These are ancillary value systems that the narrative can employ. There is also a figurative axis of synecdoche/metonymy. From the prodigal's initial demand through the slaughter of the fatted calf, Jesus' parable sets up meaning synecdochically, to present an "inner" or organic awareness of repentance, acknowledgment of the father and of his forgiveness. Yet the closure, with the father's words to the elder brother, stresses pattern, continuity, and discipline. The elder's parallel return, his refusal to enter the house, and his father's enigmatic

"Thou art ever with me, and all that I have is thine" are metonymic. Metonymy stresses the systemic, the mechanistic, the extrinsic; hence discipline, savings, sexual restraint, endogamy, and xenophobia are presented through the elder brother.

Spending, sexual excess, forgiveness, desire versus discipline—all these topics of the fabula become extremely prominent in narratives of the 1920s and 1930s. I have taken the phrase "consciousness of guilt" from the Sacco-Vanzetti trial as a point of entry in presenting tensions of the fabula present in 1927; I examine both the trial's and *The Jazz Singer*'s use of this consciousness. The latter used the fabula to tell a narrative of improvement, the former a narrative of deterioration.

If 1927 was a watershed in "consciousness of guilt," it seems clear that the fabula thereafter began to be interpreted according to the demands of a new technology and economy. As I explain in chapter 2, when the automobile and the electric light replaced the streetcar and the gas lamp, they did more than improve mobility and visibility; when the telephone and the radio replaced conversations and concerts, more than personal contact vanished. The perceptive and figurative habits of millions of Americans changed in the 1920s. To assert a simple economic or technological determinism is not my intent, however, for I think the imagination chooses among, combines, or invents the structures by which it understands the world but that lived experience offers the most immediate and vivid possibilities. Technology and the economy offer themselves to artistic figuration and, in turn, seize upon cultural values to endow themselves with "momentum." This idea I have borrowed from historians of technology in order to show how technology tends to be self-cloaking, to feign ideological neutrality. In the roman noir, it found a perfect Trojan horse.

As technology was shifting, the economy entered a phase of extraordinary growth, in which getting rich seemed to depend on spending money, leading in the United States to unparalleled speculation. When this spending was no longer directed at artifacts of use, of intrinsic or synecdochical value, it began to chase "qualities" of color, lightness, and newness. Momentum shifted from mass production (Henry Ford) to mass marketing (General Motors) and then to consumers. The shift from synecdochical to metonymic values, from systems of desire to those of discipline, from speculation to credit, is clear in technology and the economy, but it is most visible in the field of product design, which evolved to promote and regularize consumption. Design had to arbitrate among the values, and it frequently made, if not narratives, choices based on figurative assumptions. Design embraced art nouveau, then art deco and Streamform. The open, exposed mechanics of Victorian artifacts were covered with fairings in the Toledo scale, Coca-Cola dispenser, and Coldspot refrigerator of Norman Bel Geddes. The gaunt, black, "efficient" Ford Model T lost out to the colorful sheathed Chevy, which was replaced by "fast" Streamform autos like the Marmon 16 of W. D. Teague. Even Rube Goldberg's critique of technology ended up acceding to the new values.

The perceptual revolution required by this change occasioned enormous anxiety. Consumers did not immediately adopt the new; they had to be won to it by designers and legions of young advertising writers like Dashiell Hammett. But buyers had to be cautioned about the limits of consuming things (and sex) by those intimate with their tastes, like editorial writer James M. Cain. Eventually they had to be shown the autoeroticism of self-discipline by Raymond Chandler, a prodigal returned to the fold. This advocacy was taken up by young or disenfranchised writers with ambition and nothing to lose—no university education, no alliance with modernism, no commitment to family, and often no steady job. They were in and of the conflict, attracted to and alienated by the changes for which they provided narratives.

Their frequent decision to ally the fabula of prodigality with the detective novel owes to a correspondence in story structure that narrative analysis makes clear: both contain a narrative of deterioration embedded within a greater narrative of improvement. Just as the prodigal son's dissipation of his inheritance is contained and ameliorated by his reintegration into the family (and his father's reassertion of genetic and financial control), so the detective novel develops an apparent story of the crime within a revealed story about what really happened. While the revealed story's outcome may be macabre or gloomy, it is always reintegrative. At the end of The Big Sleep, Marlowe finds that vixenish Carmen Sternwood murdered Rusty Regan and left him to rot in an oil sump—not pretty. But Marlowe's final prospect on the crime integrates the decline of the Sternwood family oil fortune, warning about the cost of financial and sexual prodigality. In both types of narrative, some emphasized feature of the saga of deterioration (the apparent plot), usually from the axes discussed above, corresponds to the thematization of the saga of improvement (the revealed plot). *The Big Sleep*'s anxiety about "sexual spending," for instance, is linked by the apparent plot's outward search for gambler Rusty Regan (the prodigal brother of Marlowe) and the revealed plot's discovery that he was actually killed at home because of insufficient sexual caution. But it is hardly necessary to have a detective to create such value systems and noir narratives, as James M. Cain showed.

The utility of the overlap in "genres" first becomes apparent in Dashiell Hammett's *Red Harvest* (1929), which is as much a Western as a "detective" novel: the fabula is frontier prodigality. The revealed story is nil, but the containment of deterioration by the anonymous prodigal-hero (who labors to discover his own innocence) depends finally on his repentance and a forgiving Old Man. In its ebullient materialism and telegraphic style, *Red Harvest* is typical of the mid-1920s and Hammett's own roots in what he called the "meiotic" (metonymic) discourse of advertising. Apparently set in Montana, the novel is actually a local California narrative, a feature of the roman noir that increased in importance through film noir.

The Maltese Falcon (1930), on the other hand, is already an art moderne parable about metonymic style as prodigal raiment. The consciousness of design values evinced is a separate level of the story. Sam Spade's suppression of his sexual desire for Brigid on behalf of his business points the way to a nexus central to most subsequent roman noir and paramount in film noir: desire must serve economic ends. Hammett added thin/fat to the contemporary axes of the fabula with Casper Gutman (based on Fatty Arbuckle), and his "objective" point of view anticipated film noir's emphasis on technology, while making it seem invisible.

James M. Cain fully understood the implications of desire in an economy based on endless consumption. Retelling the Snyder-Gray murder trial of 1927, Cain developed minor insurance details into a statistical worldview and then seized on Depression-era anxiety about tramps. *The Postman Always Rings Twice* (1934) narrates the end of the open road, the penalties for lust and failure to work. Cain was able to discard the detective as arbiter of axial values because of his extraordinary technique. He created the sensation of speed through elisions of dialogue and of emotional and intellectual sequence, discovering how to signify desire metonymically. His retrospective confessional frameworks not only suggest double jeopardy and provide the suspense of the revealed plot but also anticipate the voice-over narrator and confessional form of film noir. In *Double Indemnity* (1936) Cain realized his theme in pure form: insurance agent Walter Huff, spurred by sexual desire, decides to rebel against his employer and is tracked down by his best friend, an actuary. The progressively darker tone of the two novels owes to Cain's refining his theme of technology, law, and government as statistical games played by inhuman sportsmen while he incorporates these games into the narrative of improvement. What Cain dares to lay out is an improvement only possible through blind obedience to techno-economic imperatives. The contrast of this novel with Cain's journalism about California (he found it bucolic) provides a clue to why this state became the favored setting of roman noir: as the first postindustrial economy, it seemed to preview the future.

It remained for Raymond Chandler, a romantic and a factotum in the oil industry, to develop the stylistic level of the fabula. Unlike Hammett and Cain, Chandler overlaid his subject with hyperbole, litotes, overstatement and understatement, and trope of every variety. But all of his figures depend on a scientific rationalism that undercuts efforts at self-determination, that mocks attempts to escape the local and the California, that frustrates romantic impulse and declares mechanical, autoerotic simulacra the only personal freedom. In *The Big Sleep* (1939) Chandler extends the implications of Hammett's portrait of Spade to show that technology has changed the semiotics of sexuality. If Freud was the governing authority in Hammett, in Chandler a post-Lacanian name-of-the-despot is everywhere present in the system of consumption. It is part of the sexual and monetary "flow," a metonymy natural in the age of Keynesian economics and huge California water projects. In *Farewell, My Lovely* (1940) Chandler's narrative arrives at something like economic and sexual schizophrenia. Marlowe's apparent story includes the economic scapegoating of women and minorities and his alienation from the local bourgeoisie. It implies that we will never get beneath the "smooth shiny" surface of people or things, never repent or know love, never return home. The only escape, a covert narrative of improvement, is in the style of our darkness. But while Chandler's most brilliant metaphors are figures of ideological resistance to the unrestrained desire that he feared in a consumer economy, he sketches the potential within the emerging economy for an erotic "celibate machine."

Style and improvement are the promises of technology, which developed the perfect vehicle in film noir. Though there were other precedents, such as the gangster movies of the 1930s, film noir developed from the roman noir, particularly the works mentioned. But it added a level of technology, because new lights, lenses, cameras, dollies, films, techniques, and economic pressures of the Depression demanded optimization, and the law of optimization—Eliminate steps!—is fundamentally metonymic. Thus the technique of film noir's directors became the locus of the narrative of improvement. Just as the name-of-the-despot is dispersed everywhere by Chandler, film noir made immanent the narrative of improvement *as technique*. Drawing on Hammett's portrayal of the protagonist's desire/discipline dilemma, on Cain's confessional narrators and doubled plots for its "double time demands," and on Chandler's schizophrenic style and autoeroticism, film noir became the optimal vehicle: an infinitely consumable narrative of deterioration, invisibly balanced by the techniques and technology of a narrative of improvement. With film noir we realize that now we all trust the surface of things, read the system in the metonymic hint, value discipline, and admire saving. It is this illusion of retrospective self-understanding that has made the American roman noir so durable. We may look back and see the crisis of adaptation, the perils avoided, and the "success" that technology has afforded us. The American roman noir teaches us that things could be much darker. It prefigures our prodigality, so we can imagine that we have avoided it.

Earlier versions of some of the chapters in this book appeared in *Literature/Film; LIT: Literature, Interpretation, Theory; Proceedings of the West Virginia University Colloquium on Literature and Film; Proteus; Semiotica;* and *Style.* The readers and editors of these journals supplied many helpful comments.

The American Roman Noir

Introduction: 1927

Let's call 1927 the apogee of the Roaring Twenties. It was a year rife with epochal events. In March the Federal Reserve cut the re-discount rate, igniting speculative fire in the stock market that culminated in the Crash. In April Henry Ford retired the Model T. In May, while the nation was still hyperventilating over the sex-and-murder menu of the Snyder-Gray trial, Lindbergh flew the Atlantic. In August *The Jazz Singer*, the first movie with recorded music and dialogue, opened in New York City, and two weeks later Sacco and Vanzetti were executed in Massachusetts.

Life changed in small, fundamental ways too. Take electricity: the screw-base light bulb was introduced in 1927, and suddenly light gleamed from dining rooms and auto headlamps, from streetlights and theaters, which were air-conditioned. Electrical consumption increased 54 percent between 1922 and 1927, as power lines followed the streetcars, infiltrating new suburbs, where washing machines, stoves, and refrigerators became standard. By 1927, sixteen million houses had been wired for electricity out of eighteen million possible (*Americana Yearbook* 262–75).

Such a broad but common change, David Nye writes, altered the social construction of reality, as electricity became a "metaphor for action" (178). It collapsed the difference between here and there, a perceptual revolution noted by painters such as Edward Hopper and Joseph Stella. When Robert Frost discovered in the woods a "resurrected tree," he worried that this telephone pole was "dragging yellow strands / Of wire with something in it from men to men" (125).[1] With innovations from high-speed presses to sound film, from vacuum tubes to the photoelectric cell, the 1920s began to move faster, more easily. The *Americana Yearbook*, which in 1923 covered all electrical topics in three pages, by 1928 devoted thirteen pages to electrical inventions alone.

Electricity made possible synthetic materials like plastic and aluminum and fed the catalytic cracking processes behind phenolic plastics (radio cabinets), rayon (stockings), and cellulose acetate (film). It spread the as-

I

sembly line and promoted piecework, drawing women and blacks into the labor force (Nye 216–17; Allen 83). Recognizing a symbol, Ford put a power plant at the heart of his Model T factory, but by 1927 GM had leap-frogged him with its Chevy. Ford then conceded that his new Model A would have to be advertised extensively, come in colors like "Arabian sand," and boast such amenities as a starter motor. Even he found mass marketing and advertising unavoidable by 1927 (Hounshell 279). As Jennifer Wicke writes, these forces changed the nature of social discourse about things, posing a challenge to traditional narrative forms like the novel (see Wicke 3–17).

After 1927 it was not enough to make a good product cheaply. Manu-facturers found themselves making what people wanted, so they redoubled their efforts to influence people's wants. The textile and fashion indus-tries had tried to force long, cloth-consuming skirts on women in the early 1920s, but women cleaned out stores that carried short skirts. By 1927 the light shirtwaist and the knee-length skirt were national standards; sales of corsets and bras had declined by 11 percent since 1920, and petticoats had vanished (Allen 88, 90, 219, 223).

Nowhere had life changed more dramatically by 1927 than in relations between men and women. A shift that began in wartime factories reached a threshold with ratification of the Nineteenth Amendment, granting women the right to vote in 1920 elections. Popular psychology, mass marketing, and advertising sanctioned a "liberating" of emotions. Restraints on sexual activity began to decline among youth, according to testimony as various as Fitzgerald's *This Side of Paradise* (1920) and Robert and Helen Lynd's study of Muncie, Indiana, in *Middletown* (1929). All married women of the white-collar class interviewed by the Lynds used or approved of birth control, but less than half of working-class women did (113, 123, 136–40).[2]

The white-collar family was likely to have an enclosed car, which quickly became a private room on wheels, movable to a darkened lane or alley. They rented hotel rooms where the sexes mingled as they smoked cigarettes and drank bootleg gin. Simplified forms of these consumption rituals, popularized by confession and detective magazines and movies, descended to the working class. Such narratives codified the consumption of sex, alcohol, and cars or other status objects and the resulting guilt one was to feel (Lynd and Lynd, 236–42).

By 1927 the idea that women stayed at home until married had been discarded by the white-collar class. Construction of suburbs freed urban flats, and blocks of "efficiencies" were built. Into these moved young women, particularly if they had attended college, who worked outside the traditional domains. This change was initially reflected in the novel as problematic (Edith Wharton's *The House of Mirth*, 1905), but was approved by 1929 (Ursula Parrott's *Ex-Wife*).

Men, recently behind department store counters (Harold Lloyd in *Safety Last*, 1923), at first shared such jobs. Then they moved into sales, real estate, managerial, or insurance positions. Fewer people and none of the swelling white-collar class worked in agriculture or industry, which were becoming mechanized. Women in this recently all-male world adopted a style that Raymond Chandler called the smooth shiny girl. Its value was "youth," its form slender. Rubenesque figures and buxom lasses were out: the smooth shiny girl was long-waisted, flat-breasted, and tight-skirted, with bobbed hair—the type of lithe angularity that suggested the art moderne fairing of an expensive new machine. Parrott described her as "ineffably slim yet sufficiently curved" (61). The sheathed look is usually traced to the 1909 introduction of the French *directoire* gown in Chicago, where it provoked a riot. But by 1927 this style, which featured high heels, rayon or silk fishnet stockings (daringly rolled below the knee), the cloche hat, and flaunting makeup, had spread to small towns (Urdang 279). The smooth shiny girls, wrote Frederick Allen, "worshiped not merely youth, but unripened youth: they wanted to be—or thought men wanted them to be—men's casual and light-hearted companions; not broad-hipped mothers of the race, but irresponsible playmates" (89).

Among the new activities men and women shared in 1927, dancing, smoking, and drinking stand out. It is difficult now to perceive the foxtrot as lewd, but a newspaper of the 1920s called it that and a "syncopated embrace." There were complaints that in the new body-to-body dances, men always chose the women without corsets (Allen 74–75). Such tactile experience offered people a heightened consciousness of content and sheathing, of mechanics and masking, of inner and outer. There was a craze for "animal dances," with new versions appearing every few months, so that dance, once a form of religious ritual, became a product, in need of newer, more flagrant motions.

If the offenses of the dance hall escaped the view of upright Americans, smoking did not. In 1920 only the bravest women claimed a right to smoke, but by 1927 women smoked in restaurants, in theater lobbies, and at parties (Allen 99). As Bryan Holme's *Advertising: Reflections of a Century* shows, much cigarette advertising was pitched specifically at women by 1927. But cigarettes began to appeal to men too, as a convenient and even measuring of time.

The Eighteenth Amendment, effective January 16, 1920, was so disregarded as to be ludicrous by 1927. Alcohol flooded American society, nowhere deeper than in the swelling white-collar classes so important in establishing consumption as a way of life. The federal government fielded only two thousand agents, who interdicted only 5 percent of the liquor smuggled into the country. Everyone knew a service station or a drugstore that sold alcohol, if not a speakeasy. Yet because the traditional male domain at the corner beer emporium was gone, by 1927 the drinking of liquor was done in mixed company. "Our new-found freedom," wrote Parrott, "arrived too late for tavern-owners" (65). Hip flasks and hotel rooms took drinking out of the range of chaperons and corner bartenders.

"Listen with a detached ear to a modern conversation," wrote Mary Agnes Hamilton in 1927, "and you will be struck, first, by the restriction of the vocabulary, and second, by the high proportion in that vocabulary of words such as, in the older jargon, 'no lady could use'" (Allen 92). Everything that had been "grand" was "lousy," said Lady Brett Ashley in *The Sun Also Rises* (1926). A mock toughness copied from bootleggers replaced nuance, politeness, and precision. Telegraphic brevity was the style; speakers competed in terseness, toughness, and unshockability. Everybody was tough. H. L. Mencken had no doubt about argot's source: "The vast upsurge in crime brought in by Prohibition made all Americans familiar with a large number of criminal words and phrases, and many of these . . . have entered into the everyday speech of the country" (*American Language* 716).

There was a striking disdain for material property. Waste as the sign of success was a subject of Ring Lardner, F. Scott Fitzgerald, Ben Hecht, and Dorothy Parker. In Lardner's "Old Folks' Christmas," the children whine about gifts and lay waste to the household. Parker chronicled the guests who arrived ridiculously late and refused to speak to the host. The gate-crashing that Fitzgerald depicted in *The Great Gatsby* (1925) had become accepted practice at smaller affairs by 1927. Fitzgerald's typical hero, wrote Vernon Parrington, was "a bad boy who loves to smash things to show how naughty he is" (3: addenda, 386). The "house parties of flappers and wide-trousered swains left burning cigarettes on the mahogany tables, scattered ashes light-heartedly on the rugs, took the porch cushions out in the boats and left them there to be rained on, without apology," reported Allen (99). Men and women unmoored from tradition seem to have found one prearticulation of their vague sense of guilt in destroying things.

These hungers, fears, and fads launched a search for new narratives. No high cultural voice really answered demand, not even if we include Fitzgerald's. Readers turned to the news media, fascinated by crimes in the new style of prodigality, while ignoring those in the older vein of acquisition. Stock manipulations and streetcar and utility scandals, even on the scale of Teapot Dome, played below the newspaper's fold. The favored narratives combined sex, material waste, and perhaps bootlegging with dinner parties at the Ritz, as the protagonists tried to outwit society only to be crushed by it.

Sensational trials with these themes hypnotized the nation. The first of these, in 1926–27, dealt with the execution-style murder of the adulterous Reverend Edward Hall and his choir leader back in 1922. Five million words were telegraphed from the trial during its first eleven days. Dashiell Hammett, then writing the serial "Red Harvest," buried his story's mystery in a character resembling the trial's Jane Gibson, who was dying of Bright's disease, and John Dos Passos made notes for his *U.S.A.* trilogy. When Gibson was exposed as a fraud, writers drove to Long Island to join D. W. Griffith, Will Durant, and others covering the equally lurid Snyder-Gray trial.

A social and narrative turning point was passed in 1927. It seemed impossible, the Lynds implied, that cheerful Edgar Guest had been America's favorite poet in 1924 (238). Weary of traditional, Victorian values, anxious about technology, writers looked for narratives other than romance, adventure, love—something that could be played against the new technologies and consumerism for an evocative contrast. They also looked for something that newspapers and magazines could not do. World War I had formed one reading public from many provincial readerships, and it had created the competitive value of being first with a story. By 1921 newspapers faced unprecedented competition, and only the well capitalized could afford foreign correspondents, copious telegraphy, and the high-speed presses that beat the competition to the street. Lesser papers bought syndicated stories or folded, mostly the latter: between 1914 and 1926 the number of dailies dropped from twenty-six hundred to two thousand, while circulation increased from twenty-eight million to thirty-six million (Allen 157). The Hearst, Pulitzer, and Scripps-Howard chains benefited from syndication, mass purchasing, and new color rotogravure and offset, multiple-unit presses. Their favorite device for attracting readers was the ongoing crusade, scandal, or trial. It had heros, villains, complications, and reversals, much like a conventional narrative.

The same technology permitted an expansion of magazines, from Henry Luce's *Time* (1923) and *Fortune* (1930) to Bernarr McFadden's *True Story*, which had almost two million readers in 1927 (Allen 84). Little magazines, from *Broom* and *The Double Dealer* (1921) to *The Criterion* and *The Fugitive* (1922), were also made possible by faster, cheaper printing. There were changes in the infrastructure of distribution, which by 1927 could place and remove more than two hundred detective magazines printed in New York on newsstands in Los Angeles every week. A comparable number of sex and confession magazines appeared, with titles like *Indolent Kisses*, only to be superseded by movie magazines. The formula of these genres was to focus graphically, usually in the first person, on the temptations that led down the road to perdition, but to provide a moral ending with appropriately pious sentiments, making the narrative one of improvement. Consciousness of guilt was a vicarious experience, eminently consumable, and there was a ruthless competition in ways to make the limited number of plots seem new.

In 1920 there was no radio, but two years later radios would be a $60-million-a-year business. Radio was everyman's luxury; the stock of RCA was the pet of speculators, rising from $94 a share to $505 between 1928 and 1929 (Allen 286). As potent as its economic impact, however, was radio's centralizing and standardizing power. It was singled out by the Southern Agrarians of *The Fugitive Anthology* (1928) as being destructive of regional identity. Radio spoke like the voice of God: it standardized national events, beginning with the drama and intrigue of the Democratic convention in 1924, which introduced Al Smith. Then radio set the whole nation humming "Barney Google" and "It Ain't Gonna Rain No More." Radio taught receptive habits compatible with mass production: segmentation, standardized roles, the value of newness, supersession of models, and surface seamlessness—"all timed to the split second," wrote Chandler, "just like a radio program" (*Big Sleep* 185).

It was argued that radio encouraged a short-term, sequential focusing of attention. While the roots of this phenomenon are diffuse, radio certainly played a part by disseminating narrative in the highly consumable form of scheduled "shows." It fomented an expectation of periodicity in popular narrative. Syndicated radio shows were built of ten- and fifteen-minute musical or narrative segments, segues to "commercial breaks," and predictably scaled exposition, complication, and resolution. The threshold and ceiling of narrative durations became closer. Competition drove this standardization, for the audience had only to turn the page or dial if the "voice" it heard was not attractive. Radio changed expectations for all popular narrative: comic strip character Andy Gump was also expected to resolve crises in a standard number of panels every week.

Silent film was already an established medium in the early 1920s. Indeed, some of its autonomous masters were already exploring social issues. On balance, however, moviegoers saw far more of lighter fare; Lillian Gish, Mary Pickford, Douglas Fairbanks, Gloria Swanson, Clara Bow, and Rudolph Valentino were the matinee stars. The epics of Cecil B. DeMille, the antics of the Keystone Cops, and melodrama like *The Jazz Singer* played longer, on more screens, than did our classics.

The figurative habits of both radio and film were still largely synecdochical in 1927, though technological advances like sound film were about to shift them toward metonymy. Mediating this shift was film's appeal to a kind of consumable alterity: "Before you know it you are *living* the story— laughing, loving, hating, struggling, winning!" said an ad in the *Saturday Evening Post* (Lynd and Lynd 265). An eighteen-year-old college student wrote of one film, "These passionate pictures stir such language, desires, and urges as I never expected any person to possess. . . . even my reacting to a scene does not satisfy any more. I cannot believe that I am 'I' any more" (in McQuade 727). As Donald McQuade has suggested, "Many Americans were learning their morals and manners—and in some cases their modes of misbehaving—from the celluloid" (726).

In 1927 movie technology reached a turning point. Casting about for a gimmick to boost sales, Warner Brothers premiered *The Jazz Singer* on August 6, 1927, creating a Great Divide for all narrative (Baxter 50– 51). "Sound," as Akira Kurosawa remarked, "does not simply add to, but multiplies, two or three times, the effect of the image" (in Giannetti, *Understanding Movies* 183). What had been a moving cartoon became a powerful new form of storytelling, and written narrative had to adjust to it.

Another kind of sound—the voice on the telephone—also influenced narrative. In *The Mechanic Muse* Hugh Kenner noted how the telephone quickly evolved from "a facilitator of business, like the cash register" to a mechanism of partial presence for people who "had acquired the habit of attending to disembodied voices, and returning them routine answers" (35–36). All white-collar families the Lynds interviewed in 1924 had telephones. But everyone sensed an estranging quality to the telephone: "Radios and telephones make people farther apart," said one informant. "Instead of going to see a person as folks used to, you just telephone nowadays" (Lynd and Lynd 275). The same year T. S. Eliot put a phone in Doris's flat in "Sweeney Agonistes," and Sweeney complained, "I gotta use words."

Intellectuals saw the sum of these changes as a fall into philistinism, most notably in Harold Stearns's *Civilization in the United States* (1922). Sinclair Lewis's *Babbitt* made the narrative case in the same year, providing a personification for the condition. Parrington could then write about "swelling forces of industrialism" taking over, "while Babbitt, regnant, infests the country with his blustering agents" (3: x). Charles and Mary Beard charged that "the war which called for patriotic duties was seized upon by emotional conservatives as an opportunity to blacken the characters of persons whose opinions they feared" (276).

The important magazine of 1927 was *American Mercury*, edited by Mencken and George Jean Nathan. Walter Lippmann said that year that Mencken was "the most powerful personal influence on this whole generation of educated people" (Allen 193). That Mencken was chiefly against things has obscured the extent to which the sum of his iconoclasms was pro-science. This was more manifest in his writing style, which had an enormous influence. In his direct syntax, Anglo-Saxon diction, and epigrammatic opinions, Mencken set the trend, a discourse of neologisms and metaphors: Appalachian migrants were "lintheads," the middle class a "booboisie," and Roosevelt a "popinjay" (*Mencken Chrestothamy* 242–43). While Mencken aimed to renovate, his use of rhetorical and lexical elisions, reflecting the values of speed and directness, encouraged the cycle of linguistic production and consumption that he professed to detest.

Intellectuals only came together over the Sacco and Vanzetti case in 1927, asserted Malcolm Cowley in *Exile's Return* (1934). It "was another crisis in [their] development" (219). The case dramatized the disparity between events and ideals and was the "one political event of the later 1920s that brought [them] together for a common purpose." Its theme was "the old story of innocence endangered," which Cowley thought appealed to intellectuals who had felt threatened during General Palmer's Red raids (218–19). The issue was not so much who was guilty but who had custody of national innocence—cosmopolitan intellectuals or media-manipulated consumers.

The case against Sacco and Vanzetti spanned the period 1919–27, which is one reason so many people eventually had an opinion on it. It didn't conclude in a month; its accusations and its defenses changed against a changing social and economic backdrop. It was available as a figurative example of how things were evolving. But 1927 was also the year of the enormously popular *Jazz Singer*. Its consciousness of guilt contradicted the intellectuals' interpretation of 1920s America, and while it was an immediately popular narrative about change, it was not naive. It too figured the recent past, the stigma of alienation and foreignness. The nation was ripe for new narratives, ones that could fold alienation into a narrative of progress without being pious or dull, with all the suspense and thrills that had become customary and a moral lesson about change at the end.

On the sabbath-days, I could look upon the sun and think how people were going to the house of God, to have their souls refreshed; and then home, and their bodies also; but I was destitute of both; and might say as the poor prodigal, "He would fain have filled his belly with the husks that the swine did eat, and no man gave unto him."
—Mary Rowlandson, *A Narrative of the Captivity and Restoration* (1682)

The Prodigal's Tale

The American consciousness of prodigality is deeply informed by the Puritan opposition of soul to self. "The advantage of self-knowledge," Sacvan Bercovitch has written of the Puritans, is that "the terror it brings may exorcise our individuality. It may drive us to 'desire to be found, not in ourselves.' It may teach us that to love our neighbors as ourselves is to realize how drastically 'self is against the good of our neighbors'" (18). In Rowlandson, this impulse found purely allegorical form: she is the prodigal, caught in self. Nor should we think that American Deism ended this informing opposition. It is present for Benjamin Franklin in *The Way to Wealth* (1757): "If time be of all things the most precious, wasting time must be the greatest prodigality" (362). What is Franklin's concept of time, if not the "desire to be found, not in ourselves"? Hector St. Jean de Crèvecoeur detected the encroaching self when he surveyed frontiersmen whose "new manners, being grafted on the old stock, produce a strange sort of lawless profligacy, the impressions of which are indelible" (555–56).

Over time, however, the allegorical meaning of *prodigality* relaxed, and romanticism particularly effaced the stigma of self. It became a form of "consciousness of guilt," of mutual obligation, so that we find Walt Whitman in *Song of Myself* writing, "Prodigal, you have given me love— therefore I to you give love" (21.25). Self may be put in motion, transformed, elided, or suspended by an emphasis on reciprocity. This partakes of the ritual practice of oblation, a giving to God so that God may give back, which underlies the resolutions of all stories of prodigality. In the most dramatic narratives of high culture, the return to individual or social wholeness and well-being (soul) is gained by placing everything material (self) at risk. In popular literature, the narrative of material progress (self) is balanced by a secondary one about disaffection and alienation (soul). The net effect of such dual movements is to provide a way of going forward into the future. Most emplotments share the same fabula, or underlying set of narrative events, familiar to us as the parable of the prodigal son.[1]

It is doubtful that the prodigal's tale originated with Jesus, who appears to have been recasting an older narrative for his own ends. In any case, the author of Luke arranged it in a thematic triptych. Jesus tells it after parables about a shepherd who leaves ninety-nine sheep in the wilderness in order to rescue one and the owner of ten coins who spares no effort to find a lost coin. As the summation, the parable of the prodigal son reiterates Jesus' points about the comprehensiveness of his Church and the availability of God's mercy to the repentant sinner. These have become Christian commonplaces, obscuring the economic tension underlying all three parables. All begin in plenitude, proceed to a situation of lack, and end with a recovery—of the sheep, the silver piece, the "lost" son—that reveals a societal drive toward completeness, toward assimilation and the exaction of conformity from members. In each case material well-being is wasted or placed at risk on behalf of the lost member. The disproportionate consumption of energy by one individual is thus highlighted, then chastened by a recovery that, ironically, involves no minor expenditure of resources. In all three parables the recovery is followed by a feast. Why the individual is lost and guilt about inequity are topics never addressed. The parable of the prodigal son, unlike the two that precede it, has become a figure of Western consciousness because of its deft presentation of socioeconomic conflict from opposed points of view, as well as from a mediating one. This allows the issue to be reinterpreted as the age demands. Examining the parable in detail, we can see how this process works.

The first eight verses (Luke 15.12–19) describe, from the prodigal's point of view, his request that his father divide his "living" between his two sons. With his share, the prodigal journeys into a "far country," where he "waste[s] his substance with riotous living." A famine erupts there, and the prodigal is reduced to being a hired servant. Sent to feed husks to the swine, he reflects that the beasts eat better than he does, and he remembers that his father's servants never hungered. Repenting, he decides to ask his father for a place as a servant and returns home.

Then the narrative perspective, or focalization, shifts to the father, who has already forgiven the prodigal, establishing the religious allegory.[2] Before the prodigal can ask for a servant's position, the father peremptorily forgives him and summons a lavish robe, fine jewelry, and footwear. He orders the fatted calf slaughtered for a feast (Luke 15.20–24).

A third focalization appears when the elder son, who is returning from the fields, hears the music and dancing of the feast. He stops outside and asks a servant what is going on. He refuses to go inside when he finds out the reason for the festivity. His father emerges to explain his joy at the prodigal's return, but the elder son replies that the younger has "devoured thy living with harlots." Jesus does not allow the father to address this charge but depends on a verbal paradox—"Thou art ever with me, and all that I have is thine"—to elevate the father allegorically over the secular, material resentment of the elder brother. Then the parable ends, with a lack of closure that even traditional interpreters concede to be striking (Luke 15.25–32).

Commentators on the parable have long deemed the allegorical intent more important than narrative or economic issues. The works of Joachim Jeremias (*The Parables of Jesus*), Eta Linnemann (*Gleichnisse Jesu*), Charles W. F. Smith (*The Jesus of the Parables*), and Joseph Fitzmyer (*The Gospel*

According to Luke) form a kind of received interpretation of the parable.[3] Among these interpreters, Jeremias has been most influential, but he pursues reading strategies that are problematic for modern textual analysis. When the text does not say how the prodigal son got food during the famine, Jeremias concludes that "he must have stolen" (130). Jeremias will not have narrative omissions questioned, and he justifies many sections of the text as mimetic reflections of its audience without so much as a footnote. But material issues sprout like weeds from his explanations. The prodigal's seemingly selfish demand that the father divide his "living" between himself and his older brother is ameliorated by Jeremias's explanation that younger sons often emigrated because of "the frequent occurrence of famine in Palestine" (129). He authorizes the division of the patrimony by laws set forth in Deuteronomy: While he is alive, the father can give away his "living," or capital, though not the interest it earns. Nor can the son dispose of the capital while the father lives. The elder son gets two-thirds of the estate, the younger one-third, and the father enjoys the interest. The problem for Jeremias is that the younger son defies this law and turns his third into cash, then goes into a "far country," where he "wastes" it. Why? More opprobrium seems heaped on his action by the famine and his reduction to working as a swineherd for a Gentile, which Jeremias calls "the lowest depths of degradation." To explain this, Jeremias has to switch to the allegorical level, where theology and emotions can be emphasized: "The parable describes with touching simplicity what God is like, his goodness, his grace, his boundless mercy, his abounding love" (131).

But issues abound. Why is the father the only character who is not potentially a locus of realization? Presumably because he functions allegorically as God. But this causes problems, since the forgiveness of sinners comes later, according to doctrine, through the sacrificial death of Jesus, who is telling the story. Then there is the elder brother, the skeptic. Jeremias claims that he is an allegorical representation of Jesus' audience: "The parable was addressed to men who were like the elder brother." How about the ending? "The parable breaks off abruptly, and the issue is still open. No doubt this is a reflection of the situation which confronted Jesus" (131). Isn't it time to face the material issues?

Why include an elder brother? Dan Otto Via Jr. was among the first to recognize the problems inherent in treating him simply as a blocking character. While secular, Via's critique focused on the "self-discovery" necessary to grace; that is, he still found the theme in the prodigal's vantage. He differed from his predecessors in claiming that the elder brother "is given a certain stress by the fact that the section dealing with him comes last" (166). But he tacitly acknowledged the flaw in his analysis— he thought the parable an example of Northrop Frye's "comic" mode— when he admitted that "the elder brother . . . is too realistically like us to be absurd in the sense meant by Frye" (166).

Via invoked the comic mode of Northrop Frye to explain the parable as moving from decision to dissolution to well-being and restoration. The father's feast seems the ritual sign of a comic ending and of unity, since metaphors of eating and food characterize the viewpoints of both brothers. But the elder brother refuses to eat. Via waffles. The elder son represents law, says Via, when the parable is really about "contextual freedom." In his view the elder brother is "in the wrong place" spiritually and physically; but Via's suppressed insight, with the emphases on law, feasts, and symmetry, turns out to be important (170).

Although Frye did not deal with the parable directly, in *The Great Code* he pointed out that the early books of the Bible frequently use the overthrow of primogeniture as a dramatic situation:

> The firstborn son of Adam, Cain, is sent into exile, and the line of descent goes through Seth. Ham, the rejected son of Noah, is not said to be his eldest son, but the same pattern recurs. Abraham is told to reject his son Ishmael because a younger son (Isaac) is to be born to him. Isaac's eldest son loses his birthright to Jacob through some rather dubious maneuvers on Jacob's part, some of them backed by his mother. Jacob's eldest son Reuben loses his inheritance . . . Joseph's younger son Ephraim takes precedence over the elder Manasseh . . . the first chosen king, Saul, is rejected and his line passed over in favor of David. (180–81)

Frye follows the pattern forward through Milton's *Paradise Lost*, where the "archetype of the jealousy of an older son, Lucifer or Satan," rankles at the "preference shown to the younger Christ" (181). Such a series argues that "the deliberate choice of a younger son represents a divine intervention in human affairs." Only later, "with the Romantic movement there comes a large-scale renewal of sympathy for those rejected but at least quasi-tragic Biblical figures, who may be sent into exile and yet are in another context the rightful heirs" (182). Frye linked this to the rise of the "theme of the rejected rightful heir" with its "nostalgia for aristocracy," an important connection of the material and economic with the political and historic.

The involuntary exile and disinheritance of an elder son, like Satan, against all conventional expectation, is clearly the inverse of the voluntary, willful departure of the younger son with his inheritance in cash. What change in social context during the Romantic era would prompt valuation of the parable from the elder brother's viewpoint? Frye points out that firstborn sons are technically a "first fruit" to be given back to God; thus Abraham is commanded to sacrifice Isaac. "The original motive behind human sacrifice was doubtless a *do ut deus* bargain: I give that you may give" (*Great Code* 183). The material sense of giving back is stressed here because it meshes with Frye's next point: "The theme of the passed-over firstborn seems to have something to do with the insufficiency of the human desire for continuity which underlies the custom of passing the inheritance on to the elder son. All human societies are anxious for a clear and settled line of succession: the intensity of this anxiety is written all over Shakespeare's history plays" (182). In other words, reciprocity in giving— father gives to elder son, who supports father—is traditionally related to the desire for certainty of genetic descent, so that deviations from primogeniture must be explained by divine intervention. But in more modern economies a younger son could prosper without patrimony, so genetic descent and reciprocal giving declined as concerns, a reversal that could be narratized as the disenfranchisement of the elder son.

James Breech's skeptical approach to the parable in his 1983 book *The Silence of Jesus* was among the first to strip the additions of Luke and mistranslations from the older "Q text." "Scholars who assume that Jesus uttered his parable in situations of controversy have apparently not noted that *in every single case* the controversy has been created by Christian editorial work," writes Breech (185). In the core parables Jesus never attributes emotion to his characters: "The only modes of valuation are those expressed by the characters" (188). This stripping away of "motivation" exposes a narrative that predates the demand for mimetic characterization and opens Breech's analysis to economic factors. "Give me," he notes, are the younger son's first words: "Give me the share of property that falls to me." The younger son's request treats "his father as already dead . . . in the sense of no longer requiring a livelihood" (189). Challenging Jeremias, Breech notes that in the most prevalent legal arrangement, an inheritance could not be given until the death of the father. "The storyteller calls the property the man's *living* . . . the property provides the man with his means of livelihood and support," writes Breech. "In the thinking of the ancient world, questions regarding ownership of property and questions regarding father-son relationships were inextricable. What the man does—allowing himself to be treated as though dead and giving away his proprietary rights—is utterly unparalleled in any of the parabolic narratives which survive from antiquity" (190). The younger son turns the land into cash, by selling it, and treats future generations of the family as nonexistent. (The land should be kept as the basis of their livelihood.)

Breech's retranslations are also important. Previous commentators deemed the elder brother's accusation, in the Greek, that the prodigal "consumed [the father's] living with harlots" an exaggeration, for how would the elder brother know? Breech points out that the Greek word translated as "riotous living" refers to gluttons, voluptuaries, and transvestites, thus reinstating sexual excess as a theme. Suspicion of the elder brother's sexual charge is typical of the modern preference for motivation in characters. This was not a concern, according to folklorists, of ancient narrative.[4]

Breech views the prodigal's job as swineherd in economic terms, noting that he "contributes in an absolutely minimal way to his own maintenance, for feeding swine requires no competence. . . . he is not doing productive work in exchange for pay; he has attached himself to the citizen" (193). But Breech absolutely will not accept the lack of a reconciliation scene: the father "preempts the listener's as well as the younger son's expectations" (196). The "issue" of prodigality that the parable uses as its vehicle is never resolved, Breech says, but dropped in favor of allegorical meaning.

In Breech's view, the elder brother, speaking first and at length in the last section, points out that he has maintained his father as paterfamilias and giver "these many years," even after the latter abdicated that role, "yet you never gave me a calf." He questions the spending of their economic surplus (the calf) on "this son of yours . . . who has devoured your living with harlots." The elder brother's alienation from the prodigal and his metaphoric use of eating are notable. He seems disillusioned about the roles of tradition and law: "I never disobeyed your command." Breech avers that the hearer or reader was invited to identify with the sense of injustice felt by the elder son, who "now realizes that his father has taken him for granted all these years." Breech argues that the elder brother has been "mistaken" about his property obligations and "freely recognized human bonds" (203).

A literary comparison at the end of Breech's analysis proves unexpectedly illuminating. In both Shakespeare's *King Lear* and the parable, Breech notes, conflict is created by a father who decides to divest himself of his property while retaining "the name, and all th' addition to a king" (*Lear* I.i.136). In return for his patrimony, Lear demands an expression of affection from his daughters. He wants to remain a king and a father, without the responsibilities. Goneril and Regan tell him what he wants to hear; Cordelia does not. Breech says that in this respect the older sisters "differ not at all from the younger son" (208).

But wait: Are they not older and women and married? "The elder son's position and behavior, on the other hand, are analogous to Cordelia's" (Breech 209). This is not exactly true, because Cordelia is unmarried and offered without dower to suitors, the first of whom rejects her, whereas the elder son seems highly marriageable. But her older sisters are like the prodigal son in their sexual excess (Goneril commits adultery), which links them to Edmund and Edgar in the parallel plot. Here we note that Gloucester's bastard son, Edmund, and his legitimate son, Edgar, do indeed exemplify the plot that Frye calls "the rejected rightful heir," for Edgar is justly ascendant at the end. In fact, *King Lear* uses a double prodigal son/daughter plot, which reveals the sexual politics of the underlying fabula: a woman could not occupy the position of the elder brother (though she may seem to, she is always unmasked), and in order to occupy convincingly the position of "prodigal" (rather than that of "whore"), a woman should be married. Since married prodigality most obscures genetic descent, it makes the most emphatic statement about prodigality's dangers.

The best way of getting at the dynamics of prodigality is narrative analysis. As scholars since Vladimir Propp have pointed out, such a parable as the tale of the prodigal son consists of an initial situation and a series of events that may occur in various orders. Narrative analysis calls this the fabula. As Propp noted of Russian folklore, the exact setting and the descriptions of characters, their motivations, and their inner lives are unimportant in the oldest forms of narrative. But in all versions of "Tom Thumb" a boy tricks a giant.[5] Fabulae may be divided generally into those showing improvement and those showing deterioration. When the fabula appears to show both, as in this parable, one process is embedded within the other, and the embedded process reveals the central issue. The order of events, the attributes of settings, appearances, motives, and dialogue are features of a second level, the story. Tom Thumb's size, the number of his siblings, what he says to the giant—these details may vary. When printed, hence read rather than heard, such a story can be analyzed at a third level, that of the text, where style, rhetoric, and other lexical features can be assessed.

The parable of the prodigal son, as Frye showed, employs a fabula used widely in the Bible. The initial situation—"There was a man who had two sons"—describes Adam and many subsequent patriarchs. The request for, division of, and jealousy over the patrimony constitute a series of initial events as old as Isaac or David and as recent as last week's soap opera. This fabula usually involves a journey, often to a distant land; the departure of one actor is always a deletion or inversion of the normal process of gathering or of expending energy in order to get something. Other actors may focalize the journey as a process of deterioration, but the journey could result in a miraculous transformation, a return home, and a process of improvement. Each possibility tends to have an actor associated with it. All actors who share the same relation to the telos of the fabula belong to the same actant: Goneril and Regan are actors in the same actant.[6] Now, none of the principal actors in the parable were female, but women appear to have played an important part in the original fabula. The parable is just one story, and in it women are a submerged concern, represented initially by the "foreign whores" of the Greek but effaced by Luke. Over time they were reinstated in the roles of the three principal actants, as Breech showed in *Lear* and as Frye suggested of the history plays.

The fabula of prodigality is at base about the social reservoir of energy:

who owns it, how it is accumulated, who maintains it, and who gets to spend it. The initial situation of two brothers lends itself to such a thematics, structuring the meaning by contrasting actions and by binary logic. The brothers must be functional equals at the outset, except that one, usually the younger, does not inherit the means of attaining the object of his desire. So he departs to find his fortune elsewhere. The "unfair" advantage of the stay-at-home brother, who is somehow "unworthy," is almost as likely to be chastised (Jacob and Esau) as the spendthrift nature of the younger. Nor is the father's actant exempt from critique, for being someone who gives foolishly.

The most thorough narrative analysis of how this fabula works is Daniel Patte's 1975 attempt to examine it by four parallel models.[7] Breaking apart all the sequences of action, their interruptions, and the parties posited as senders, receivers, helpers, and such, Patte revealed the extent to which this fabula concerns individual volition and social constraint. It moves from a "situation of lack" (the father lacks his prodigal son) through a type of fabula called villainy to a restoration of both sons to the father. In this view, the father is the central actor, first losing and then regaining each son in symmetrical embedded plots. This analysis produces interesting results: the prodigal son's request, the division, and his departure (vv. 12–13) are actually subsequences of the clause "and there wasted his substance with riotous living." Why should this event, narrated later, dominate? It fulfills the earlier lack of an "opponent" in the parable at the line "And he divided unto them his living." Why shouldn't the father have done so? He has no clear opponent. The subsequences of the prodigal's journey read forward in time but lead actantially back to reveal that the father's unstated nemesis is a general notion of waste. Patte contends that "the father . . . indirectly participate[s] in the villainy" (86); he creates his situation of lack. For Patte, however, the father is the hero of two symmetrical villainies, in each of which he reincorporates a son into his own scheme of things. He overcomes their waste, and things improve.

Patte's second analysis, deriving from Claude Lévi-Strauss, shows the extent to which giving, consuming, and working are thematized. Their importance becomes clearer when Patte (137) arranges them in his third analysis in a semiotic square, or "grid" of A.-J. Greimas (see figure 1).

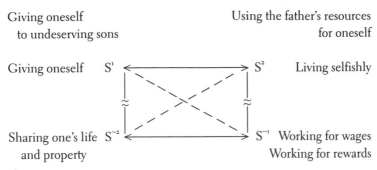

Giving oneself   Using the father's resources
to undeserving sons   for oneself

Giving oneself S^1 ⟵   ⟶ S^2 Living selfishly

Sharing one's life $S^{\sim 2}$ ⟵   ⟶ $S^{\sim 1}$ Working for wages
and property   Working for rewards

Figure I

Here are revealed the material tensions underlying not only the parable but also the fabula. Unfortunately, neither of Patte's models accounts for the shifts in focalization.[8] Left unexplained are the elder brother's values and his structural position. It is difficult to resolve his appearance at the end, where a "realization" or insight linked to him receives the validation of narrative closure. That neither the father nor the prodigal changes or is involved in events other than customary giving/receiving roles compounds this conundrum. And if the three points of view are progressive, rather than parallel, the parable's use of time poses a problem.

What can be said about the elder brother that would begin to explain his function in the fabula? Does he merely provide a symmetrical contrast with the prodigal? Is he tricked by his father? On the Greimas grid, his position is at the corner labeled "Working for wages / Working for rewards." In more basic economic terms, he represents the working/saving function. The events associated with him, giving rise to his actantial value, are distinct from those of the father (giving) and the prodigal (spending). Contrary to what we might assume, these actantial values are not opposed but are in a triangular flow of stability and implied completion. These economic values coincide with the conception of time employed. Patte's universalized "situation of lack" was too simple; materially speaking, each actant seems to lack the object of its desire, but it is finally shown to be blind to some aspect of the power of having it too. The prodigal lacks the object of his desire (the patrimony), but having it, he squanders it. His relation to the giver is clear, but his relation to the savings function is now

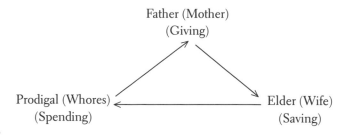

Figure 2

one of lack. The father subsequently lacks the object of his desire (one of his sons, that is, the complete family, and someone to whom to give) because he exercised his power to give foolishly; therefore he forfeits his power and becomes a dependent of his elder son. That he continues to try to give in this status, the problem that has troubled so many commentators, indicates his need of the elder son and the savings function. It would be peculiar if the elder son were the only member of the triad not lacking, though his actantial value (savings) is clearly the answer to preceding lacks. Only his earlier absence prevents us from realizing that he too lacks the prodigal, whose departure diminishes the family socially—in its ability to make alliances through marriage—and economically, since the cashed-out patrimony, probably land, reduces its means of production. In context, then, the elder brother illustrates the lack of a proper object of savings, which is integration or familial wholeness. His is the perspective of one responsible for shepherding familial unity into the future—for creating and maintaining capital. The proper sequence of these actors and their actantial values is triangulation (see figure 2). (The implied female counterparts are added for subsequent discussion.)

Each node is the object of each other node in some context, but with a change of context each could be antithetical. If someone told the narrative from the point of view of the elder brother's lack, it might be titled "The Father's Last Lesson," for the third section develops the relation between saving and giving as instruments of social cohesion. Socially, the elder brother learns about the flexibility required in father-son relationships, and theologically, the availability of the Father's grace binds the Son to him. But in economic terms the elder son learns about the generosity, or expenditure, necessary to a giver, that is, the relation of giving to prodigality (Patte's S^{-2}, sharing). Savings have as their point the maintenance of the social whole, the family. The creation of an economic surplus has no point without descendants. To ensure the coherence of society, it is sometimes necessary to indulge the whims of prodigal members who do not respect the law that the elder brother will soon embody.

SECULAR ANALYSES

The elements of the fabula that overlap the Freudian motif of sibling rivalry are too obvious to ignore. Should that be the basic category of the fabula, of which the parable of the prodigal son is but one type of story? This notion is seconded by the variant forms noted by Frye and Breech, but most commentators take pains to deny the obvious. Breech writes, "The story does not deal with sibling rivalry" (210).

The range of psychoanalytic commentaries on sibling rivalry exceeds the space available here to discuss it, but it tends to be limited by recourse to the family drama. Freud saw the issue as a grievance "against the mother [that] flares up when the next child appears in the nursery" (123).[9] Erik Erikson later developed a second focus in "the power of the newborn." The relation between siblings was neither naturally protective nor antagonistic, in his view, but "grown" out of "the power of the baby (and of small children in general) to evoke patience and protectiveness in older children" (572–73). In the work of Jacques Lacan, the *nom-du-père* overwhelms the relations of the siblings to each other or to the mother. The mother is important, if only implied, as the co-actant of the father. But she often plays an important role in the machinations of one brother against the other (Jacob and Esau) or in tricking an enfeebled or deluded father, as in novels by James M. Cain and in much film noir.

In *The Uses of Enchantment*, now viewed as less than original work, Bruno Bettelheim defined the common ground of psychoanalysis and narrative analysis in this fabula.[10] Most versions of the fabula belong to a type that he termed "tales of two brothers," the oldest written versions of which date to Egyptian papyri of 1250 B.C. Bettelheim cites Kurt Ranke's estimate of over 770 distinct stories based on this fabula. The central actors are "the stay-at-home brother and the adventuresome one" who "remain in touch through magic," wrote Bettelheim. "What all these stories have in common are features which suggest the identity of the two heroes, one of whom is cautious and reasonable, but ready to risk his life to rescue the other brother, who foolishly exposes himself to terrible perils; and some magic object, a life token, which usually disintegrates as soon as one dies, serving as the sign for the other to set out on the rescue" (91).

While many versions simply dichotomize these tendencies—Sinbad the Sailor versus Sinbad the Porter is Bettelheim's example—others develop into multifaceted oedipal dramas. Bettelheim points out that in one Egyptian papyrus version, the elder brother's wife attempts to seduce the younger brother, to whom she represents his (absent) mother. In fact, in other papyri, sons writing to their mothers is a common narrative situation. Thus in the Michigan papyri, Valerius writes to Samaphes, "I hope soon to change my way of life and sail up to you. For I know your zeal to make me less distraught; for when I give heed to you I live in less anxiety." In a letter to his mother, Nilous, Antonius Longus abases himself: "I was ashamed to come to Karanis because I am going about in rags. I write to you that I am naked. I beseech you, mother, be reconciled to me. For the rest, I know what I have brought upon myself. I have been punished in every way. I know that I have sinned. . . . Don't you know that I *would* rather be a cripple than be conscious that I am still owing anyone an obol?" In many of these papyri, clothes are the tangible form of wealth, as accompanying pawn tickets testify.[11] Unlike the parable, however, these versions of the fabula show women as important actants. They are also the recipients of the story, a metanarrative function that would later be focalized through the voice-over in film noir, just as the role of such "inner scripts" would be reinstated in roman noir by Raymond Chandler.

We may gain some idea of the originary historic and social context of Luke's story by considering those details the Lucan author appears to have added to the fabula. Chief among them is the attempt to make the prodigal's fall culturally resonant by having his benefactor raise swine. This would be an environmental paradox, however, for studies have shown pork to be the most expensive form of animal protein; indeed, anthropologist Marvin Harris has postulated that the ban on pork in the Jewish dietary laws stems from the ecological ravages of swine. Unable to digest grasses, swine forage for roots, berries, and acorns in the woods, which they quickly destroy, causing soil erosion, flooding, and desertification. Harris suggests that these catastrophes led to widespread bans on raising pigs across Mesopotamia between 2400 and 1700 B.C. (*Cultural Materialism* 190–94).[12]

If one continued to examine the story from Harris's vantage, distinguishing between objective data and internal social explanations of data, the "far country" that the prodigal describes is either a figurative exaggeration (his hunger stands for a famine; swineherding stands for the lowest occupation) or the far country is a society in which extreme oligarchic stratification occurs during economic crises (a rich man raises pigs for personal consumption but starves his servants).[13] We can see that the parable and its fabula unite two narrative movements, one internal and subjective, the other external and objective, making it an unusually apt vehicle for the concern in the 1920s with inner/outer. But it is not ecologically probable that the famine occurred only in the far country. If famine was widespread, the two interpretations are compatible, for a society that experiences difficulty maintaining the material status quo, because of population pressure or ecological depletion, often rejects outsiders, except as a source of capital. Despite his patrimony, the prodigal might have been unable to join the corresponding class in the far country, hence representing himself figuratively as spending, bereft of working/saving or giving.

The prodigal's penniless return reverses the usual folkloric motif. No marvelous issue, no new kingdom, no precious knowledge come from his journey—nothing save poverty and humiliation. This is hardly an endorsement of foreign investment. Auditors who drop their identification with the prodigal son, as they cast about for understanding, are rescued by the reappearance of the enigmatically generous father. He is problematic only if we fail to recognize that the position of principal actor is progressive, coinciding with the progression of desires. The fabula entails a dynamic conception of time, in which the function of each actant implies the next actant.[14]

Many interpretive problems arise from a refusal to drop the father's focalization of the issue then, after it has entailed the elder son's. For example, whether or not the father legally owns what he gives the returned prodigal is secondary in the dynamic time of the fabula to the fact of the father's giving. What is important to the fabula is that he occupies the economic position that anthropologists call the "big man" (see Harris, *Cannibals and Kings* 104–8). He maintains his power and status by giving the surplus they create back to his family and followers, thus obligating them and expanding credit. The slaughter of the fatted calf and the feast of reincorporation are not just festivities. They demonstrate his control of society's store of energy. By an expenditure that is relatively minor compared with the half or third of his estate that has been lost completely, the father gains greater control than before of manpower and of his line of descent.

This leads us to see that exogamy is an unstated threat to the father and to giving. It is an additional "opponent." Each male has an explicit or implied female partner. The prodigal squanders his genetic seed with "foreign whores," casting into doubt the line of his father's descent. From the father's point of view, there is no need for alliances outside the immediate clan, for they would demand unrequited (and perhaps greater) giving. Indeed, the absence of a famine in the father's land, his servants' better condition, and the surplus that is the calf argue mimetically and figuratively for the prosperity of the father's society.

The elder son represents the third and seemingly most parsimonious focalization. His prudence and restraint contrast with the spending of the prodigal son and with the giving of the father. The conversation between the elder son and his father explains giving as a form of saving. Control of land, herds, and capital, the father implies, rests with the unimpeachably stable members of society. The prodigal has returned, but the Big Man understands that he is a spendthrift for whom a kid or calf must be slaughtered occasionally for the sake of social coherence. Small prodigalities, the father suggests, forfend the danger of social disintegration. One is reminded of Edmund Burke's remark that "economy is a distributive virtue, and consists not in saving but in selection. Parsimony requires no providence, no sagacity, no powers of combination, no comparison, no judgement" (530). [15]

Were he an anthropologist, Burke (or the father) might put it this way: "Endogamy and concentration of wealth are more likely if you increase the rewards for standing pat, if you give when the law does not require it. Economic surplus should be used to maintain social wholeness. Emigration and exogamy represent a threat not just to the lineage but also to the wealth of those who stay home in power, since the labor they could command, representing an investment of capital, has fled." We never learn if the elder son apprehends this last lesson in being a father-giver. Successfully apprehended, it would make him the economic father of his father, as well as of his younger brother. Such a resolution would be structurally sound, since the level of material awareness manifested by each succeeding focalization increases. It would make a grim narrative, though; often, as in Chandler, it is subsumed by problematizing or dichotomizing the identity of the father.

An ancillary goal of the fabula seems to be to reinstate the prodigal under the power of the giver for his sexual as well as material needs. There is a strong implication that he will be "given" an appropriate wife and proceed to a phase of conjugal, social saving. In the parable, not much of this is developed, but sexuality as pure consumption, the analogue of material spending, became more common as stories based on the fabula developed in the roman noir.

The relative absence of women from the best-known versions of the fabula, except as "harlots" who "devour" a "living" in a "far country," marks this as one of the core patriarchal as well as economic texts. In all of the stories discussed, the negative actants are filled by women, from "foreign" and "wasteful" through "unlawful" and "barren." The metaphors about eating are figured to evoke such primal male images as vagina dentata, a favorite of Raymond Chandler. Not even the foreigner who hires the prodigal as a swineherd, to say nothing of those men who doubtless took his money, are as stigmatized as foreign women are.

Modern distance on the economic issues of the fabula quite likely began in the Renaissance, when large market economies developed. The elevation of trade from an ancillary activity to a primary one extended the legitimation of reciprocity outside the family. Younger sons were no longer predestined to fail in far countries; in fact, we may suspect that elder sons occasionally envied their brothers' newfound freedom and wealth. An inversion of the traditional fabula is not difficult to imagine: the elder son is disenfranchised and turned out, to myriad adventures, until he unmasks

the "seeming loyalty" of the young usurper before their father. Milton
and Shakespeare demonstrate the potential appeal of focalizing the fabula
through the elder brother for a mercantile audience. Concomitant with
economic liberalization, we begin to find women as "long lost heirs" and,
with the rise of the novel, as prodigals. The role of giver is so close to
the heart of patriarchal authority, however, that women had for centuries
to seem givers only to be unmasked. But a side effect was that who the
father was became cloudy. The elder brother was less a problem when the
fabula was inverted (the shrew, the spinster) but off-limits in the original
form. The study of links between gender and economic fabulae, touched
on here, has barely begun.[16]

The extraordinary economic and religious ferment in Europe at the time
of American colonization may account for the settlers' frequent use of the
parable of the prodigal as a vehicle for ideological purposes. From William
Bradford's *Plymouth Plantation* (1651) through Cotton Mather's *Magnalia
Christi Americana* (1702), we find examples of proud or profligate individuals struck down (Bradford's "lusty seaman" being the best known) on
behalf of social unity. King Philip's War promoted an identification of
Indian lands as the "far country" and Puritan captives as "prodigals," of
which Mrs. Rowlandson's and Hannah Dustin's accounts are the most famous. Variously attired, the thematics of prodigality are also evident in the
work of William Byrd (*Secret History of the Dividing Line*, 1709), Royal
Tyler (*The Contrast*, 1787), and Susanna Rowson (*Charlotte Temple*, 1791).
Rowson explicitly thematizes sexuality. Her prodigal daughter plot repli-
cates such details of the fabula as repentant letters to the mother and the
preoccupation with genetic descent (Charlotte is seduced by a foreigner).
In the era of Franklin (*Autobiography*, 1818) and James Fenimore Cooper
(*The Pioneers*, 1823; *The Last of the Mohicans*, 1826), prodigality became
an explicit intellectual topic.

Prodigality is a form of disaccumulation, which can be rendered by
other fabulae. While American literature has nothing like the potlatch
of the Kwakiutl Indians, the fall of the wealthy family, often in tandem
with the decline of the great house in which they live, served honorably
in the 1800s. From Charles Brockton Brown's *Wieland* (1798) and Poe's
"Fall of the House of Usher" (1839) to Hawthorne's *House of the Seven*

Gables (1851) and Howells's *The Rise of Silas Lapham* (1885), nineteenth-century authors haunted, imploded, and immolated the bourgeois solidity that American patriarchs associated with their dwellings.

In contrast to these high cultural narratives of deterioration, however, there were always popular cultural narratives of prodigal improvement. That frontier profligacy Crèvecoeur feared found voice in tall tales and myths. Richard Slotkin has shown the deep roots, variants, and antiquity of the Daniel Boone saga, and comparable genealogies exist for Mike Fink, Paul Bunyan, Margaret Tobin "Unsinkable Molly" Brown, and other embodiments of pioneering. These prodigals, successful in far countries, began to appear in "literature" under the guises of the "long lost heir" (Oliver Effingham in Cooper's *The Pioneers*) and the "frontier traveling woman" (the journey of Sarah Kemble Knight, 1704, and, later, Willa Cather). Many slave narratives, beginning with Olaudah Equiano's (1789), employ substantial motifs of the fabula. In popular literature, the thematics of successful profligacy fomented by Horatio Alger (Richard Hunter in *Ragged Dick*, 1867) reappeared when Dorinda Oakley, the "forsaken wife of a worthless profligate," became an economic power in Ellen Glasgow's *Barren Ground* (1925). Narratives of agricultural dispossession later on (William Faulkner, Erskine Caldwell) found the fabula valuable, and it was a mainstay of naturalists such as Theodore Dreiser (*Sister Carrie*, 1900; *An American Tragedy*, 1925) and John Steinbeck (*The Grapes of Wrath*, 1939; *East of Eden*, 1952).

As such variety indicates, prodigality has been open to different ideological investments, but at no point has there been such intense concern as in the texts about the "spree and hangover" (a revealing metaphor) of the 1920s and 1930s. As Charles and Mary Beard wrote in *The Rise of American Civilization*, "In the new order, prodigal members of the plutocracy set standards of reckless living and high living which spread like a virus among all ranks of society" (726).

The tension between the preservation of wealth and the means of its creation, between what people did with money and how they acquired it, grew hypertropically in the 1920s, from Booth Tarkington's *Alice Adams* (Pulitzer Prize, 1921) through Ring Lardner's *How to Write Short Stories* (1924) and Anita Loos's *Gentlemen Prefer Blondes* (1925). It contributed to the immediate recognition of Fitzgerald's *The Great Gatsby* (1925) as a classic. With *Gatsby* as a lens, we can see that the era had already connected two key elements of the fabula—material waste and foreignness—but had made different stories about progress out of them. In much American narrative the thread back to the native country, the difficulties of being a foreigner, the issue of foreignness and origins, accounted for a character's motivation to acquire wealth. Foreignness could be the secret of success or failure; an indication of its importance is the way the origin of Jay Gatsby in roughneck Jimmy Gatz is withheld from readers, to be delivered in narrative synchrony with revelations about his "gonnegtion" to racketeer Meyer Wolfshiem. But instead of a familiarizing source like bootlegging, Gatsby's wealth owes to a discomfiting, high-tech fencing of stolen bonds.

Two popular narratives of the era reveal the fabula's flexibility. Using the new medium of film, *The Jazz Singer* (1927), produced by five Jewish immigrants to America (the Warner brothers), took the opposite view of origins, wealth, and technology. Al Jolson, playing a cantor's son, leaves the Lower East Side of New York City and finds success as a nightclub singer because "he has a tear in his voice." His foreignness is the source, not the secret, of a success aided by telephones, trains, and recording, not to mention movies. In contrast, during the 1927 trial of Nicola Sacco and Bartolomeo Vanzetti, the state of Massachusetts advanced a traditional view of the relation between foreigners and capital—xenophobia.[17]

Both narratives involve consciousness of guilt. But in court this was a legal concept about the relation of acts, words, and evidence to motive: if the accused lied or concealed evidence, such acts led to the presumption of guilt. The emphasis of the legal system was on tradition. It embodied the principle of the conservation of material gain: Thou shalt not steal; thou shalt not covet (elder brother–ism). Its modus operandi required the reenactment of the sixth or ninth commandment. But interestingly, both the defense of Sacco and Vanzetti and the makers of *The Jazz Singer* departed from this, averring that consciousness of guilt was consciousness that economic success requires alterity. In *The Jazz Singer* such a consciousness causes Al Jolson to adopt the figurative mode of the technological world and to become wealthy. The defenders of Sacco and Vanzetti argued that consciousness of guilt was a double bind that forced the accused into self-alienation.

Not until after the election of 1922 did Sacco and Vanzetti come to the attention of intellectuals.[18] The struggle to "get the story out" took time and depended on an appealing narrative. At the trial, there was little evidence to suggest Sacco and Vanzetti were innocent and no narrative "hook." But in 1925 a fascinating complication developed, as a confessed murderer named Celestino Madeiros came forward to announce that he, not Sacco or Vanzetti, had committed the crime with the Joe Morelli gang. The state supreme court refused to upset the jury's verdict, and at that time, only the trial judge could reopen a case to admit additional evidence. Madeiros's factual contradictions soon were forgotten, and his rejected "confession" made a permanent part of the narrative of "innocence endangered" that was Sacco and Vanzetti.[19]

The narrative of the Commonwealth of Massachusetts followed the tradition of reenactment, but did not include "consciousness of guilt" in its initial accusation. Basically the state assumed that foreigners had attacked society's amassed capital, and it relied on narrative mechanisms of ritual scapegoating, especially the hypothetical power of the victim (see Girard 176). The case depended on circumstantial evidence but reenacted events in a clear, simple narrative that convinced the jury. Interviewed twenty years later, jurors cited the strength of the physical evidence, particularly the bullet, and discounted talk of a bias against foreigners. Eyewitness testimony was relatively strong, but positive identification of the defendants began to break down in the second week, when witnesses for the prosecution equivocated under skillful cross-examination.

On the trial's fourteenth day, district attorney Frederick Katzmann changed tactics, charging that Sacco and Vanzetti exhibited "consciousness of guilt," a strategy not mentioned in his opening statement. "There is no reason, if they are innocent, for withholding a single truth. There is every reason for uttering the truth if innocent," he declared. Sacco and Vanzetti had by then given several versions of where they were and what they were doing at the time of the crime. "Each falsehood uttered by way of exculpation becomes an article of evidence of greater or less incriminating value," said Katzmann (Weeks 168).

"Consciousness of guilt" sounds dubious, but the concept can be traced to Anglo-Saxon law and is prominent in the early crime narratives collected in the *Newgate Calendar*. It is a synecdoche about crime, as Stephen

Knight has explained in *Form and Ideology in Crime Fiction*: "The sense of guilt makes them act rashly afterwards, so drawing attention to themselves and to crucial evidence. . . . The idea behind this is that the Christian conscience is suddenly awakened, the objective Christian pattern reasserts itself against the subjective criminal rejection of those values" (11–12). Understood as a narrative feature, consciousness of guilt draws together two value systems and two plots, one of which becomes a subplot in which a second voice tries to construe the events in a new narrative pattern.

Thus, imputation of consciousness of guilt opened the way for a "revealed story." The defense saw that consciousness might be of some guilt other than greed. The motive of the accused could be a problem. Multiple motives would throw doubt on the question of identity. Showing that "who" committed the deed was not the "who" presumed would be extremely effective; better yet, the multiplication of "who" undercut the representation of an accusable subject. Which "who" is "conscious" of what particular "guilt"? This production of selves left its subject bereft of a "natural self"—alienated. It was the "greed" of America that had alienated Sacco and Vanzetti, whose socialism proved them to be essentially giving, sharing men. Now that greed had been "projected" onto them.

Katzmann failed to take advantage of consciousness of guilt, limiting his imputation to the defendants' participation in the robbery and murder. He did not stress Sacco and Vanzetti's politics—the transcript shows that Judge Webster Thayer usually stopped such discourse—nor did he emphasize their foreign origins, because a newsboy testified that he "knew by the way they ran they were foreigners" (quoted in Frankfurter 7). Both a skeptical Robert Montgomery and a sympathetic William Young have written in recent books that the transcript is relatively free of the Red-baiting supposed to have occurred (see also Avrich).

Yet if the jury found consciousness of guilt unappealing, it became a major feature of the story outside the courtroom. Intellectuals, many with experience abroad, had never wanted to live in a George Babbitt world. It was their insight that in this Freudian world, consciousness and guilt had many possible causes. Even H. L. Mencken admitted, "If they are electrocuted it will be because they are radicals and not because they have been actually connected with the murders" (in Manchester 120). Rather than desiring the wealth of others, the accused might be victims of the disparity between the American promise and the American reality. Rather than taking, they might have given, only to be taken. Rather than Sacco and Vanzetti, society might be the guilty party. These elements were reworked by Eugene Lyons in *The Life and Death of Sacco and Vanzetti* (1927), an extraordinary mix of the appeals Lyons had tried out as publicist for the defense. The accused were the children of "simple smiling men and women waving many-colored kerchiefs," peasants who broke into song spontaneously and shared equitably (11). When Lyons wanted to appeal to the white-collar class, Vanzetti's parents were "comfortably fixed" and Sacco's "among the more substantial portion." Elements of the fabula begin to appear as Vanzetti, portrayed as an idealist, abandons his widower father on the family farm and embarks on a search for self-fulfillment. Sacco was also a "trusted son," who paid his father's workmen and bought the supplies, until he too harkened to the call of America.

Lyons's diction became melodramatic when describing their first years in America: "prey," "fleeced," "low wages, no jobs," "bad time to arrive," "sharks," "ignominy," "uncertainty," "remembered with a shudder," "vermin," "slums and slime," and "purgatory" are among his descriptions of eastern cities. He structured the first part of his narrative by place-to-place comparison: the ancient, harmonious, noble fatherland versus the grasping, cruel, cutthroat "land of opportunity." But Sacco and Vanzetti did not "give in"; they persevered. Lyons suspended the fabula to introduce pioneer persistence and Jeffersonian natural aristocracy.

Then in a section titled "Their Loss of Caste," Lyons assigned fault to social structures: "Far deeper and more tragic are the humiliations of [Vanzetti's] changed social standing" (19). He depicted Vanzetti rummaging through garbage barrels to find a meal (though he worked in a restaurant) and surviving on cabbage leaves and rotten potatoes. Lyons recognized that his underlying fabula did not depend on a return home as much as on a change in the final interpretive register: the prodigal had to be alienated, with ambiguous father figures present. Lyons gave the American intellectual a chance to be father, to be provenient judge: "After a day in the stone quarries or before a brick furnace, Vanzetti went to his books, demanding an answer to the riddle of rich and poor" (25). Vanzetti read his way through the Great Books: besides Marx and other socialists, he finished the Bible, Greek, Roman, Italian, French, and American history, Darwin, Spencer, Dante, Hugo, Tolstoy, Zola, and countless poets. He carried William James's *Psychology* into court every day. May not such a prodigal be forgiven, nay, welcomed with open arms? The issue of "foreignness" was transformed: "Italians, Russians, Jews, Greeks accepted the fish-vendor as a brother" (43). To be an idealist, to be well-read, was to be a foreigner and to distinguish oneself from the Babbitts. Lyons invited his readers to identify intellection with foreignness, to consider a lack of it American and materialistic.

A major refinement came from the pen of Harvard law professor Felix Frankfurter, who would coach James M. Cain for his editorial on the case in the *New York World*. Far more sophisticated than Lyons, Frankfurter appealed to intellectuals through close legal reasoning, footnotes about comparable "barbarisms" in "uncivilized" cultures, and overt invocation of high cultural alienation. Frankfurter argued in *The Case of Sacco and Vanzetti* (1927) that a "role" had been forced upon the defendants in place of their "natural selves." He wrote that "Sacco and Vanzetti after their arrest were shown singly to persons brought there for the purposes of identification, not as part of a 'parade.' Moreover, Sacco and Vanzetti were not even allowed to be their natural selves; they were compelled to simulate the behavior of the Braintree bandits" (32).[20]

Among the first passionate high-brow defenders was Edna St. Vincent Millay, who wrote to the "booboisie" in *Outlook*: "You long to return to your gracious world of a year ago, where people had pretty manners and did not raise their voices; where people whom you knew, whom you had entertained in your houses, did not shout and weep and walk the streets vulgarly carrying banners, because two quite inconsequential people, two men who could not even speak good English, were about to be put forever out of mischief's way" (in Weeks 254–55). Millay ransacked her imagination for analogies: the defendants were children, were like the readers' children, were being kidnapped, were like coins and castaways. In one passage she alludes to a parable in Luke and then positions the United States as a "far country."

They are golden coins, hidden under the mattress in a very soiled wallet. The only pleasure they afford you is the rapturous dread lest some one may be taking them away. And some one is taking them away. But not the one you think. . . .

These men were castaways upon our shore, and we, an ignorant and savage tribe, have put them to death because their speech and their manners were different from our own and because to the untutored mind that which is strange is in its infancy ludicrous, but in its prime evil, dangerous, and to be done away with. (in Weeks 255)

Within ten years readers could choose among Upton Sinclair's *Boston* (1928), Bernard De Voto's *We Accept with Pleasure* (1934), Maxwell Anderson's *Gods of the Lightning* (1928), James Thurber's *The Male Animal* (1940), John Dos Passos's *The Big Money* (1936), and eight other novels that depicted the trial. In *The Sacco-Vanzetti Anthology of Verse* (1927) several poems compared the defendants to Christ crucified.[21] The Algonquin Round Table group, Heywood Broun in particular, proselytized tirelessly for the defense. Dos Passos extended Frankfurter's theme of the son alienated to a note of ecological crisis: "America our nation has been beaten by strangers who have bought the laws and fenced off the meadows and cut down the woods for pulp and turned our pleasant cities into slums and sweated the wealth out of our people and when they want to they hire the executioner to throw the switch" (in Weeks 262). This reworking combines Millay's passion and Lyons's frontier virtue. In it Sacco and Vanzetti are natives of a United States that has been invaded by industrialist "foreigners" who close off traditional frontier venues of escape. The fenced meadows and timber cut for "pulp" (magazines) combine with electricity ("the switch") to rob prelapsarian "pleasant cities" of their intrinsic wealth. By apprehending prodigality's deepest roots, Dos Passos completed its inversion, making Americans "prodigal sons" in their own land.

By contrast, in *The Jazz Singer* (1927), directed by Alan Crosland, Al Jolson played out his life story. He rose from the Jewish ghetto, where his voice and cantor-father had marked him for a traditional life, to burlesque and the stage, on which he became the most popular jazz singer of

As the black-faced cantor's son in *The Jazz Singer* (1927), Al Jolson vindicated "consciousness of guilt" for the average man. He showed that economic success requires adaptation and alterity, while defenders of Sacco and Vanzetti argued that it resulted in "alienation." (©1927 Turner Entertainment Co. All rights reserved.)

the 1920s. The similarity of his life to that of Irving Berlin, whose "Blue Skies" debuted in the film, and to those of the Warner brothers, underlines the fact that the film's mythos of adaptation for success was widespread: numbers of immigrants felt they had a stake in new technologies and art moderne settings. Film scholars have felt it significant that the cantor-father, who disinherits Jolson, is an antitechnology figure who yells to "STOP!" the sound track and that he must die before Jolson can achieve stage success. That Jolson succeeds with his mother's aid follows closely one variant of the fabula. But if the film draws heavily on elements of Algerism and the immigrant success story, it also recognizes the costs. Not only his father's death but also Jolson's deft donning of blackface after singing the Passover Kol Nidre emphasize how "other" he has become. "He belongs to the world," says his mother finally, and several titles disparage "those who are turned to the past." This narrative ruthlessly embraces new economic enterprises and technologies despite their costs. The "prodigal" need only adapt to his strange new land to prosper.

Most academic writing about *The Jazz Singer* regards the plot as a "sentimental story" of "anguished conflict" and downplays the shift in technology, circling around two scenes in which Jolson ad-libbed his dialogue.[22] In the first he speaks to the audience (and the camera) between songs in his nightclub act, delivering his famous line: "Wait-a-minute . . . wait-a-minute! You ain't heard nothin' yet!" In the second, Jolson returns from his journey to Los Angeles and revisits his mother. Sitting down at the piano, he sings "Blue Skies" while apparently improvising dialogue about his plans to move his parents to a nice apartment in the Bronx: "Lots of nice green grass up there, and a whole lot of people you know, the Ginsbergs, the Gottenbergs, and the Goldbergs and, oh, a whole lot of Bergs I don't know at all" (quoted in Slide 867–68).

His mother, played by Eugenie Besserer, becomes more and more flustered, until Jolson remarks what the audience has noticed—that she's getting kittenish. As Anthony Slide wrote, "What impresses about this dialogue is its natural, unforced, unrehearsed quality. . . . it has an ad-libbed ring to it. It is so natural, so close to reality, that it becomes almost embarrassing to hear. One feels an encroachment on the intimacy of the couple" (868). David Cook notes that "the effect was not so much of *hearing* Jolson speak as of *overhearing* him speak, and it thrilled audiences bored with the conventions of silent cinema and increasingly indifferent to the canned performances of the Vitaphone shorts" (240).

To these scenes can be added another. Mordaunt Hall wrote in 1927 for the *New York Times* that "one of the most interesting sequences . . . is where Jolson as Jack Robin . . . is perceived talking to Mary Dale as he smears his face with black. It is done gradually, and yet the dexterity with which Mr. Jolson outlines his mouth is readily appreciated. You see Jack Robin, the young man who at last has his big opportunity, with a couple of smudges of black on his features, and then his cheeks, his nose, his forehead and the back of his neck are blackened." Rich as this review is in its appreciation of technique, Hall complained about the verisimilitude of the sound that so impresses modern scholars: "There are also times when one would expect the Vitaphoned portion to be either more subdued or stopped as the camera swings to other scenes. The voice is usually just the same whether the image of the singer is close to the camera or far away" (391).

Auspicious here is the relation between technology and emotions about wealth. Is this not consciousness of guilt? *The Jazz Singer* is told from the point of view of a prodigal who adapts to and is successful in a far country. It depends on making the father a vengeful blocking character: "Now I have no son," he says. Jakie Robin travels three thousand miles, falls for a shiksa, and adapts to a life ordered by trains, telegrams, and telephone calls. If the fabula of prodigality has not suggested itself, the film's manipulation of the Kol Nidre, sung at the feast of Passover, guarantees that the point is made by formal symmetry. Jakie was to sing the Kol Nidre beside his father, but he's disowned and the redemptive feast is suspended. The structure of Orthodox Judaism is replaced by the structure of show business, which establishes its own rhythm of events, driven by technology. But the feast, as Jolson shows by filling in at the temple and singing the Kol Nidre brilliantly after his father's death, is merely postponed.

What began as a narrative of deterioration turns out to be embedded in a narrative of improvement. Jack Robin may lose his father in synchrony with his success on stage, but he sings "Mammy" as his mother sits in the audience at her first Broadway show. "Jolson puts all the force of his personality into the song as he walks out beyond the footlights," wrote Mordaunt Hall (391). That his singing in blackface was so powerful, and his technique of concealing his "real self" so hypnotizing, reminds us that audiences perceived Jolson as appropriating an Other for his advancement and that they recognized him paying the cost of his improvement. There is no fragmentation of the self by alienation here. The point about such a popular narrative of successful prodigality is that consciousness of guilt may be subsumed and conquered. The prodigal can adapt to and become a success in a foreign land.

The truth can be evoked only in that dimension of alibi in which all
"realism" in creative works takes its virtue from metonymy.
—Jacques Lacan, *The Four Fundamental Concepts of Psycho-Analysis*

Metonymic Sources

Technology

Most explanations of the impact of technology center on
artifacts and the continuity of their development, not explaining gaps or
failures or including cultural values. To incorporate these, we turn to the
"momentum" model developed by Thomas P. Hughes and others.[1] Taking
its figure from physics, often suggestive for literary theory, the momentum
model permits a "soft" determinism. It allows for failures and momentum's opposite, inertia. This breadth more nearly explains how technology
can offer figurative lineaments to the imagination, without asserting a

homology of meanings. This flexibility helps to explain how prodigality refigures itself metonymically.

Metonymy, in which a name of a part substitutes for the whole, has been explained by Roman Jakobson as "discontinuous . . . nominal." It is said to substitute the container for the contents—"They had another bottle [of beer]"—an extrinsic and mechanistic mode of figuration. On the other hand, synecdoche names a part that symbolizes some quality of the whole. Jakobson said it was integrative, emphasizing intrinsic and organic qualities: "He is all [the qualities of] heart" (in White, *Metahistory* 36). These are really two different ways of reconstructing reality, as Hayden White explains in *Metahistory*: metonymy, while "open to the charge of lack of scope and a tendency toward abstraction," writes White, "facilitates causative or systematic thinking" (17, 35). It seeks to uncover in the acts of agents their extrahistoric causes and inclines to the belief that there are laws behind processes, rather than teleological ends. But synecdoche seeks to consolidate or to crystallize dispersed events according to an intrinsic, shared, organic quality. Rather than laws, it finds principles that in the aggregate prefigure a teleological end.

In the economic boom of the 1920s, metonymic qualities became allied to "progress" and to narratives about it. This is because metonymy shares qualities with momentum. Hughes, John Staudenmaier, and other momentum theorists have shown that, first, once a technological paradigm takes hold, it usually generates further innovations in its framework. Second, existing artifacts, especially tools, have momentum, if their durability, economy, and familiarity made them part of people's habits. Third, governmental policy usually endorses the existing technology. Fourth, investment has momentum: once we have a stake, we invest more to save the initial investment and ignore or combat other technologies. Fifth, inventors, engineers, and technicians achieve a momentum as they work together that makes them reluctant to discard a process or technology they have pioneered: "solutions in search of problems" are common. Finally, "the value-laden 'embrace' of some culture is capable of giving momentum to a technical concept, an existing artifact, or a governmental policy," writes Staudenmaier (87).[2]

The momentum model explains the dynamics of technology in an apparently contradictory way—committed at once to both change and changelessness. The figuration of such a Janus-like nature is nearly always metonymic, because in foregoing a teleologic end, in finding an order that allows and even orchestrates the gaps in an organic coherence, metonymy enables the artist to avoid a completely reactionary stance: technique, paradoxically, saves the antitechnologist from philistinism.

When Cora wants to explain to Frank the reason for their love's failure in Cain's *The Postman Always Rings Twice*, she chooses a curious metaphor: "It's a big airplane engine, that takes you up through the sky. . . . But when you put it in a Ford, it just shakes it to pieces" (88). The inadequacy of Fordism is not so apparent today. How did this mythic man—who in 1906 prophesied "a light, low-priced car with an up-to-date engine of ample horse-power, and built of the very best material" (in Sward 49)—come to be perceived as out of touch in 1934? He had understood the cultural value of travel in the technological matrix so well.[3] Lobbying efforts by bicyclists had improved roads, gasoline and kerosene were available because of the commercialization of petroleum cracking, and cold forging and metal-casting techniques from gun and sewing machine factories provided Ford with precise parts. There were specialized metal lathes, drill presses, and finishing machines. The open-hearth furnace and alloy steels increased his metallurgical options, and Goodyear had invented the vulcanization process for rubber.

Ford used only a few of these but seized upon the cultural reverence for efficiency. His important innovations were in the way things were done and fell under the heading "Continuity of Production." To produce the vehicle that put Americans in motion, he banished immobility from the factory. His plant floor was arranged according to the sequence of operations necessary to make the product. Traditionally all milling machines had been in one department; there had been one furnace room and one for cooling vats. If any part needed extra milling, tempering, or annealing, it went back: this was energy efficient. But Ford put a milling machine, a furnace, or a vat exactly where it was needed, even though this meant duplication and energy "waste." He undid the organic, synecdochical "production efficiency" achieved in the bicycle industry, but he eliminated bottlenecks, and no worker, no part, was ever idle. There was an even flow of the product out the door. Fords became the metaphor of this efficiency, in part because Ford installed metonymy in the work process.

Ford's first true assembly line took men from workbenches to stand before two steel rails, down which they pushed magneto coil assemblies, each adding a part. Each of the twenty-nine workers had previously assembled about 35 coils a day, averaging twenty minutes each. On the line, they assembled 1,188 coils—one every thirteen minutes. Within a year, fourteen workers turned out 1,335 coils a day, at five minutes each (Hounshell 248). The human cost was considerable. Workers complained of backache from stooping over the line: Ford raised the level. They complained of the erratic pace: Ford installed a chain to drag the magnetos evenly along the tracks. Labor turnover in 1913 was 380 percent, according to Keith Sward: "So great was labor's distaste for the new machine system that toward the close of 1913 every time the company wanted to add 100 men to its factory personnel, it was necessary to hire 963" (249).[4]

By moving work to the worker, the assembly line made the machine central and the worker marginal; it made the elimination of entire manufacturing stages more thinkable, because they were more abstract, less human. The process stressed deletion rather than elaboration. The imagination asked how steps could be taken out of a process, a question once shadowed by the worker's resulting joblessness. Now the worker was just reassigned, because jobs were essentially alike: the worker performed a simple action at a regulated pace in attendance upon a machine. Work became homogeneous, the task of a magneto coil assembler like that of an upholstery stuffer. Work became metonymic, that is, extrinsic, discontinuous, and nominal in meaning; formerly it had been synecdochical, or imbued with intrinsic, organic, and continuous shared meaning. Some of the latter qualities shifted to the system, which became complex and was understood only by engineers. For the line worker the object simply appeared from the system at a uniform pace. His friend upstream could no more explain to him the contributing assembly than he could explain his own part to someone at the loading dock. Each worker became less a mechanic: that quality was transferred to the "system." Three understandings tended to result: that work was homogeneous, that work flowed to the individual from an incomprehensible system of upstream tributaries and hidden sources,

Work became more metonymic—uniform, regulated, and extrinsic—during the late 1920s and throughout the 1930s, a change noted and initially celebrated by writers and photographers, one of whom photographed these telephone operators for the W.P.A. (National Archives, Amer. Image no. 121)

and that improvements came from the deletion of steps, rather than from elaborations by the worker or from physical economies.

To understand Fordism's failure for Cora, we need to understand why General Motors succeeded Ford. As early as 1914 *World's Work* had detected among consumers "the fetish of 'The New Model'" and asked, "How many automobiles can America buy?" (Cleveland 679–89). Ford refused to comprehend the effect of metonymic habits on consumers, resisting installment buying—it was morally vitiating and un-American, he thought—and cars in colors, to say nothing of such doodads as the electric starter that Charles Kettering introduced at GM. The cultural values of travel (status, education, economic improvement) conflicted with Ford's "efficiency."[5]

Ford plunged on, stressing backward and forward integration, building his own steel mills and buying a railroad, until the cost of a 1916 Model T

General Motors's 1927 Chrysler gave consumers a choice of styles and colors, forcing Ford to retire the Model T. (The Western Reserve Historical Society, Cleveland, Ohio)

had dropped 66 percent from its 1910 level, to $360. It came in black, in four cylinders, with a crank, for cash (Hounshell 258). But Ford's synecdochical aesthetic—his auto was not only efficient itself but a metaphor for its system of production—was incommensurable with the advent of what Daniel Boorstin has called "the search for novelty" (7–9) typical of American affluence. Faced with a flood of inexpensive, homogeneous products, consumers no longer made buying decisions based on efficiency. They faced decisions about style, and having "no peasant traditions to give them character," as William Carlos Williams remarked (201), they fell upon the novel, the up-to-date, and the easy to use.

By 1920, writes David Hounshell, the Model T had become a popular metaphor for changelessness. By 1927 Ford's share dropped to 25 percent, while Chevrolet sold more than one million cars in colors (261). This moment marks the eclipse of technological production values by the cultural factors of mass marketing. Consumers embraced the "tradition of the new" because it offered built-in assurances of the "latest" technology along with social status. The momentum of efficiency, simplicity, and reparability faded when consumers perceived that all choices were "good

The 1934 Chrysler Airflow perfected Streamform styling, associating speed and smoothness with social status and wealth. (The Western Reserve Historical Society, Cleveland, Ohio)

enough" technically. Competition then shifted to surfaces, kinesthetic and status values, provinces of the young advertising men.

The rise of flexible mass production, in which cybernetic adjustments between consumer preference and mass marketing determined what was produced, was the era of General Motors and Alfred P. Sloan, though no special foresight can be attributed to either. As late as 1925 Sloan said, "While the bringing out of yearly models results in many disadvantages and, for that reason, we are all against yearly models, I don't see just what can be done about it." He often railed against "the 'laws' of Paris dressmakers in the automobile industry" (in Hounshell 263, 267). Yet Sloan's decentralization of plant and authority was better at adapting to consumer wants and at adopting new processes and products.

Charles Kettering and William Knudsen represent two important trends at GM. Kettering invented the electric starter motor, which increased the convenience of the car and made it more usable by women, opening a vast new market. "Keep the customer dissatisfied," Kettering said, urging the continual adoption of "features" such as shock absorbers, pneumatic tires, electric lights, and windshield wipers. He proposed heavy advertising to create demand for these improvements. GM hired Knudsen to figure out how factories could adapt to continual style changes. He began to use stamped metal wherever possible, learning to form without wrinkles or thin spots the sharp and shallow curves that would dominate the Streamform styling of the 1930s. He also pioneered the welding of large, thin pieces of metal formed on huge hydraulic punch presses. These stressed skin panels became a basic feed stock of industry, used subsequently for everything from skyscraper facades and locomotive fairings to airplanes and refrigerators. Ford ignored these processes.[6]

The new cars were fast, but trains and airplanes were faster. The metonymic pattern created was "acceleration," which began to establish itself as a value. Propelling acceleration were radically new engines based on the turbine's principle of eternal circularity. Intellectuals took note but had a hard time aestheticizing this. Harriet Monroe in "The Turbine" (1925) personified the turbine as a woman, explosive if crossed, who "sits upon her throne / As ladylike and quiet as a nun." According to the poem, "She'll burst her windings, rip her casings off / And shriek till envious Hell shoots up its flames" (37).[7] The competition for speed and distance records, a mania in the age of Lindbergh, led to bigger, more powerful engines. The availability of hangars, airfields, and sunny weather made flight popular in California, which became the mecca of aerodynamics. Wind-tunnel testing, pioneered by Glenn Curtiss in Los Angeles, revealed the high resistance of cloth and wood wings and showed that the weight of a smooth metal wing, aerodynamically shaped, could be overcome by a powerful engine to achieve even greater speeds.

"Speed" was a potent point of contact between technological momentum and cultural values. The desire to perform operations faster drove a great deal of invention, yet speed was only a relative efficiency. A savings of time, it could be an expense in materials and energy. The selection of speed from the spectrum of efficiencies is a cultural choice, understandable for a people with a history of much space to cross to do their daily work. But other cultures facing similar spaces have not so chosen, and the elevation of speed into a national fetish in the United States during

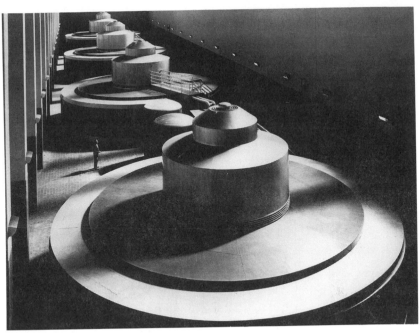

The turbine revolutionized production and use of electricity but resisted literary appropriation; however, these at Pickwick Dam yielded a metonymic series to a CCC photographer. (National Archives, Amer. Image no. 134)

the 1920s reveals a cultural preoccupation with transformation. "Speed" came to be the concomitant of personal change, the consumer's arrival at the new and better state that has long characterized the American project. This process of inner amelioration seemed easier, given the mind's propensities, among bright new things. As Jackson Lears has pointed out, such selections often proceeded under the guise of antimodernism, in the name of a therapeutic traditionalism (306–7). "There has been nothing like the airports," remarks Cecilia in Fitzgerald's *The Last Tycoon* (1941), "since the day of the stage stops . . . [or] stops on the great trade routes" (14).

NEW MATERIALS

Aluminum was the quintessential new metal: it was ductile, smooth, shiny, light, strong, and nonoxidizing—a solution in search of a problem. The Pittsburgh Reduction Company could find no major market until the advent of the aluminum camping trailer, which improved on the mobility, privacy, and ease of autos. Then the metal spread to railroad cars and airplanes and found its way into auto pistons and connecting rods. Soon cast aluminum cookware, radio bodies, and foil five thousandths of an inch thick were seen in households. By World War II, 75 percent of the weight of an airplane was aluminum (Oliver 583).

Skilled craftsmen had produced most glass before World War I, but the perfection of the Owens bottle-making machine automated the work of seven men, producing 240 perfect bottles per minute. Next applied to light bulbs, an Owens machine tripled production. Transparency was the primary kinesthetic quality of glass: glass became distortion-free and symbolically linked to the light it transmitted. From light bulbs to skylights to bottled drinks, glass transmitted the "truth" about content.

Plastics found scant employment in the United States until Dr. Leo H. Baekeland patented phenolic plastics that he called Bakelite. Bakelite replaced wood cabinetry during the radio revolution and appeared on many electrical products, because it was fireproof and an insulator. Rayon, nylon, and synthetic rubber followed, and around 1930 white urea-based plastics for dishes, tabletops, and appliance coatings appeared. So contemporary were they that Percy Marks titled his novel about college youth *The Plastic Age* (1924). Alkyd resins became the basis of thermal-setting lacquers and paints for cars, permitting quick-drying and brilliant colors. Philip Marlowe would note the "sweet and sinister" smell of "hot pyroxylin paint" in Chandler's *The Big Sleep* (173).[8]

Aluminum and rubber permitted rotogravure, printing from an etched, or depressed, surface. First used by the *New York Times* in 1912, rotogravure led to colors and to use of acetate photographic "screens" that could break down the solidity of images into thousands of tiny dots, replicating by an optical (metonymic) illusion the tonal values of photography. As finer dot matrices developed, news photos grew in size and number. The *Los Angeles Times* began to devote several pages on Saturday to recapping the week's lighter side in photos and captions. Such photo pages were initially exempla of the commercial class, but the press soon discovered that photos could connote speed, conflict, smoothness, and other emerging values.

By 1925 the United States had nearly 70 percent of the world's telephones, with the highest per-capita concentrations (after Washington) being in Los Angeles, San Francisco, and Pasadena.[9] The telegraph, with its per-word charges, had already encouraged *le style télégraphique* of Hemingway. The telephone too was initially expensive. Not only brevity but also the ability to leave the obvious implied were forms of communicative economy that became aesthetic values in the slang, ellipsis, and laconism of "tough talk."

The Jazz Singer was made possible by acetate cellulose rolled to thousandths of an inch, flexible and inexpensive. Then Lee DeForest used a photoelectric cell to convert sound to light, which was printed as a pattern on film. The condenser, microphone, amplifier, and vacuum tube came together in a General Electric laboratory in 1926, and in a few years Americans had established such a hegemony in motion pictures that 70 percent of the films shown in England and France were American-made. Like news photos, films quickly improved in visual resolution. From muddy images of static figures emerged a universe of crisply delineated men and women, buildings, animals, and landscapes. Film, which had initially imitated the Victorian stage, where emotion was elaborately mimed, reinvented narrative (e)motion. Griffith pioneered close-ups and crosscutting to reveal emotions by juxtaposition; then explanatory prefacing and titles dropped away. Though Griffith claimed to have taken this technique from Charles Dickens, intellectuals were shocked by the popularity and efficacy of emotion suggested through technique.

As a way of understanding life, film fomented an extraordinary shift. While using such conservative elements as character "types" and melodramatic plots, it invested narratives with the values of its materials (speed, light, ductility) and technologies (continuity, model change). Light and dark, plasticity and brittleness, the smooth and the rough, became nodes of filmic value. Above all, film promoted supersession, relentlessly disillusioning audiences about earlier narrative events and scenes; each movie, in turn, seemed to exaggerate a feature of its predecessor. Becoming the analogue of the annual model change, film accelerated narrative consumption. With a new film weekly, the sense of an original in human experience grew distant.

Technologies must be adopted before they foment shifts in popular understanding. Natural gas was a promising form of artificial light in 1910, but within twenty years no American understood the solution to darkness in terms other than electrical ones. Look at the figurative meanings such terms acquired: "turned on," "plugged in," "live wire," and "blown a fuse" (Nye 155–56). Such technologies infiltrate the ideology of daily life. Because they have been conceived as fulfilling a role in a process, automobiles, typewriters, and light bulbs stand only one remove from the technology that made them. In the hands of users, they can even induce the ideology of their production. But when an object's tool value is secondary, when its decorative function equals its utility, the technologies by which it was created fade behind its kinesthetic qualities, which become self-referential.

A molting of forms is the nature of technological impact on the appearance of common artifacts. The first automobiles looked like carriages or bicycles, the first telephones like speaking tubes, the first radios like end tables. Radically new forms, regardless of their function or efficiency, are seldom adopted by consumers immediately. Over time and by incremental changes, as they accept the function of the artifact, consumers adopt the new form.

The dominant kinesthetic trend between 1910 and 1940 was lightness. Weight, formerly a guarantee of value, became a problem because it increased shipping costs. From this came reductions in the weight of clothing, crates, cars, and all types of materials. There was an analogous change from the opaque or dark to the transparent. Advances in glass, lights, and interior design overthrew the serious, somber Victorian palette. Transparency led to a shift from tactile roughness to smoothness. Lightness under the fingertips, lightness on the tongue, and lightness in the ear replaced woolens and iron, corn liquor and hoe cakes, John Philip Sousa and organist Clarence Eddy.

The segmented, incremental, isolated, individual, or occasional gave way to the seamless, continual, uninterrupted, or scheduled. Welds replaced rivets; zippers replaced buttons; monocoque fairings replaced bolted plates; the twenty-four-hour cafeteria (invented in Los Angeles) upstaged the restaurant; sans serif typefaces such as Universal, Gill, and Futura replaced Gothic and Roman; in the "funny paper" the single panel of "Old Doc Yak" gave way to the comic strip of "Gasoline Alley."

High and low culture reflected technology differently. In high culture, as Hugh Kenner points out, the principles of mechanization were abstracted from machines, as the telegraphic "distance" of Eliot's voices, the "scientific organization" of Pound's sources, or the diagrammatic complexities of Picasso's cubism (8–9).[10] In popular culture, the objects produced by new technology were regarded asystemically, often with a faux naïveté, as wondrous or problematic. More attention was paid to their kinesthetic qualities. There is less narrative comedy about machinery in the workplace (Chaplin excepted) than about machinery in daily life. The ubiquitous auto humor and cartoons of Rube Goldberg treat artifacts in isolation.

The new materials, since they had no synecdochical meanings, tended toward their absolutes. Once it no longer had to refer to wood, plastic could be as light as possible: cutlery, airplane wings, and even auto bodies were formed of it. Radios could be sold not by their similarity to furniture but by their lightness. Most radical were the shapes of prestressed, reinforced concrete bridges, dams, and buildings. The rapid supersession of artifacts and the shift to lightness occasioned distressing overlaps, in which vestigial and new paradigms were in circulation at once. A critically important conflict of function and surface arose, epitomized by the 1932 Toledo scale. While consumers did not object to Streamform cars, chairs, or stoves, they wanted to see the mechanism of "honest weight."

Such supersession and overlaps accustomed the populace to design as an arbitration of value conflicts, and then as a value apart from function. Design, in turn, amplified the metonymic trend. The quoted style or the referred-to original were understood to valorize consumer items and even some tools, as much as their functionality did. This "referring-to" overcame the foreignness of new materials until their kinesthetic values became familiar, but it was also the basis on which mass marketing cultivated the annual style.

The continual supersession of the "new" led finally to designed obsolescence. After Kimberly Clark introduced Kleenex in the 1930s, disposability became part of some products. Paper cups, ballpoint pens, paperbacks, and clothing were designed for discard, leading to what Ann Ferebee has called "the dematerialization of the product" (98): the tool or artifact is replaced by a system. Eventually columns of hot, forced air would replace department store doors, so that a sensory value, like heat, replaced a material object, the door. This represents the arrival of consumerism at a purely metonymic state.

The Economy

Legions are convinced that when the stock market crashed in 1929 suicidal investors leapt from high windows. Yet as far back as 1954 John Kenneth Galbraith pointed out that "the number of suicides in October and November [1929] was comparatively low—in October, 1331 suicides in all the United States, and in November, 1344. In only three other months—January, February and September—did fewer people destroy themselves. During the summer months, when the market was doing beautifully, the number of suicides was substantially higher" (134).

Economic change seems to demand narrative explanation. In the case of the broken speculators, Galbraith noted that "suicide" became a figuration for the Crash: "At a time when broken speculators were plentiful, the newspapers and the public may simply have supplied the corollary. Alternatively, suicides that in other times would have evoked the question, 'Why do you suppose he did it?' now had the motive assigned automatically: 'The poor fellow was caught in the crash'" (135). As Galbraith pointed out, financiers also committed suicide by asphyxiation and immolation, but these do not appear in narrative. There are reasons in the figurative process: asphyxiation lacks the salient features of a man jumping from the window of his office, which always happens to be in a skyscraper. Symbolic setting, dynamic action, and axial values make good figures. In a better economy, such action would be demented. In one worse, such as that of 1932, leaping does not figure either. Rather than reality, narrative about the economy usually reflects figurative processes. The "Roaring Twenties" and the "Hard Times" of the thirties have figured those decades so long, so persuasively, that it is difficult to see the economy of the period whole or to recognize the infiltration of the metonymic into narratives about it. It is good to begin with economist John Garraty's reminder:

During the Great Depression, people who had full-time jobs were usually better off, at least economically, than they had been before 1929. This was true because in nearly every nation, the cost of living fell faster and further than wages fell. It is also worth noting that at all times, a large majority of the work force was employed. Put the other way around, the unemployed, although unprecedentedly numerous, were always a minority. Another important fact to remember is that unemployment, for a majority of those who suffered the experience, tended to be a temporary condition. (86)

The Depression, in other words, was not an economic inversion; it was multifaceted. The nature of market economies encourages multidirectionality, new industries being created while old ones die. But in extraordinary times the imagination begs for figurative comprehension, and in the twenties and thirties it begged forcefully. It was easier to see the figure in the carpet than the warp and woof of a changing economy.

Between 1900 and 1914 in the United States, Peter Fearon points out, "the employed farm labor force was static in number, while non-farm labor expanded from 16 million to 25 million" (3). Swelling the flow to cities were record numbers of foreign immigrants. This growing urban population formed a motivated industrial workforce and a body of avid consumers, but their tastes and purchasing power were not initially important in determining what was produced. It was the age of Ford and the logic of efficiency.

World War I buoyed farmers and brought unprecedented wages to city dwellers, who in turn increased their investments. The value of the steel, autos, cotton, flour, meat, and electric appliances produced by Americans doubled in five years. Production of petroleum and rubber quadrupled; shipbuilding increased tenfold. In feeding Europe, Americans raised the prices for cotton, corn, and wheat more than 200 percent in forty-eight months, creating a prosperity that came to seem normal. Europe's purchases were financed by American loans, turning the United States from the world's greatest debtor nation in 1914 to its largest creditor by 1925. Ironically, while international trade made them rich, Americans embraced isolationism.

The end of the war provoked a minor recession in the United States. Returning soldiers, like Harold Krebs of Hemingway's "Soldier's Home," found few jobs: unemployment rose from a rumor to 5.2 percent by 1919. But Krebs's parents had prospered, and their demand for cars and houses exploded in late 1919, stimulating a boom that carried into 1920. This was to be the pattern of the decade: a year of recession followed by two of expansion.[11] It was to be repeated three times, each cycle sharper than the preceding, creating the explanatory figure of the "roller coaster." The first drop came with the recession of 1920–21. Unemployment hit 11.7 percent, but consumer prices and government spending fell, and the problem seemed to correct itself. In 1921 the period designated as "normalcy" by President Harding began. Radios crackled everywhere, unemployment was 3.3 percent, and prices were stable. Krebs found a job and got married. Dexter Green expanded his dry-cleaning chain, while Jay Gatsby launched a "drug store." The gross national product grew at a rate that would average 3.4 percent over the decade, with four-fifths of that growth in consumer goods, which George Babbitt admired in Floral Heights.

The recession of 1924 was short and sharp, with stocks falling back 15 percent, to 1922 levels. But by 1925 another boom began that lasted through 1926. Enormous war loans were repaid by France and Great Britain with reparations from Germany, which borrowed from the United States. This acceleration of the money supply kept the 1927 recession short. "An increasing number of persons," wrote Galbraith, "were coming to the conclusion—the conclusion that is the common denominator of all speculative episodes—that they were predestined by luck, an unbeatable system, divine favor, access to inside information or exceptional financial acumen, to become rich without work" (x). As an economic figure, "speculation" had never been adopted so widely, in such anxious defiance of older economic understandings.

Among economists, 1927 is historic, Galbraith explains, because the central bankers of Great Britain, France, and Germany came to the United

States to lobby for easy money. The Fed obliged, cutting the rediscount rate from 4.0 to 3.5 percent. Funds flowed to the stock market, especially through margin accounts at brokerage houses and banks that required only 5 or 10 percent down. "Speculation on a large scale requires a pervasive sense of confidence and optimism and conviction that ordinary people were meant to be rich," Galbraith noted. It "must be nourished in part by those who participate. If savings are growing rapidly, people will place a lower marginal value on their accumulation." Speculation "is most likely to break out after a substantial period of prosperity" (174–75). Speculation is the shortcut by which prodigality seems to create savings.

Speculation was organized by "pools" (another new figure) that manipulated the prices of more than one hundred prominent stocks by 1929. In popular imagination (with a basis in fact), a hidden coterie controlled each pool, and from chauffeur to society matron, the public walked with its ears alert for clues to this coterie's intent. Prodigality depended on information, which, like money, was recycled; the nearer one stood to the source, the more the recycling enriched one. "Inside stuff" coming down and value rising, despite their opposition, became speculation's axial values.

The quest for easy money lasted until 1929. The price of the average common share doubled; unemployment was low (3.2 percent in 1929), inflation negligible, and the GNP rosy. But the markets for housing and autos were saturated, and inventory filled department stores and grain elevators. In March 1929 there were days of panic when some bankers wanted higher reserve and margin requirements, but popular sentiment for easy money prevailed. As Galbraith noted, "This was a world inhabited not by people who have to be persuaded to believe but by people who want an excuse to believe" (175).

According to scholars, the economy was already headed into its cyclical recession when the market crashed on October 29, 1929. Even the salesman interviewed by Studs Terkel for *Hard Times* knew something was amiss. "Up to [1928], people were buying very good and paying very good. But they started to speculate, and I felt it. My business was dropping from the beginning of 1928" (423–24). The causes of the Crash are still vociferously debated by partisans Left and Right.[12] But the stock market actually rebounded. "By the end of 1929," notes Garraty, "the October collapse no longer seemed particularly significant (except to those who had lost their shirts)" (31–32).

The shirts lost ranged from a dozen to a haberdashery, but the white-collar class felt *sans chemise*. The epitome of being caught short, as Galbraith noted, was the extraordinary rise in employees arrested for embezzling, presumably trying to meet their margin calls. Embezzlers "were far more common than the suicides," he writes (139). But they got no narrative.[13] Painful experience in speculation led some people to retreat to older types of economic understanding, from hoarding to primitive communism. But these turned out to be temporary retreats from a technological momentum that was rolling forward. Telegraphy and telephones provide an example. On October 21, 1929, the stock ticker was an hour behind at noon, an hour and forty minutes behind at 5:00 P.M. Many investors did not find out their stocks dropped until brokers liquidated their holdings for margin requirements. An ice storm in the Midwest knocked down telephone lines, so other investors got out while they could. In the following days, the ticker ran two hours behind. October 29 began at a thirty-three-million-share-a-day rate, triple the record. The rest is history. Did people perceive technology's failure? No. Rather, as Faulkner showed in *The Sound and the Fury*, the Jason Compsons blamed "eastern Jews" who controlled "information" about what was going on "at the top" (150).

Four months after the Crash, President Hoover proclaimed the "recession" over. Indeed, the fortunate majority that Garraty cites continued to buy. Automobile sales, off their peak of 1.1 million in 1929, never fell below 600,000 a year in the 1930s. A Chicago printer and his wife told Studs Terkel that in 1934 "we just stopped in, give 'em $600, all we had with us, and bought that [Studebaker]" (*Hard Times* 353). The number of cars on the road increased, and the production of cigarettes, shoes, and textiles changed little. The number of boilermakers dropped, but the number of switchboard operators increased (Lester V. Chandler 23). American longevity, 57.1 years in 1929, rose to 63.7 years by 1939 (Garraty 104).

The Depression was heterogeneous. Farmers, prosperous during World War I, had not shared greatly in the wealth of the 1920s. The 1930s left Detroit and Chicago devastated, but Richmond, home of the tobacco industry, went unscathed. Even in Michigan the unemployment rate was highest (34.3 percent) for fifteen to nineteen year olds and lowest (13.1 percent) for the thirty-to-thirty-nine-year-old men who might be expected to head families. Among black women in Detroit, however, the jobless rate was 75 percent, versus 19 percent for white women (Lester V. Chandler 37, 41). Black women got no narrative, while white family men did.

The bottom fell out in 1932, with unemployment reaching 23 percent. Hoover embraced the balanced budget, leaving relief to the private sector, but Franklin Roosevelt, taking office in 1933, was experimental, committed to "doing something." Initially he too wanted to balance the budget, but pressure to aid the states' relief efforts, his own public works projects, and the end of the gold standard in 1934 made for an expansionary atmosphere.

By 1937 industrial production had regained its 1929 level, but it was accompanied by inflation. Alarmed, Roosevelt cut expenditures and talked of balancing the budget just as new Social Security taxes reduced spendable income. "American industrial production slackened . . . then plummeted," writes Garraty. "On the stock exchange, the shares of manufacturing corporations fell about 40 percent in less than two months. By June 1938, national income was down by 13 percent, more than 11 million workers were jobless, and business profits were running at less than a quarter of what they had been the previous September" (243–44). Oddly, Roosevelt's misstep and this depression within the Depression seldom appear in narrative. Casting about for something that would work, Roosevelt's advisers embraced Keynesian economics at a moment when the specter of Germany on the march was forcing France, then Great Britain and the United States, into deficit spending for rearmament. From $7.4 billion in 1937, total federal government expenditures rose to $20.5 billion in 1941 (Lester V. Chandler 137).

No item changed America in the 1920s and 1930s as much as the automobile. The number of cars increased from 1.9 million in 1919 to 5.6 million in 1929. Putting America on the road demanded massive investment, consumed raw materials prodigiously, and made opulent profits. It urbanized northern cities and established satellites on the prairies. It sent recruiters to farming regions and the Black South to garner labor. It fostered secondary industries in glass, rubber, machine tools, electrical goods, and paint.

The dirt and plank roads that carried earlier traffic became insupportable. Streetcars were too limiting. The motorized American demanded all-weather highways, the Lynds reported, for by 1924 he used his car as much for business as for pleasure. State after state embarked on ambitious road-building programs. The extent and surfacing of streets became such a point of civic pride that Sinclair Lewis would feel obliged to prick it in his novels. Over 275,000 miles of new surfaced roadway supported the Motor Age, notes Lester Chandler, making a life beyond the radius of streetcar lines possible for an urban middle class that was struggling to find material situations commensurate with rising expectations (16). What to do about Depression unemployment? Put 'em to work building roads!

The auto even changed economic life among the poor. Workers that the Industrial Workers of the World (IWW) once organized by "riding the rods" by the 1920s "became 'rubber tramps' in broken down flivvers," an organizer reported to Terkel. By 1926 his members were "living in nearby towns, if there were decent roads between town and job. The automobile made it possible for a man to live a fairly settled life and fill these out-of-town jobs. The migratory worker had practically disappeared in '26. You didn't hear about him again until the Dust Bowl days" (*Hard Times* 307).

By 1932 it was clear that auto owners were not driving less; because of hard times, they used their cars more on business, and they drove as cheap entertainment. As they drove, Americans were stopping at roadside restaurants, motels, and attractions like the lion farms that interested James M. Cain. These businesses required little capital to enter and attracted the unemployed. Roads replaced train tracks as the nation's circulatory system and in its metaphoric vocabulary, making personal mobility a form of consumption rather than of commercial utility.

Paradoxically the Depression solidified the grip of the annual model change. Despite losses, the Big Three increased advertising. Their task was to attract reluctant buyers whose cars were lasting eight years (as opposed to five in 1920) and who had an attractive range of cheap used cars to choose from. The increase in ad linage for autos and their products fueled a robust magazine industry.

Immigration had run 1 million per year before World War I but fell to 25,000 in 1919. The number of Jews, Catholics, and foreigners in labor unions and in the strikes of 1919–20 produced xenophobia. During the 1921 recession, 650,000 eastern Europeans arrived, and Congress responded with the first in a series of restrictive acts, limiting European immigration to 358,000 annually (Fearon, *War* 22–23). In 1924 immigration was cut again, and Asians were banned entirely. In 1927 European immigration was cut to 154,000, but immigrants already formed one-seventh of the population and one-fifth of the workforce in some cities (Fearon, *War* 23). There were large numbers of unassimilated foreigners in the country, and native-born Americans resented not only the newcomers' strange ways but also their economic competition. "Bohunk" and "hunky" were anxious epithets not only in the Chicago of Carl Sandburg but in the Nebraska of Willa Cather and the Los Angeles of Raymond Chandler as well.

Tensions were particularly high in the late 1920s. Political and police corruption was widespread, and Prohibition had been greeted as a business opportunity by Johnny Torio, who hired Alphonse Capone as his marketing manager. Violence shocked urbanites, who were nervous about shoot-'em-ups that sprayed their neighborhoods with bullets and unsure about how they fit into a world of speakeasies and fixed policemen. But the usual immigrant problems—language, education, social status—were compounded by the increasing rationalization of the workplace and the inflation of consumer expectations.[14]

Immigrants were greeted by suspicion and hostility, especially those from southern and eastern Europe, mostly young males without dependents. Like Cain's George Papadakis, they appeared immediately in the labor force and took, it seemed, jobs from "real Americans." Sacco and Vanzetti were perceived as part of this pattern. F. Scott Fitzgerald put a Greek coffee shop in the Valley of Ashes in *The Great Gatsby* in 1925, the year that Hemingway wrote, in *In Our Time*, "Like all Greeks, he wanted to go to America."

The narratives we have about labor in this period tend to be dominated by dramatic strikes, usually in coalfields, on which Cain actually reported. But mining was in decline, and conflict was inevitable. Coal lost out as soon as natural gas was discovered. Likewise, the textile industry faced competition from synthetics like rayon and by new machinery. Other union activity focused on fading industries like boilermaking, shipbuilding, and shoemaking (Fearon, *Slump* 25, 63).

"The bulk of the new jobs which absorbed the expanding labour force," reports Fearon, "was created in the wholesale and retail trade, in finance and related services, in construction, and in government employment" (*Slump* 25). These were not usually filled by immigrants or farmers. Rather, Fearon notes, "when workers moved up the economic and social ladder, places opened for others to take the jobs they had vacated" (67). The older, urban American labor force "adopted middle class values and expectations": the millworker's son became an engineer. The new class tensions evident in many of the era's conventional novels, from Tarkington's *Alice Adams* (1921) to Cather's *The Professor's House* (1925), were more representative of American experience than agricultural dispossession or industrial violence.

The proportion of women working had increased during World War I, as women filled positions ranging from clerical to light manufacturing jobs. From 8.3 million in 1920, Fearon calculates, the number of women working rose to 10.6 million in 1930 (*Slump* 63). The increased presence of women in the workplace raised the suspicions of men, particularly union men, who agitated to reduce their numbers. Nonsexual fraternization and nonpatriarchal structure were novel, to say the least, and were often equated with communism (Fearon, *Slump* 65).

During the Depression, migration from farms to urban centers continued, but not as quickly as before. Urban unemployment was discouraging, as Cora finds out in Cain's *Postman*. Some city dwellers went to live with relatives on farms or took up subsistence farming. Louis Bromfield later described this in *Malabar Farm* (1948) as an exercise in idealism. The number of farm families increased until 1936, contrary to the impression left by Dust Bowl narratives.

The situation of blacks, who suffered the highest unemployment rates in the North and the worst sharecropping conditions in the South, was least improved by the New Deal. Farm aid went chiefly to whites. Work relief programs such as the CCC were segregated, and the NRA paid lower wages to blacks, when it hired them at all. Nor would Roosevelt commit himself to a federal law abolishing lynching. Southern racists like Faulkner's Percy Grim, who lusts after autos (*Light in August*, 1932), are mirrored by northern racists like James T. Farrell's William Lonigan (*The Young Manhood of Studs Lonigan*, 1934).

CONCEPTUALIZING THE ECONOMY

The rise of statistics has been explained by the use of artillery ballistics in World War I, by the spread of Heisenberg's theories, and by government collection of data on the unemployed during the Depression. The spread of consumer credit contributed, as did the rise of academic sociology. Professional sports had addicted millions of little boys (such as Ring Lardner) to batting averages, to say nothing of the attention people paid to the stock market. By the late 1920s statistics were considered mental exercise. The spread of the statistical worldview led to new commonplaces, such as the metaphor of "roulette," replacing that of "cards." Hammett would plant statistics at the core of *The Maltese Falcon* (1930).

The insights of statistics were used to calculate risks and to contain them (e.g., higher down payments for used cars, title to remain with seller). Auto dealers in California organized the first credit pool for cars around 1909 out of their own funds, but growth was slow. Banks avoided buying auto debt at first, fearing that consumers would default during hard times.[15] During World War I bankers noticed that consumers paid this debt, so they made a market. Suddenly everything was available on credit. "People were getting to consider it old-fashioned to limit their purchases to the amount of their cash balance," Allen wrote of the late 1920s. "The thing to do was to 'exercise their credit'" (140).

The magnitude of unemployment during the Depression is a subject of fierce debate. "In no industrial nation were adequate figures on unemployment available," Fearon writes; "some depended on labor unions to keep track of the jobless, some counted only those who qualified for relief, while others relied on unemployment insurance data." It is agreed that unemployment in the United States was more an urban than a rural problem. Geographically, it was a northern problem: by 1939 New York, Pennsylvania, Ohio, Illinois, and Massachusetts still had not regained the number of jobs they had had in 1929. In the South and in California the number of wage earners in 1939 surpassed the number in 1929. In the anomalous case of Washington, D.C., government jobs increased, and pay held constant, while prices declined 17 percent (Fearon, *Slump* 13, 139–40).[16]

The visibility of the unemployed—their soup lines, apple stands, and street-corner congregations—was disturbing to solid citizens. "People with jobs tended to view the unemployed with mixed feelings," writes Garraty. "They sympathized with them on humane grounds and because awareness of their plight was a reminder of their own vulnerability—'there but for the grace of God go I.' Yet they also feared the unemployed as possible competitors" (96). Job security was of enormous importance to everyone working; a conforming, obedient work behavior took hold, not only on the job but also in civic life. "The social and economic mobility characteristic of the previous decade slowed to a halt," says Garraty. "Few workers could feel safe when ever-larger numbers of their colleagues were out of work" (87).

The employed took few risks. Birth rates fell by 10 percent, marriage declined by about 20 percent, and even divorce diminished (Garraty 108). The jobless were linked to crime not only in the popular imagination but also by writers such as Farrell, Edward Anderson, and Hemingway. "It is obvious many unemployed people stole things they needed but could not afford and committed crimes of many kinds because of the emotional strains they were enduring," notes Garraty (108). Illegal occupation of foreclosed or abandoned houses was widespread and troubling; before 1930 few people had visibly lacked housing. Now homeowners might have squatters next door. Merchants watched customers closely, and landlords let unpaid rent go rather than irritate occupants or risk having properties broken into and vandalized. A low-level wariness about one's fellows was pervasive, exacerbated by attention given to Capone, John Dillinger, and gangster movies, beginning with *The Public Enemy* (1931). Writers such as Nelson Algren (*Somebody in Boots*, 1935) proved they could up the ante.

The failure of synecdoche to provide figurative distinctions between cases may have presaged its decline. The vague economic link between foreclosed farmers and Bonnie and Clyde, for example, romanticized and justified the pair for some people, but the same synecdochical process linked the foreclosed corner saloon keeper who refused to move with Al

Capone. Synecdoche integrated everyone into the same telos. By the end of the decade, broadly antigangster narratives arose, such as *Bullets or Ballets* (1936). *Brother Orchid* (1940) even showed Edward G. Robinson knocking off Humphrey Bogart, then joining a monastic order!

Public anxiety settled largely on tramps. Although never numbering more than a few hundred thousand, tramps recalled the older railroad era's hobos and linked them to road-building of the twenties and thirties. Edward Anderson's *Hungry Men* (1935) and Steinbeck's *The Grapes of Wrath* (1939) use, respectively, the old and new technological backgrounds. But sympathy for tramps opened the synecdoche and demanded case-by-case evaluation, so that *tramp* became more metonymic. By the time Cain wrote retrospectively about the Depression in *Mildred Pierce* (1940), he presented the jobless as part of a mechanistic, extrinsic condition.

Those laid off were generally older, a trend already noted by the Lynds in 1924, or those just entering the workforce. Middle-aged white managers retained their cohort. There was a great deal of trading down: "Domestic service and waiting-on-table, which previously had been monopolized by blacks, now attracted white competition," writes Fearon (*Slump* 137). Acel Steckler of *Hungry Men*, an aspiring musician, is reduced to dishwasher, and Cain's "grass widow" Mildred falls to waitressing. Fearon cites a 1932 survey that shows the average salary falling 15 percent from 1929, the average wage 11 percent. Where wages held steady, hours worked often declined. Share-the-work schemes abounded, so that even among those employed in manufacturing, the workweek fell to 34.6 hours in 1934 (*Slump* 138, 140).

California had occupied an important position in economic mythology since the Gold Rush, one confirmed by its land boom in the 1880s, its oil boom in the 1920s, and its apparently recession-proof citrus, tourism, film, and retirement economies early in the Depression. "Movement generally," reports Fearon, "was in a westerly direction with California as the desired destination for many." The first migrants had plans. "Many on the move were relatively well educated compared with those on relief, had smaller families and a clear destination in mind. They were not aimless wanderers but were moving to areas where they had personal contacts" (*Slump* 141, 253).

Later waves were desperate: hobos and flivver families like the Joads of

Grapes of Wrath, who were stopped at the border. "There was a delayed re-action to the events of October, 1929," noted Cary McWilliams, a lawyer who had migrated in 1922 (McWilliams 297). "In a year or two," he told Terkel, "I saw the impact on clients—the kind of widows who are legion in Southern California. Who had brought money out from the Middle West and had invested it in fly-by-night real estate promotions. They began to lose their property. . . . There was a feverish activity in foreclosures" (*Hard Times* 241).

By 1934 McWilliams had become California commissioner of housing and immigration and estimated that there were three hundred thousand unemployed in Los Angeles County alone. No better summary of the anxiety of white-collar and retired Californians could be wished than a re-port he quotes from the State Relief Administration bulletin for June 1934:

> Unemployment due to depressions is distorted and prolonged in Los Angeles by the deficiency of productive industries. . . . It is believed that the oil boom of the early 1920s, the motion pictures, and real estate booms, the stimulations of tourist trade and migrations by the local chambers of commerce, have over-populated the county with white collar workers. Permanent jobs do not exist for them within the basic in-dustries of the county. The population is over 85% urban, concentrated in 29 cities, most of which cluster around Los Angeles. Since 1920, the population has more than doubled. The proportion of white collar workers to all gainfully employed workers has become almost double that of the United States as a whole. . . . The productive industries do not appear large enough to justify the size of the white collar class. . . . less than one out of twenty gainful workers is employed normally in agriculture, against one out of five for the United States. (297)

In fact, the lack of heavy industry saved California from the worst of the Depression. The high average age (forty-five years versus thirty-five years for the nation) meant that Los Angeles supplied fewer expensive services, such as schools, prisons, and police. The ratio of farm workers indicates that agriculture was efficient. But the report is explicable if we realize that most Californians were originally easterners and interpreted the De-pression by older figures, despite the postindustrial economy developing around them.

First the Chinese, then the Japanese, had dominated California farm labor, but the latter organized and then were successful as truck farmers. Less quick to form unions, boarding clubs, or cooperatives, Mexicans were exploited by white farm barons. Their numbers rose from 121,000 in 1920 to 368,000 in 1930 (Starr, *Material Dreams* 172–74). African Americans in number were absent from California before 1916, but after 1920 they deserted the rural South like other small farmers; their early experience in Los Angeles was captured by Arna Bontemps (*God Sends Sunday*, 1931) and Gilmore Millen (*Sweet Man*, 1932). This layering of migrant classes contributed to white-collar anxiety. Members of this class saw themselves as too numerous, without the basic industries present elsewhere. The Folks, as Bruce Barton called them, took the situation to heart: their status in utopia was uncertain. Ways of relieving this anxiety, most immediately, were political.

Upton Sinclair had moved to Pasadena in 1915 at the peak of his fame and ran for the Democratic nomination for governor in 1934. With only his pamphlet *I, Governor of California* in hand, he organized the movement End Poverty in California (EPIC). The idea was to turn over unused state land to the unemployed to grow crops and to transfer unused factories to unemployed workers to make products. Their goods would be traded for scrip that would circulate among those without money. More than eight hundred EPIC clubs were formed by "the little people," and Sinclair captured the nomination. McWilliams reports seeing "New Economy barber shops, Epic cafes, and Plenty-for-All stores in the most remote and inaccessible communities in California" (298).

Several events combined to defeat Sinclair. One was the San Francisco general strike of 1934, a manifestation of radical labor and "foreign immigrant" power that terrified the white-collar class. At least ten million dollars was raised by the California oligarchy to defeat Sinclair, with the advertising and film industries collaborating on documentaries showing hobos flooding the state. Still, if a third-party candidate had not siphoned off three hundred thousand votes, Sinclair might have defeated former Iowan Frank Merriam for the governorship (McWilliams 298).

New economic figuration centered in southern California to a striking degree, arising from the idealistic strain imported by pioneers, adventurers, religious splinter groups, and retirees. Californians felt themselves "an island apart." Los Angeles was still one of the whitest areas of the United States. Many whites had moved there to participate in utopian movements, but they were confronted by the paradox that McWilliams described to Terkel: "You saw California as synonymous with abundance. It's so enormously rich, especially in agriculture. Yet you saw all kinds of crops being destroyed. There were dumps in southern California, where they would throw citrus fruits and spray them with tar and chemicals" (*Hard Times* 242–43).

The new economic figures tried out in California anticipated many of the nation's post–World War II economic metaphors. The first and briefest of these was Technocracy, a technology-will-save-us movement. The *Los Angeles Daily News* ran a series of glowing articles on it in 1932, attracting to its pressroom doors crowds of people waving dollar bills for copies of the paper. Technocracy failed for simple reasons: no one would invest in the technology, it did not have a compelling figuration, and its most popular aspects were passwords and the secret handshake. It failed to capitalize on new economic patterns like the "flow" of credit, stock, and oil. Second was the Utopian Society, organized in 1933 by a former stock kiter for Julian Petroleum. This group appealed to the Folks and small businessmen with its Depression-era technique of chain-letter recruitment and its secret rituals mimicking the dying fraternal organizations of the heartland. By 1934, McWilliams estimates, it had five hundred thousand adherents; its first public meeting, attended by twenty-five thousand, had to be held in the Hollywood Bowl (295). Eventually it became the vehicle of Sinclair's EPIC candidacy.

Sinclair's defeat in 1934 left the field to Dr. Francis Townsend, a South Dakota migrant who dressed up a revolving pension scheme he had read about, calling it the Townsend Plan. Unlike Technocracy and EPIC, which focused on production and exchange, the Townsend Plan was about consumption. Every American over sixty would receive two hundred dollars a month in scrip, with funds to be raised by a transactions tax. The scrip had to be spent within a month, accelerating the velocity of money and stimulating production. Not unexpectedly, the Townsend movement was based in Long Beach, where thousands of retirees from Iowa lived. The Republican nominee for governor, Merriam, adopted the plan as his response to Sinclair's EPIC movement. Elected, Merriam abandoned the plan when he found it would cost twenty-four billion dollars a year, half the national income (Garraty 153; McWilliams 294–300).

It is instructive to compare this scheme with the one most popular in the East, the Share the Wealth program of Senator Huey P. Long. Whereas the Townsend Plan was a metonymic figure of the circulation of credit, Share the Wealth renovated the old dream of seizing the money of the rich. Long proposed to confiscate all fortunes over eight million dollars, to enact an income tax reaching 100 percent at one million dollars, and to give all families a stake or "homestead" of five thousand dollars and an income of two thousand dollars. The rich, said Long, are "pigs swilling in the trough of luxury" (Garraty 172).

Long's plan was too crude for Californians. "In an area without smoke-stacks where the sale of real estate has been the major industry," McWilliams noted, "there are no visible symbols upon which the distressed masses can vent their fury" (303). It made more sense to figure life in the patterns of local climate, geography, migration, and autos—circulation. The scarcity of water stood out; Los Angeles's water had a distant origin, flowed through aqueducts, and was pooled behind dams. Speculation in stocks and real estate had prepared a swelling middle class for the idea that "credit" was analogous to this flow. In their apprehension of the watercourse way of credit, Californians were Keynesians before Roosevelt. They saw no shortage of goods; unharvested vegetables rotted on the ground, and wells burned off excess oil. The flow of production and consumption had been interrupted somewhere.

Los Angeleans knew about dams and pools. The Los Angeles Aqueduct had them, as would the Hoover Dam, completed in 1936. Sometimes after a rain, flash floods brought a cannonade of boulders down dry watercourses, as an astonished Raymond Chandler noted at La Crescenta in 1934. In March 1938, eleven inches of rain made the Los Angeles plain into a sea, an event that novelist Rupert Hughes turned into the local classic City of Angels (1941). Invariably it was trouble upstream. As McWilliams saw, however, there was no one Californians could point at, since these water projects were their own. The impetus for a metonymic elision grew.

Some Californians were prepared to believe that the crisis owed to the

"This is our last night together, until I return from my honeymoon."

Cartoons from *Americana* magazine attacked the rich savagely during the Depression but were too crude for Californians, who were mostly middle class, had no smokestack industry, and saw no obvious villains.

"We must hire some new servants; I've borrowed the cook's last dollar."

"Of course we could live cheaper in France but we can only get credit in America."

Addition

Subtraction

eastern bogeymen who had caused them to head west—the corrupt politician and his counterpart, the gangster. The *Los Angeles Times* relentlessly alleged a connection between Tammany Hall, Al Smith, and Democrats generally. The gangster as economic villain also had a local angle: it put the source of evil outside California and made the villain a migrant. "Some very tough people have checked in," Chandler explained, "the penalty of growth" (*Big Sleep* 67). In contrast to the murders in eastern gangster narratives, California versions favored blackmail, kidnapping, and bootlegging. A threat against reputation, blackmail appealed because it actually happened in Hollywood and because Los Angeleans, as migrants, depended on the stability of the reputations they brought. Kidnapping intensified this threat, and the Lindbergh baby kidnapping created a referable master narrative.

Bootlegging existed in Los Angeles, but certainly less than in other major cities. Los Angeles had voted itself dry long before the Volstead Act and had fewer saloons and more churches per capita than any other West Coast city. Much of the liquor that was bootlegged in came by boat, giving rise to a romance of moonless nights and deserted coves that Chandler used in his short stories. Metaphorically, liquor fit the California templates of water and flow; the flow had been cut somewhere above, and a "gangster" was controlling the downward drip.

Dust Bowl migration to California started another paradigm. First the hobos, then the Okies, were discovered to import a pestilence. The Folks wanted everyone to stay where they were. Chandler made clear in *The Little Sister* (1949) that the disease started back in Iowa, in Kansas, or in Nebraska. This appealed to those who, like Chandler, arrived earlier and felt that that fact conferred status. Consciousness of this double standard was keen, but it was represented unevenly. In Cain's narratives, the new Californian was the victim of "double jeopardy."

The inevitability of economic downturns also complemented a latent Puritan sense of self versus soul. The durability of such oppositions is evident in the writing of economists: Wesley Clair Powell, in *Business Cycles* (1913), wrote that "prosperity engenders a crisis, by which crisis turns into depression, and by which depression finally leads to . . . a revival of activity" (Garraty 7). As late as 1932 Stuart Chase described economic cycles as "the spree and hangover of an undisciplined economy" (Garraty 7). The Depression, in short, was commonly understood as punishment for the twenties. Even James Agee, who made a painstaking effort to see without prefiguration, reverted to his childhood Anglicanism: "You never know what is enough, until you know what is more than enough," he concluded in *Let Us Now Praise Famous Men* (418).

That popular culture was less dour and more disposed to self-reliance is hardly surprising. There was "an almost universal liveliness," wrote Josephine Herbst about the 1930s, "that countervailed universal suffering" (776). "Most of us wore clean shirts and shined our shoes," wrote T. Owen Horan. "There was a general sense of optimism: 'Things may be tough now, but they are going to get better'" (4C). From a renewed interest in Horatio Alger's novels to the success of Disney's *Three Little Pigs* (1933) and the upbeat films of Frank Capra, audiences were looking for the bright side. Hard-boiled optimism dominated new professions like advertising, as pioneer William Benton told Terkel: "With more men out of work, we'd have an easier time finding good salesmen. By multiplying our salesmen, we'd have an offset to the fact that there are fewer people to whom to sell" (*Hard Times* 65).

One self-reliant alternative was small-scale entrepreneurship. While larger retail outlets failed, thousands of small cafés, bars, and restaurants opened, many along popular highways. The 1933 Census of Business reveals that 25 percent of service businesses then in operation had begun after 1929. They included beauty parlors, hand laundries, repair shops, furniture refinishing shops, and shoe-shine emporiums (Fearon, *War* 144–45). Their owners have a special status in oral tradition, for they and their chroniclers note repeatedly that they were ashamed to accept charity. But in high culture representations, such "little people" on the make, from Faulkner's Snopeses to Nathanael West's Greeners, were portrayed with that hustling attitude that had been deplored by intellectuals since *Babbitt* (1922). The mass readership during the Depression rejected this view, however, turning Dale Carnegie's *How to Win Friends and Influence People* (1938) into a best-seller year after year.

Another figurative shift concerned women, whose gains did not contract, as one might expect. Garraty notes that "proportionately fewer women were laid off than men. This was true partly because most women were paid lower wages than men for the same work. Employers tended to keep them on when it was necessary to cut back. Also, the kinds of work that women did were not as hard hit" (115–16). The common effect of male unemployment was to increase the influence of women, as wives and as mothers. G. H. Elder Jr.'s study of Oakland households (*Children of the Depression*, 1974) describes the "mother's centrality as decision maker and emotional resource . . . among deprived households" (in Garraty 114). Garraty reports that attendant problems were the father's loss of status with his children, resentment at his wife's economic dominance (when she got a job), sexual dysfunction due to poor nutrition, apathy, or fear of pregnancy, and isolation from neighbors or social cohort (115). Terkel heard from a psychiatrist that miners in Pennsylvania "were loathe to go home because they were indicted, as if it were their fault for being unemployed. A jobless man was a lazy good-for-nothing. The women punished the men for not bringing home the bacon, by withholding themselves sexually. By belittling and emasculating the men, undermining their paternal authority, turning to the eldest son" (*Hard Times* 196). This fits the fabula of roman noir, evident in, for example, the "unemployed husband" in Cain's *Mildred Pierce*, and "emasculating women" became a staple of film noir.

Design

In the opening lines of *The Maltese Falcon*, Dashiell Hammett described his hero's face as "a V *motif.*" His mouth, nose, eyes, brows, and hair repeated that pattern to suggest a "blond satan." It was one of the first conscious uses of art nouveau in American popular literature, and it epitomizes the complex of technological and economic forces affecting the mass of Americans. The V-motif is a design that finds the overlap in two systems, or patterns, and attempts to go forward by eliding their differences.

To understand the newness of Hammett's character, we must look at what went before. In the early 1900s Americans saw new designs only on radically new objects, such as the Hoover electric vacuum cleaner of

1909. In architecture, furniture, tableware—objects with histories—consumers chose among neo-Gothic, Greek revival, and Romanesque styles, the traditional imprimaturs of quality. Neither consumers nor intellectuals in 1900 saw anything wrong with new technologies and materials imitating handicraft and traditional materials. In fact, they exulted in the contradictions of plywood Louis XIV chairs, cast-iron flatware decorated with Renaissance cabbage roses, and automobiles advertised in Egyptian typefaces. The cultures and values quoted were not only supposed to ease anxiety about quality but also to invoke a legitimating narrative. Synecdochical mottoes were stitched into samplers, carved into chairs, embossed on mirrors, and enameled on shaving mugs. A chair might feature picturesque curved arms and legs, a suggestive rococo back, and upholstery decorated with emblematic flowers, angels, vines, and animals, yet be stamped in steel and painted to simulate wood grain. The influential "dog chair" of A. Jones shown at the Crystal Palace Exhibition in 1851 was typical of Genteel Age America. It had arms formed by greyhounds and the motto "Gentle when stroked, angry when provoked" carved into the back. The same exhibition popularized H. Fitz Cook's Daydreamer chair, whose ornamentation required an explanatory pamphlet: "The chair is decorated at the top with two winged thoughts—the one with bird-like pinions, and crowned with roses, representing joyous dreams, the other with leather bat-like wings—unpleasant and troubled ones. Behind is displayed Hope, under the figure of the rising sun. . . . The style is Italian" (in Ferebee 26).[17]

Manufacturers did not deny the underlying processes or materials of Victorian objects due to a reticence about technology. Rather, the late nineteenth century had been relatively good to Americans, so they continued to draw their values from it. Late Victorian taste ran to silk, wood, ivory, horn, or stone; cast iron was de rigueur for stoves, tubs, and kitchenware. Yet these materials per se and their uses were often overshadowed by their decoration, as buyers legitimated their taste and status through ornamentation. Thorstein Veblen decried this "conspicuous consumption" in *The Theory of the Leisure Class* (1899), but once initiated, buyers wanted filigree, turrets, embossing, cherubs, and gold leaf. The essence of objects became their surfaces, and in retrospect we see that the excess of Victorian style provided the fissure in which modern design took root.

The "dog chair" of A. Jones from the 1851 Crystal Palace Exhibition typified late Victorian taste in the United States, blending the picturesque, the rococo, and the synecdochical. The Daydreamer chair of H. Fitz Cook even required a pamphlet to explain all its emblems, animals, and symbols.

New technologies were at first employed to produce old forms quickly and cheaply. Iron-framed buildings had appeared in the United States in the 1850s, but their cast-iron facades resembled stone. The new steel typefaces of William Morris (called Troy and Chaucer) imitated calligraphy. The electroplating of cast-iron "silver" reduced the cost of flatware and permitted a high degree of ornament. Snag-proof rubber boots imitated the look of leather without its permeability or cost.

Improved rail transport and the growing network of roads introduced truly national markets for these items but made weight and durability critical. Demand for heavy, brittle materials such as cast iron fell, and the decline of Europe's colonial empires reduced the supply of horn, ivory, leather, and rare woods. Manufacturers turned to advertising to promote demand between 1900 and 1915, affecting the American notion of textuality, as Jennifer Wicke has argued (3–15); illustrations and then photographs were featured in ads, not to mention product "promise" and the testimonial. Ads "cannibalized" narrative forms and usurped the discourse of daily life. In this realm, objects were fragmented into advertising "qualities" and lost their organic, synecdochical wholeness. In the 1930s George Gallup and scientific surveying gave manufacturers the ability to measure such qualities, and advertising became a feature of all products, making them metonymic equals except as advertising could put one feature forward. But this was only half of a cybernetic process, for consumers wanted ever more "features."

"Functionalism" describes the period marked by the advent of the Ford Model T in 1908 and its end in 1927. New mass production techniques affected new artifacts first, so new forms typified autos, typewriters, telephones, radios, and washing and sewing machines. At first engineers designed these new products, because efficiency was more significant than appearance. Utilitarian products seemed to need no "style," or else they inclined buyers to the native wisdom of Horatio Greenough that "form follows function." Many items were destined for the kitchen, which engineers deemed a "women's factory floor" in need of labor-saving devices. For the nascent aesthetic of functionalism to spread and to influence design generally, however, it had to make peace with the public preference for ornament. The plaint about ugliness was not unique to Ford's Model T: it was uttered of Frigidaires too. Manufacturing needed a style that mediated between the organic, decorative, and narrative forms of late Victorianism and the aesthetics that arose from efficiencies of production.

Art nouveau was to be this style. Aubrey Beardsley and Oscar Wilde may seem to link it to fin de siècle decadence rather than to the machine aesthetic, but "their difference was in taste rather than technique, in content rather than style," writes design historian Ann Ferebee (58). Art nouveau emphasized lightness and space; rather than decoration, it favored emphatic outline. In place of the object ornamented, uniform patterns dominated surfaces. Symbolic peacocks, lilies, and swans replaced specific cultural quotation and narrative contextualization. White or empty space became a positive design value, flattening surfaces and reducing the importance of perspective, symmetry, and background. The geometric forms, straight lines, and pedestals of Victorian design were replaced by the whiplash, the spiral, the arabesque, and biomorphic motifs borrowed from the Celtic revival. The whiplash, as though curled by electricity, particularly expressed the era's tensions; it could be multiplied, lengthened, or shortened to cover entire surfaces, as Beardsley demonstrated. But even with the familiarity of nature, art nouveau was more metonymic than Victorian design.

In spite of the organic suggestion, most objects given art nouveau style were quintessentially functional. Witness Hector Guimard's wrought-iron entrances to the Paris Metro or Louis Tiffany's electric lamps fashioned to look like trees. The art nouveau typography pioneered by Eugene Grasset, Otto Eckmann, and Henri van de Velde created new curvilinear typefaces that were more readable and connoted more speed. In poster work and illustration, Arthur Mackmurdo's biomorphic patterns covered whole surfaces, and Beardsley's Yellow Book emptied white spaces to stand in dramatic contrast to black masses. Art nouveau had a pseudoaesthetic expressed by Oscar Wilde: "All art is at once surface and symbol. Those who go beneath the surface do so at their peril. Those who read the symbol do so at their peril" (in Ferebee 61). Consumers couldn't have cared less about such peril, as their habits of perception skated over the surface.

The first art nouveau designs that found wide application were for furniture. Michael Thonet, a Vienna designer, anticipated both their style

LE GRASSET

DANS l'évolution actuelle des arts de la décoration, la plus importante lacune restant à combler était celle d'un caractère typographique synthétisant, pour l'Imprimerie, le goût moderne, comme jadis les Alde, les Elzévir, les Didot furent, typographiquement, l'émanation de l'art de leur époque.

The art nouveau typography of (*from bottom left*) Henri van de Velde, Otto Eckmann, and Eugene Grasset was more readable and connoted speed, while Arthur Mackmurdo's biomorphic designs, as exemplified in this title page, provided a familiarizing hint of nature but were easily mass produced.

The change from synecdochical to metonymic design appears even in the spot illustrations used by newspapers and magazines. The set on the left, from the early 1920s, reflects an organic, static, Victorian, and highly detailed visual worldview; the set on the right, from the 1930s, is streamlined, smooth, dynamic, and metonymic.

and production techniques with his bentwood chairs, which he produced using lamination, heat-molding, and untrained workmen. He built factories near beech forests and established a worldwide distribution system that sold fifty million Vienna café chairs before World War I. These light, open, curvilinear forms were copied by other designers for staircases, balconies, pillars, candelabra, and desks.

Just as electric lights in houses suggested sunshine, skylights and picture windows of improved glass flooded interiors with real light. In such radiance no one needed the Victorian palette of red and gold to suggest sparkle; the new interior decor combined gray, pink, light green, and olive. The chemical synthesis of aniline purple in England, dubbed *mauve* by the French, produced an immediately popular pastel and spurred development of the dye industry. With new color schemes, interior light, and curvilinear furniture, a unified style was created that overturned Victorian taste.

Art nouveau quickly became an international movement. The lean designs of Peter Behrens, who is credited with being the first "industrial designer," were displayed at the 1912 exhibit of German applied art in Newark, New Jersey, and caused excitement. That they could be adapted to mass production was not lost on American visitors. Within eight years an American named Joseph Sinel had coined the phrase "industrial designer" and had stamped it on his letterhead.[18]

The term *art deco* originated with the 1925 Paris Exposition des Arts Décoratifs. While that show failed to define a unified European style, it did present a grammar of design perfectly suited to new manufacturing processes and materials in the United States. *Art deco* is used here to signify the late stage of art nouveau, sharing its emphasis on lightness, surface pattern, outline, rhythmic line, and the pastel palette, but straightening the curvilinear line and discarding the hint of symbolism that recalled synecdoche in art nouveau.

As early as 1919, a young French émigré named Raymond Loewy had noted that the products of American manufacturers were "absorbed, by an eager public, on performance alone and in spite of appearances. The country was flooded with refrigerators perched on spindly legs, and others topped by clumsy towering tanks. Typewriters were enormous and sinister-looking. Carpet sweepers when stored away took the greater part of a closet, and telephones looked (this is no pun) disconnected. I felt that the smart manufacturer who would build a well-designed product at a competitive price would have a clear advantage over the rest of the field when things would become tough" (76–77). Loewy's sense that "things would become tough" eventually proved correct. Macy's, where he began work as a window trimmer, was overstocked at the end of the 1926 boom, while Americans "doing" Europe on the strength of the postwar dollar brought back Bentleys, Swiss kitchenware, and Italian clothes, introducing a status disdain for domestic manufacture.

Loewy, W. D. Teague, and Norman Bel Geddes—the pioneer industrial designers—were hired in the mid-1920s by manufacturers anxious to redesign their products to make them more attractive. One of the first fields of battle was, ironically, duplicating machines. Loewy, whose training was in commercial illustration, found his first assignment in reshaping the Gestetner. At about the same time, Teague, also an illustrator, was hired by Mimeograph. Their designs employed new, smooth housings, and although no victor is recorded, some smaller firms dropped from the business.

A graduate of the Chicago Art Institute, Geddes had worked in commercial illustration before turning to Broadway, for which he designed the sets, props, and costumes of some ninety productions. In 1926 he decided to become part of the larger world, designing things people used. That frantic manufacturers paid ten times what he earned illustrating was no disincentive. Geddes designed Toledo scales (1929), Oriole stoves (1932), and National cash registers (1935), as well as buses, cars, and the J. Walter Thompson advertising offices. This range of products, with a focus on "white goods" and electrical appliances, was typical, as was the alliance with advertising. Unlike the Europeans, American designers were employed from the start, in the words of designer Harold Van Doren, to "make things irresistible" (in Sparke 96).

American designers took important elements from architecture. The steel framing of skyscrapers allowed "curtain walls" to be hung from their skeletons, a technique that required lightness and uniformity of sheathing material. No longer were blocks, cornices, or ornaments cut for specific niches: instead, steel blanks were stamped to accept rivets. These "million-windowed" skyscrapers, as Dos Passos called them, were among the first truly modern designs to find popular and intellectual welcome in the United States. Writers from Henry Blake Fuller (*The Cliff-Dwellers*, 1893) on employed these buildings in narrative, while photographs by Margaret Bourke-White and Alfred Stieglitz iconized them. The curtain wall made the exterior the easiest part of the job. The "sheath" was tall and smooth: verticality was its essence. Architects emphasized this height by "stepping back" the body of the building every ten or twelve stories. This ziggurat appearance broke the line of visual perspective, tapering to suggest an ultimate summit out of sight, like a mountaintop.

Curtain walls and "step-form" were immediately deployed by the new industrial designers on commercial objects, from furniture to radios and clothing. For most Americans, step-form *is* art deco. Its spread fomented a change in the way consumers perceived objects. The "accelerated perspective" of step-form is a discontinuous linearity that moves in a discernible direction. The eye and imagination can be habituated to the rhythm of the step, anticipating the next segment; one might say this is the style's pleasure. While the acceleration is principally visual, suggesting that the series of jumps will result in a finale—the skyscraper's pinnacle, the mountain's summit—the perceptual paradigm is actually broader. The "grace and slenderness" that Loewy emphasized derive not so much from the profile of step-form as from narrowly spaced parallel lines and rhythmic repetition of complementary geometric forms. The mode of perception suggested by step-form is both episodic and telegraphic. It hints that design need not be continuous; a series here and another later are enough to suggest the general direction. The resolution is only a metonymic part of a whole, over which meaning is evenly dispersed. This is the style of Jay Gatsby, of whom Fitzgerald wrote, "If personality is an unbroken series of successful gestures, then there was something gorgeous about him" (8). This is something very different from the Victorian predilection for synecdochical heroes or heroines or quoted mottoes that invoke legitimating narratives.

Sheathing (curtain walls) was the other important element of this new design grammar. The rationale for its incorporation in consumer goods, given its origin and function in architecture, was dubious until Glenn Curtiss conducted his streamlining experiments on automobiles. Aeronautics

A steel skeleton and curtain walls made possible Ralph Walker's design for the Barclay-Vesey Building in 1922. The narrowly spaced parallel lines and rhythmic step-forming suggest a mode of perception both episodic and telegraphic. (Syracuse University Library, Department of Special Collections)

was among the most visible design practices, and hints that it offered were regarded as irrefutable. In one experiment, Curtiss purchased a showroom auto that ran seventy-four miles per hour, removed the body, and placed it on the chassis backward. Then he drove the same car eighty-seven miles per hour. The smoothly tapered trunk created less drag. In later tests Curtiss showed that the speed of practically any car could be improved by 20 percent at twenty-five miles per hour through streamlining (Geddes 40).

Since the "speed" of mechanical objects was an important cultural factor in their sales, manufacturers redesigned their products to take advantage of this "free" increment of function. Streamlining was highly compatible with drawn aluminum and stamped steel blanks, which could be hung on frames and riveted or welded together. Streamlining items made of iron also reduced labor and weight, hence their cost and shipping expense. Speed became an absolute value, apart from functionality; if that was what consumers wanted, bread boxes and vacuum cleaners could be made to look fast. Sheathing soon acquired the metonymic value of speed, to the extent that a woman wearing a sheath dress was a "fast woman" or a "speed." Designers were of paramount importance in this perceptual reorientation, for the battle was waged during the Depression. Less visible was the shift in power from manufacturer to consumer that the infatuation with styling marked: manufacturers who once designed objects by production logic, like Ford, found they had to cater to mass taste, as Sloan did.

STREAMFORM

After designing the award-winning 1934 Hupmobile, Raymond Loewy defined Streamform as "the elimination of cracks, joints, rivets, screws, etc. Another thing to be avoided is the feeling of boxiness. The general mass should be flowing, graceful, free of sharp corners and brutal radii. This within the bounds of restraint, of course, as many a designer overdoes it and the end result is bulbous, fat and without character: what we call the 'jellymold school of design'" (213). The advantages of such design to a manufacturer using steel stamping technology are obvious. Loewy's locomotives were monocoques, welded into one piece and lowered over the engine and chassis. He and his colleagues spread Streamform to objects for which it posed no advantage. In his Gestetner duplicating machine and the Sears Coldspot refrigerator, Loewy justified sheathing by the reduction of noise, dirt, or visual clutter. Soon objects from toasters to typewriters—including Loewy's famous Coca-Cola dispenser—appeared in aerodynamic fairings, as if prepared for takeoff.

His competitor Norman Bel Geddes, because he redesigned the Toledo scale, was among the first to discover that sheathing created an inner/outer conflict. Geddes changed the scales from cast iron to stamped steel easily enough but was stymied by the advertising claim "No springs—honest weight" emblazoned on the open mechanisms of the scale. To cover the innards with a fairing would cast doubt on the integrity of the tool and its synecdochical promise. Such fairings had succeeded on automobiles, whose engines had bothered their owners until they gave up repairing them, and on telephones, which were not self-serviceable. But scales determined monetary value; hence their integrity required that inside and outside be consonant. Geddes's ingenious solution was sheathing with a glass viewing port.

In his design for the Oriole stove in 1932, Geddes took on a related problem. The manufacturer wanted to use the same basic oven from the top to the bottom of the stove line and to enclose all of them in the new white enameled steel blanks he touted as more sanitary. But the enamel was brittle, spalling or cracking during assembly. Geddes took his cue from architecture, designing the stove as a steel skeleton with a skin of panels that bore no weight and were clipped in place. Thus Geddes overcame "brittleness" by subdividing the sheath into many panels, each independently mounted. This implied that sheathing was another metonymic series, a step toward the dematerialization of artifacts into systems. About this time consumers became eager to participate in the "newness" suggested by Streamform's dissociation of surface from interior. The sheath was understood as the perceptual and emotional "outside" in the tension between inside and outside.

New designs in new materials alone did not win consumers to industry. "The intensity of competition during the Depression years," writes Penny Sparke, "caused manufacturers to develop increasingly sophisticated sales tactics and, to this end, advertising was extended into 'styling' as a means

Norman Bel Geddes solved the problem of aerodynamic fairings that covered essential inner mechanisms with a glass window that showed the inner workings of the 1929 counter scale. (Courtesy of Edith Bel Geddes)

of selling the products of the new industries in an increasingly stagnant home market" (94). The "design" of objects thus came to include their advertising—an expansion that left the object itself only one part in an overall system of consumption.

W. D. Teague, designer of the widely admired automobile Marmon 16 (1931), reassured everyone with his books *Design This Day: The Technique of Order in the Machine Age* and *Good Design Is Your Business*. He seemed to espouse neoclassicism even in his chapter titles: "Rhythmic Relationships," "Dominance, Accent and Scale," and "Balance and Symmetry." He invoked George Santayana, John Dewey, and Leonardo da Vinci and included an appendix on the proportional scheme of the Parthenon. But actually he was an exegete of technological momentum, extolling the designs of status items such as the Halliburton aluminum suitcase, the Shakespeare fiberglass fishing rod, and Eames plywood chairs—modernity that intellectuals could approve.

Teague was soon writing about the dangers of "under-consumption." Taking his data from the Brookings Institution, Teague alleged that in 1929 "78% of our whole population had incomes providing for none of the luxuries of life and only the minimum comforts, if any!" (*Design This Day* 275). This peculiar vantage on one of the great boom years in American history became popular in Progressive planning circles. Ten years into the Depression, Teague would write, "It is obvious that what we are now suffering from is not over-production but underconsumption" (277). As in the vindication of "credit" despite "speculation," "consumption" now gathered momentum despite "over-production."[19]

Whatever its rhetoric, design had come to be about mass taste: Russel Wright's American Modern dinnerware, Geddes's Philco radios, and Teague's little Kodak cameras. The confirmation occurred at the 1939 World's Fair in Flushing Meadows, New York. At Alfred Sloan's behest, Geddes designed the General Motors Futurama—a glimpse of interstate freeways and floating airports that cost seven million dollars (Sparke 102). But the impetus was still shifting in 1939. The annual model change, the democratic department store, the service station chains, the batch production of General Motors—these concessions to the consumer began to achieve momentum, and avant garde designers found themselves ignored.

The idiosyncratic Loewy, lover of fast cars and French cuisine, began to satirize consumer taste, which he called the "Most Advanced Yet Acceptable." He wrote, "The adult public's taste is not necessarily ready to accept the logical solutions to their requirements if this solution implies too vast a departure from what they have been conditioned into accepting as the norm. In other words, they will go only so far. . . . Mass production of a successful given product by a powerful company over a period of time tends to establish the appearance of this particular item as the *norm* in its own field" (278–79).[20]

The ascendancy of the consumer, the redesign of everyday objects to his and her taste, was resented by intellectuals, artists, and writers. Retracing the career of the era's preeminent cartoonist gives some hint of how such resistance turned into accommodation.

THE METAMORPHOSIS OF RUBE GOLDBERG

Reuben Lucius Goldberg, born in San Francisco in 1883, went to Berkeley to study engineering and design at the behest of his father, even though his first love was drawing. As a young engineer, Goldberg helped to design the San Francisco sewer system and other public projects. He won recognition for his drawings, which he had to retrieve from the garbage cans of the *San Francisco Chronicle*, only when he went east in 1907. There his syndicated "Weekly Invention" caught on. This one-panel burlesque of industrial design as applied to ineluctably human situations made him the most popular cartoonist in America by 1922, and he earned more than one hundred thousand dollars a year (Goldberg 7). At once a critic of technology and a designer himself, Goldberg showed how the metonymic systematization of life confused the consumers who demanded it, but only so much of it.

Goldberg's technique, at the height of his popularity, was to mechanize a human activity such as walking on icy pavement, squeezing toothpaste, or finding galoshes. The parody arose from the inappropriate application of technology. Goldberg would segment this into four to ten steps, actually reversing the design dicta of continuity and simplicity. These steps involved animals, plants, or other unpredictable elements arranged to act in an ostensibly predictable sequence. To this upending of technology's pretension to repeatability and uniformity, Goldberg then added strings, levers, balances, and other flimsy connections that emphasized the improbability of the invention's fulfilling its design. These "chance" elements are actually a pro-industrial design critique, because the implicit criteria are convenience, smoothness, and sheathing, in which each "Weekly Invention" is wanting. Goldberg was not, in other words, an antitechnologist as much as an early proponent of "human factors" and cousin of Charles Kettering.

Over his career, Goldberg relied more and more on an increasingly sophisticated reader awareness of the visual and perceptual habits inculcated by technology and design. The change may be seen by comparing the early and late cartoons. The "can-opener" of the early twenties is incomprehensible without its Victorian-style narrative context of 134 words (see p. 90). Its caption describes the sixteen labeled steps of the panel, which is packed with artistic detail about shadow, sound, motion, and texture. As a critique, this cartoon relies on older habits of comprehension: a narrative context for the image, a step-by-step causal connectivity, and a high degree of particularization or ornament. As an illustration, it relies on late Victorian habits of representation such as perspective, balance, weight, and ornament; objects appear on pedestals or suspended, advancing their claims to viewer consideration.

By 1930 Goldberg's critique, as well as his style, incorporated some of the consumer habits encouraged by technology. The antimugging device is as inappropriate an application of technology as the can opener, but as a mechanism it is far more integrated: it is portable, integrated on its human pedestal, and its parts are mechanically causal, rather than dependent on the whim of mice or dragons. It uses an independent source of explosive energy (the harpoon gun) and concedes completely to the consumer demand for personal mobility. An equally significant change has taken place in the perceptual matrix of the cartoon panel. The narrative context has shrunk to forty-nine words (necessary to explain the ether). Most of the context is implicit in the cartoon itself. The mugger is designated by the high number of clashing surface patterns: the checkered hat (identifying the "loser" from commedia dell'arte onward) and the texturing of one side of his coat and the dramatic shadowing of the other. His hands, one of

WEEKLY INVENTION

HOW TO PROTECT YOURSELF AGAINST A HOLDUP MAN...
WHEN YOU LIFT YOUR HANDS STRING (A) LOWERS MATCHIE WHICH SETS OFF HARPOON GUN (C) FIRING BOXING GLOVE (D) AT HOLDUP MAN'S JAW. IF HE IS ALERT ENOUGH TO DUCK HE WILL STICK HIS FACE INTO ETHER-SOAKED SPONGE (B) AND FALL GENTLY TO THE SIDEWALK

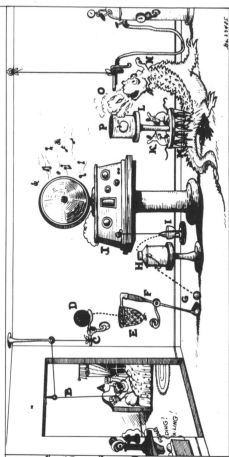

PROFESSOR BUTTS FALLS ON HIS HEAD AND DOPES OUT A SIMPLIFIED CAN-OPENER WHILE HE IS STILL GROGGY.
GO OUTSIDE AND CALL UP YOUR HOME. WHEN PHONE BELL RINGS, MAID (A) MISTAKES IT FOR AN ALARM CLOCK - SHE AWAKENS AND STRETCHES, PULLING CORD (B) WHICH RAISES END OF LADLE (C). BALL (D) DROPS INTO NET (E) CAUSING GOLF CLUB (F) TO SWING AGAINST BALL (G), MAKING A CLEAN DRIVE AND UP-SETTING MILK CAN (H). MILK SPILLS INTO GLASS (I) AND THE WEIGHT PULLS SWITCH ON RADIO (J). WALTZING MICE (K) HEARING MUSIC AND PROCEED TO DANCE, CAUSING REVOLVING APPARATUS (L) TO SPIN AND TURN, SPIKES (M) SCRATCH TAIL OF PET DRAGON (N) WHO IN ANGER EMITS FIRE IGNITING ACETYLENE TORCH (O) AND BURNING OFF TOP OF TOMATO CAN (P) AS IT ROTATES.
WHEN NOT OPENING CANS, THE DRAGON CAN ALWAYS BE KEPT BUSY CHASING AWAY INCOME TAX INVESTIGATORS AND PROHIBITION OFFICERS.

Reprinted with special permission of King Features Syndicate

In the early 1920s (opposite, top) Rube Goldberg's Professor Butts satirized mechanical complexity within a visual frame that was still Victorian. By 1930 (opposite, bottom) his subjects and style reflected the changes in technology and design that he supposedly critiqued. At the height of his fame in 1947 (above), when he won the Pulitzer Prize, Goldberg depended completely on the metonymic habits fostered by the new techno-economic climate.

which caricatures a primeval grasp while the other merges into a revolver, figure his motive. These conventions of the graphic depiction of crime make him immediately understandable. The rest of the narrative context comes from the background, where a policeman is suggested to be leaning against a streetlight and blowing bubbles. Behind the policeman an urban skyline rises. The criticism that the police forces of large eastern cities were in league with organized crime was common, but here the suggestion is that private citizens need means of protecting themselves. Like the mugger's, the policeman's dress suggests an older style. Contrasting with these characterizations is the smoothness and solid black and white blocking of the "hero" and the flapper on his left. Though his glasses, bulbous nose, and fringe of hair suggest a bumbler, the hero wears an unmottled white shirt, evinces a high degree of symmetry, and is linked to the chic woman by his defensive posture and the repetition of the white area of his shirt in her dress. She is the most *moderne* figure, an asymmetrical, curvilinear form of high-contrast black and white masses. Visually, this tableau can be read left to right, from the most modern to the most old-fashioned. It is cropped at the subjects' waists. No "presentation" of objects on pedestals or by suspension is necessary; a more cinematic way of seeing is presumed, without need of foreground or continuous background.

By the time he won the Pulitzer Prize for editorial cartooning in 1947, Goldberg's illustrations partook of the same instant legibility as billboards and advertisements. Labels provided the narrative context, and the image was a single visual metaphor presented in dramatic chiaroscuro. By this point Rube Goldberg depended completely on the perceptual habits proposed by the technology he had once lampooned. His themes of fear, alienation, and death are those of film noir, and his representational habits are completely metonymic.

To write of washing machines in terms of yachts is not to be too
literary. It is to be not sufficiently literary. The disproportionately
florid, the gaudy, have worse reputation in literature than ever they
have had in advertising. There are few literary points on which there
is general agreement, but I know of no first-rate writer or critic who
does not call that style most perfect which clothes ideas in the most
appropriate words.
—Dashiell Hammett, *Western Advertising*, 1926

Dashiell Hammett,
Copywriter

By 1927 Hammett was again the enfant terrible of San Francisco advertising. A year earlier he had lain hemorrhaging in a pool of
blood, felled by chronic tuberculosis and alcoholism. But in 1927 he was
reviewing new books and writing essays for the West Coast's leading advertising magazine, while turning out a barrage of successful newspaper copy
for Albert Samuels Jewelry. Samuels depended on a volume business, and
Hammett's long, chatty banners of copy drew customers. Hammett succeeded in advertising because he "understood the values of the world of
the twenties," observes biographer Diane Johnson, "in which men bought
diamonds for women and a good watch for themselves, and an engaged

couple was a new stable social unit, and people wanted to trade 'up' and 'amount to something' and they wanted other people to know how well they were doing" (39).[1]

Hammett's ads may seem distant from the hard-boiled prose style he helped to create, but the gap only indicates a vanished context they shared. His detective style was an advance on his ad style, its meaning an extension of his insights into stylistic change, advertising and its textuality. In this matrix he had honed an ability to narratize the concerns of the "average man," in ads such as this:

> She loved him dearly—there was no doubt about it. If she had not respected his feelings so much she might have given him some intimation of her disappointment regarding the diamond he had placed on her finger when their troth was plighted.
>
> But she just could not think of hurting him. So she smiled bravely, and assured him that she was the happiest girl in the world. However, she was *ashamed* to compare her dull, lifeless stone with flawless brilliant, blue-white diamonds that her girl friends had received from their intended husbands.
>
> How had he come to unwittingly place her in this humiliating position? It was simply an error in judgement. He could not afford to pay over a certain sum and he had bought "size" instead of "quality." If he had only asked her, he would have learned this fact: All intelligent women of refinement prefer small gems of fine quality to diamonds that may be larger yet not so pure and scintillating. (Johnson 39)

Copywriters like Hammett had to find product promises other than biggest, newest, or most or least expensive, as the measurement of life on a material, Victorian scale disappeared. This decline of synecdochical meaning put consumers at risk of "error[s] in judgement." Metonymic substitutes, promoting an awareness of invisible "quality," played on the difference between exterior and interior. Hammett, for example, sells his diamonds not by their material value, but as one invisible quality (her secret shame) is replaced by another (her intelligence and refinement). This imputation of a metonymic succession was necessary because, even when the sheathing did not hide the mechanics of the product, the "need" for it was not obvious. The consumer had to hunger for invisible things.

This rhetoric of the invisible, however, capitalized on a presumption that the nation still held many values in common, such as "pep" and pride of place. Using the older consensus, much could be elided for the hearer to supply; *sheba* and *giggle-water* conveyed a worldview. The modernist prose style encouraged readers to fill in the missing content, and by 1927 successful advertising employed a related tactic: "There's Something About Them You'll Like" (Tareytons), "Even Your Best Friend Won't Tell You" (Listerine), and "Be Nonchalant, Light a Murad." Hammett's understanding of a relation between this elided style and the new anxieties of mass audiences would be his strength.

It's nothing unusual to find a man of position and excellent standing who is temporarily short of cash. The average man figures a long time ahead on the spending of his income. Besides his fixed expenses of rent, meals, clothing and recreation, he usually carries some kind of an investment, a savings account or life insurance, that pretty well takes care of all he earns. So when he finds himself engaged he may not have the cash necessary for the ring. We try to take care of men like that. (Johnson 39)

When he wasn't writing such copy for Samuels Jewelry, Hammett was approximating today's consultant. He wrote articles and reviewed books for *Western Advertising, Saturday Review, Forum*, and *Stratford Magazine*. By most accounts, he was an extraordinary success. The publisher of the Oakland *Post Enquirer* wrote to Samuels that Hammett's copy was the best advertising his paper had ever carried. The future noir novelist dismissed this as "applesauce, since he knows I'm thinking about cutting down the space used in the Oakland papers" (Johnson 66).

Hammett worked half days for Samuels, devoting afternoons to his own writing. Besides the reviews, he engaged in what he called Blackmasking: he wrote detective stories, at two cents a word, for *Black Mask* magazine, one of three pulps begun in 1920 by H. L. Mencken and George Jean Nathan to fund *Smart Set*. That was where Hammett preferred to appear, beside F. Scott Fitzgerald, but the editors apparently counseled him to aim lower. He began to read *Black Mask* during his second convalescence from tuberculosis in 1921, after his employment by the Pinkerton Detective Agency.

Therein lay his unique capital. Hammett had joined the Pinkertons in 1915 when he was twenty-one years old. The agency was the largest private law enforcement concern in the United States, originally created to bridge the gap between the federal government's small law enforcement arm and local police forces. In an age of increasing legal, technological, and commercial complexity, the Pinkertons systematized crime prevention, pursued criminals across local jurisdictions, and tackled cases that were essentially economic. In the West, the IWW and smaller radical unions had followed the railroads into mining and timber camps. Called in, the Pinkertons deployed their vaunted union-busting abilities: they beat up strikers, burned headquarters, and safeguarded strikebreakers.

Hammett had been a good Pinkerton. His family in Baltimore had been relieved when he found this job. Not only was it the first he kept more than a month, but the Pinkertons, something like the Marines today, were reputed to have a salutary effect on prodigal youth. *Prodigal*, by most accounts, underestimates Hammett's precocious knowledge of liquor, prostitutes, and gambling. He "began to row with his father and come home drunk," writes Johnson, when he was seventeen (16). After the death of Hammett's grandfather, the family expected an inheritance to lift them from poverty, but they received only $67.70. Pay from a railroad job melted in Hammett's hands. "He bet his money on horses, trains and fights," Johnson writes. "Whores hung around the bars near the railroad yard, and he went with them sometimes and came to like them, though he caught gonorrhea when he was twenty" (16–17).

No record of Hammett's Baltimore casework survives, but we can assume the Pinkerton routine prevailed. Operatives were on twenty-four-hour call, but the nature of their work involved patience; they watched houses for days on end, trailed suspects for weeks, and read old files and composed new ones. The agency had that curious discipline of martial organizations that also encourages repose. An agent who could not sit quietly to watch for evidence was fired; one who could not tail a suspect inconspicuously all day was second-rate. The starting salary for this work was twenty-one dollars a week in 1915.

The assistant manager of the Baltimore office was James Wright, who became the model for Hammett's Continental Op. Short, thick-bodied, and rough-talking, Wright taught Hammett the Pinkerton methods and code, and he appears to have informed his pupil that morality was strictly personal. The bad guys did not live by a civil or religious morality, so to be bound by any rules in dealing with them was to put oneself at a disadvantage. In Wright's view, a detective might lie, cheat, steal evidence, and emotionally manipulate suspects. He lived in a realm of deferred repentance. Such a moral code, writes Richard Layman, is essentially self-serving: "The essential quality which a detective must develop to avoid being consumed by his job is objectivity—an emotional distance from the people with whom he deals" (*Shadow Man* 12). This code finds its analogue in the axial values of inner/outer that Hammett later exploited in his advertising. But it was the close knowledge of human nature gained as a Pinkerton, treated as objective, manipulable material, that furnished Hammett's estimate of human nature as a copywriter and novelist.

The Pinkertons sent Hammett west on a temporary job in 1917, and he liked it. It was his first experience of frontier, probably Montana, and he enjoyed the boardinghouses, trains, and streams of young strangers living by their wits. It was the year when a Butte boardinghouse owner, Mrs. Nora Byrne, said that Pinkertons awakened her tenant, Frank Little, an IWW organizer, in the middle of the night and carried him off, despite his broken leg. In the morning he was found, castrated and hanging from a railroad trestle, with a warning note pinned to his underwear. As Hammett later told it, he had been offered a five-thousand-dollar bonus to participate in the lynching and declined (Johnson 20).

World War I intervened. Hammett joined the Motor Ambulance Company in 1918, but the worldwide flu epidemic felled him in October. The flu gave way to tuberculosis, which had afflicted his mother; he would be in and out of hospitals for ten years, always expecting to die, always amazed that he lived on. Discharged in May 1919 with a medical disability, Hammett returned home with a forty-dollar-a-month pension. "The Hammett residence resembled a boarding house in 1920," writes Layman (*Shadow*

Man 15). Mother and father, young sister, and ambitious brother Dick worked to make the family ends meet. Dashiell contributed only when he could and then resentfully. Most of his money went to gambling, liquor, and whores. Upbraided by his father and brother (the steadiest worker in the house), Dashiell left home during a remission and applied to the Pinkertons again. Although he stood six feet one and weighed only 140 pounds, they accepted him and sent him to Spokane, where they needed men for the mining fray. But Hammett's tuberculosis reappeared, and he ended up in the Public Health Service Hospital in Tacoma.

There he met a young nurse from Montana named Josephine Dolan. They flirted, arranged dates, and eventually rented an apartment where they met when Hammett could get weekend passes. Soon she was pregnant, but Hammett wasn't ready to marry, so Jose went home in disgrace. Despite the damp weather, Hammett's tuberculosis went into remission. He moved to San Francisco, where he liked the raw immigrant masses and bawdy miners, the full-throttle attitude and gull-flecked docks. Pinkertons were needed, so he found as much part-time work as his health allowed. In the spring of 1921 he sent for Jose. They were married on July 6, and their daughter Mary Jane was born in October.

From this period of his Pinkerton employment, he repeated the details of one case until they became apocryphal. The event happened at the regal St. Francis Hotel, where in 1921 Roscoe Arbuckle, the three-hundred-pound film star, was charged with the death of would-be actress Virginia Rappe, whose bladder he reportedly broke with his huge mass while raping her. An ambitious district attorney prosecuted Arbuckle in print, and the Hearst newspapers helped, printing rumors that the actor was impotent and had raped Rappe with a champagne bottle (Starr, *Inventing* 326). The Pinkertons were hired to prove Arbuckle's innocence, today universally acknowledged. Hammett knew it at the time: "The whole thing was a frame-up, arranged by some of the corrupt local newspaper boys. Arbuckle was good copy, so they set him up for a fall" (Nolan, *Life* 18). Hammett claimed to have been among the agents assigned to develop new evidence for Arbuckle, but in a sketch of the affair titled "Seven Pages" his irony reveals a disconcerting sympathy for Arbuckle's persecutors: "It was the day before the opening of the second absurd attempt to convict Roscoe

Arbuckle of something. He came into the lobby. He looked at me and I at him. His eyes were the eyes of a man who expected to be regarded as a monster but was not yet inured to it. I made my gaze as contemptuous as I could. He glared at me, went on the elevator still glaring. It was amusing. I was working for his attorneys at the time" (MS at Humanities Research Center).

It turned out that Arbuckle was the victim of an extortion plot and that Rappe's death resulted from a slipshod abortion and a history of venereal disease. "The funniest case I ever worked on," commented Hammett in "Seven Pages." "In trying to convict him, everybody framed everybody else." Even allowing for hyperbole, why should this have been "the funniest case" Hammett ever worked on? The text provides only the disparity between an innocence that he acknowledged and was paid to prove and a mistaken public condemnation that he despised but with which he enjoyed feigning sympathy. This is Hammett's first probe of the inside/outside, appearance/content dichotomy.

In fact, Arbuckle touched a deep chord in Hammett, who shared the broad conception of humor in Arbuckle's plight that derived from his films. The Fat Boy was a national butt of humor in the 1920s, reviled in novels—Fatty Pfaff in Sinclair Lewis's *Arrowsmith*, a 1925 Pulitzer Prize winner, is representative—as belonging to an inept rural past. Arbuckle was film's great Fat Boy, the epitome of a sloppy body, a disgusting buffoon. To an increasingly urbanized nation, the fat farm boy represented not health but the disregard of personal image and hygiene typical of the farm, which had been left behind. Nor did Fatty have to work at the role. Anita Loos reports that he considered it the height of wit to throw pats of butter at the ceiling of the Hollywood Hotel dining room and see how many would stick. Being fat was his only talent, she said (Starr, *Inventing* 325). That everyone "framed" everyone else to profit from his misfortune followed the Keystone plot line, but the newspapers added a retributive justice. The *San Francisco Chronicle* reported that "Roscoe Arbuckle owns three Cadillac cars, one special built, valued at $25,000, and a house on West Adams Street for which he paid $100,000. . . . [And yet] Arbuckle never aided his family" (Johnson 33–34). He was not just fat. He was a prodigal. The fabula called for him to lose all, repent, and return home.

Roscoe "Fatty" Arbuckle of Smith Center, Kansas, shown here in the film *Coney Island,* found he could not escape his persona when accused of raping Virginia Rappe. Dashiell Hammett was among the detectives assigned to show Arbuckle's innocence but called it "the funniest case" he ever worked on. He styled himself as "The Thin Man" for this cover photo of his 1934 novel.

This much could be perceived by any moviegoer, but Hammett's irony includes a local context. San Francisco and Los Angeles were engaged in a long-standing battle for regional supremacy that dictated their positions on everything from presidential politics to library levies. For San Franciscans, Arbuckle was not just an actor, but the most hedonistic example of southern California's most successful new industry. By the mid-1920s movies were America's fifth largest business. San Francisco, founded on mining, was emphatically a material city but thought of itself as a cultural capital, looking askance at the film industry and the arriviste European Jews who dominated it. Where did they go to enjoy their profits? To San Francisco, with its opera, fine food, and art museums. But could San Franciscans ignore the grossest buffoon of this presumptuous "industry" when he raped and murdered in their midst?

The Arbuckle trial was also a crisis for Los Angeles. There had been widespread dissatisfaction in the heartland with Hollywood's sophisticated sexuality, with its presentation of divorce and extramarital sex as options. The trend in Cecil B. DeMille's films *Male and Female* (1919), *Why Change Your Wife?* (1920), and *Forbidden Fruit* (1921) summed it up. Such a scandal could bring down an industry that ranked with tourism and oil as one of the city's economic foundations. Adolph Zukor realized that Arbuckle had to be sacrificed. "California's top criminal lawyer," notes Kevin Starr, "turned down an offer to defend Fatty, remarking that no jury could be expected to sympathize with a fat man" (*Inventing* 325).[2] It took three trials for Arbuckle to be found innocent, but the last jury apologized: "Acquittal is not enough for Roscoe Arbuckle. We feel a grave injustice has been done him" (Starr, *Inventing* 326).[3]

Hammett, a thin man but also a prodigal, could be ironic about Fatty's innocence because he shared the public disgust. As Johnson notes, "Fat villains were to appear in his tales" (35). Hammett would be the svelte, unseen Clyde Wynant of *The Thin Man* (he posed for the book's cover) and would portray himself as the emaciated lunger Dan Rolff (*Red Harvest*) and the lean Owen Fitzstephan (*The Dain Curse*). Opposed to him would be bulbous Casper Gutmans and rotund Chang Li Chings. The fat man was a Jew, Greek, Los Angelean—fat, smelly, and attracted to lucre.

Hammett understood prodigality not only from the son's vantage, having gone away himself, but also from those of the father and the stay-at-home brother: he had felt their ire. For him the fabula was about the tension between individuals who have and spend, apart from talent or ability, and the self-enforced social conformity of the working class that formed the audience (father and brother). Repentance and reconciliation were token. The core was that a hyperbolic subject escaped from the mass and then fell to its egalitarian demands. The working classes understood the fabula as failed escape—the prodigal rejoined to his geographic or class origins. When Arbuckle refused to fall, he defied the social forces that had created him and became guilty of an insupportable arrogance.[4]

The short fiction that Hammett was writing at the time is full of characters who come into an inappropriate consciousness that exposes to them the mechanics of working-class customs. In 1922, when Arbuckle was in his second trial, Hammett managed to combine the prodigal son theme with the egalitarian dynamics of the workplace in the unpublished story "An Inch and a Half of Glory." A nondescript worker named Parrish, who saves a child from a burning house and becomes an overnight hero, saves his newspaper clippings and lives out a role:

He began to keep to himself. After all, what had he in common with the people around him? An uninteresting lot: the lesser inhabitants of the world, unimportant cogs in not especially important machines. He himself was a cog, true enough, but with the difference that on occasion he could be an identity. The last drop of ancestral venturesomeness had not been distilled from his blood. He experimented with this thought, evolving a sentence he liked: "All their ancestral courage distilled by industrialism out of their veins." He would look at the world over his sign that said "Information" and repeat the sentence to himself.

His next position was in the basement of a wholesale drug house, but he quit this place after two weeks. He was done with working at a desk. He had reasoned things out. Desk jobs were well enough for a man who could not rise above them. But nowadays there was a scarcity of— hence there must be a demand for—men whose ancestral courage had not been distilled out of their veins. He meant to find and fill such an opening. (MS in HRC)

As he reaches his nadir, Parrish encounters another burning house. He rushes in and saves a kitten, but he loses his clippings in this fire and refuses more publicity. Sunrise finds him far away, happy and energetic in anonymity, signing up to do day labor. It is important to understand Hammett's irony. Parrish has balanced his account, has refused what the world gave freely, feeling a satisfaction in saving himself from a false consciousness of exceptionality, in wresting his living from the same material as everyone else. To be prodigal in this manner is to find repentance not under the Christian law of forgiveness, with its enduring sense of sin (soul), but under the elder brother's law of compensation, with its happy anonymity of socialized endeavor (self). This will become important to film noir.

In another unpublished story, "Nelson Redline," Hammett reveals the depth of his insight into the social and psychological rules of the emerging economy even as he introduces the narrator: "Myself: two months before, I had ceased being associated with a worker's paper that had killed itself by a shortsighted policy of specialization upon the case of the unemployed, who couldn't give it the material support it needed." Hammett's observations of working-class behavior are so skeptical as to make his later membership in the Communist Party seem quixotic. His narrator notes that "each day's task equalled each other day's task, with no allowance for our becoming more expert with practice, so that toward the end of our term, by carefully concealing our increased proficiency, we had rather an easy time of it. . . . We were sitting idle late that afternoon, the day's assignments completed, except for the bits we habitually saved so that we might have something to be busy with when [the boss] returned." Then the blowhard Nelson Redline enters, "elaborating fancifully upon an already fanciful theory that . . . the elimination of all international differences was to be brought about by an interchange of children—only orphans, I think, until the system was perfected—between neighboring nations for periods of 10 or 15 years." The irony accorded internationalism hints not only of California's xenophobia but also of the social Darwinism Hammett shared with his Pinkerton employers: "These men who refuse to—or for one reason or another are unable to—conduct themselves in accordance with the accepted rules—no matter how strong their justification may be, or how foolish the rules—have to be put outside. You don't know approximately what they will do under any given set of circumstances, and so they are sources of uneasiness and confusion. You can't count on them. They make you uncomfortable" (MS in HRC).

Hammett pushed his understanding of the tensions between the prodigal and the group farther yet in "Faith," another unpublished story. Here he focused on the role of "conventions" in group solidarity:

> Without conventions any sort of group life is impossible, and no division of society is without its canons. The laws of the jungle are not the laws of the drawing room, but they are as certainly existent, and as important to their subjects. If you are a migratory workingman you may pick your teeth wherever and with whatever tool you like, but you may not either by word or act publicly express satisfaction with your present employment; nor may you disagree with any who denounce the conditions of that employment. Like most conventions, this is not altogether without foundation in reason. (MS in HRC)

Consciousness of the social conventions—and the need to acquiesce to them—are the ultimate point of Hammett's contempt for Arbuckle. Having lost sight of these conventions, Arbuckle became their victim instead of manipulating them to his advantage, as Hammett later imagined his protagonists doing.

In his Blackmasking, Hammett by 1927 deployed this swelling knowledge expertly. Like advertising, Blackmasking was something he did for money. His purer, more idealistic efforts he kept sending to *Forum* and *Smart Set*. In his detective stories he wrote for readers recently urbanized, new to the shop and office, who longed to rebel against their powerlessness but feared the loss of material advantages. They were attracted to urban life and feared a return to the farm or homeland. They wanted a protector as hard as James Wright, but of almost Franciscan simplicity and poverty, who would chronicle a drama of disaccumulation in which a rebellious prodigal lost all, justifying their adherence to the multiplying conventions of urban work behavior.

In July 1926 coworkers found Hammett unconscious, lying in a pool of blood. His tuberculosis had caused his lungs to hemorrhage. Doctors put him in bed, ordered his wife and daughters to move out so that they would not fall ill, and declared him 100 percent disabled. The Veterans Bureau, which disputed Hammett's medical condition his entire life, concurred this once and awarded him a pension of ninety dollars a month. He moved to a small apartment on Post Street—he would never again live with his family—and began his richest artistic period. The tuberculosis cleared, and he began to write advertising and to review a few detective novels for *Saturday Review*. At *Black Mask* there was a new editor, Captain Joseph Shaw, a flamboyant former saber instructor for the army, who admired Hammett's work and came to visit. Hammett began a serial about a place called "Poisonville" in Montana. The lens of his advertising insight began to bring the experience of his travel into narrative focus. The first installment appeared in November 1927, the last in February 1928. In 1929 Alfred Knopf published the four parts as *Red Harvest*.

Red Harvest

Let *Red Harvest* be our watershed in the history of the American noir novel. On one side lie the older traditions of dime novel detectives, such as Old Cap Collier and Nick Carter. There too stand the erudite detectives of Poe and S. S. Van Dine. These detectives functioned in societies portrayed as organic, Victorian wholes. They had the social coherence found in the earliest English crime stories, in which an organic figuration held that the body politic could cure its own infections. Stephen Knight has described how the first crime stories did not have criminal catchers at all: "Society itself is so tightly knit that escape will not be possible. . . . If there has been a murder, 'some gentlemen' will come along and take the criminal to a magistrate" (in Most and Stowe 271). When the individualized criminal catcher appeared, he merely employed the commonplace wisdom of his society in order to defend it. His original anonymity is related to two features of earlier social ideology, writes Knight. First, reality was empirical: appearances revealed truth. A man found running down the road with blood on his hands was guilty of something. Stories about crime focused on circumstantial evidence without bothering to establish proof, because the consensual view of reality was external and shared by all readers. Second, the truth of visible evidence was reinforced by the Christian belief that guilt afflicted the author of a crime, whose conscience then caused him to act rashly, to draw attention to himself, or to reveal evidence—"consciousness of guilt."

On the other side of the watershed, society was becoming corporate and efficient. The erudite intellectual Victorian hero wasn't: he lost potency as alter ego, and eventually he became an anachronism. Urban commercial forces were also commodifying the crime story, retaining its ideological function but placing it in competition with other forms of entertainment.

Ideological modes often overlap. *Red Harvest*, for example, contains some of the oldest features of crime stories. Hammett made his Continental Op nameless, without background or significant human relationships. His sloppy physique (he is five feet six, 190 pounds) and quotidian habits (he drinks, counts his pennies, uses slang, likes women, boxing, and cigarettes) signal an Everyman. His commonness and anonymity are a nostalgic assertion that America is still homogeneous enough to throw up a representative of its standards, some of which are easily seen. When the Op notes on the novel's second page that "the first policeman I saw needed a shave," readers supply the series of ensuing policemen, as well as the link between shaving and honesty.

In *Red Harvest* the Op is hired by Donald Willsson, a newspaper crusader who is killed before the Op can meet him. The four plot sections involve the Op in tracking down and unmasking different prodigal sons, as commissioned by Willsson's patriarchal father, Old Elihu. A bank teller named Robert Albury turns out to have murdered Donald, not because of his anticorruption crusade, but over a gold-digger named Dinah Brand. She and her current beau, Max Thaler, fix a prizefight, which the Op undoes, leading to the murder of boxer Al Kennedy in section 2. Thaler involves the Op in his dispute with corrupt police chief Noonan, which, after raids and counterraids and a prodigal subplot involving Noonan's younger brother and Myrtle Jennison, leads to Noonan's death in the third section. Having carte blanche from Old Elihu to "cleanse" the town, the Op promotes a final melee pitting Pete the Finn against ultimate tough guy Reno Starkey. After the carnage, the Op, highly conscious of his own guilt, writes "reports" to "the Old Man" (his boss) in San Francisco. The most interesting characters are Old Elihu, Dinah Brand, Max Thaler, and Chief Noonan (this novel's Fatty Arbuckle).

Chance predominates in the formal plot of *Red Harvest*, the criminals killing each other with minor prompting from the Op or whenever the action needs a frisson. Motivation is minor. There's no real reason for Albury to kill Donald Willsson, nor an indication of what Willsson would have had the Op investigate. The implied importance of Willsson's French wife or Old Elihu's murder of a burglar are never followed up. In one sense this is bad plotting, but in another, it doesn't matter, for the main point in the older crime story is social coherence and the restoration of uniformity after chance events disturb society. "Sometimes just stirring things up is all right," the Op says, "if you're tough enough to survive and keep your eyes open so you'll see what you want when it comes to the top" (79). The Op knows what he is looking for, as though he lived in a village where everyone was known and socialization was public. Personville, the locale of *Red Harvest*, is conveniently small—hiding there is impossible—but it has been infected with prodigality—thus the homology of *person = ville*.

That Hammett looked out his San Francisco window as he wrote about "Poisonville" is evident in the novel's setting. A "town of 40,000," Personville has little to do with Butte (the only Montana town that big) or its smaller neighbor, Anaconda. Sinda Gregory presciently observed that "Hammett telescoped the geography of several American locations to create his own mythic setting" (31). How else could frontier Personville have streetcars that run at night, telephones, or a city hall where crowds loiter waiting to see famous criminals? (Hammett, *Red Harvest* 6, 39). During its famous mine strikes of 1914 and 1921, Butte did not have morning and evening papers, a Consolidated Press office, Stutz touring cars, professional boxing, or a city directory (7, 184, 11, 70, 87). Hammett's Personville reflects the commercial currents of San Francisco in the 1920s. Hammett set the novel shortly after 1921, which is to say it most likely refers to the 1924 miners' strike, an event that was recent to readers in 1929 (9).

An autodidact, Hammett wrote in his tiny apartment from a lived experience of San Francisco and its daily concerns, advertising, his reading, and his memories of the Pinkertons. The materialism of Hammett's world is difficult to appreciate today, but San Francisco was a city founded on mining wealth, augmented by the trade of its port and railroads. Early on, it found entertainment in drink, gambling, and brothels. Mark Twain wrote of it in 1863, "We fag ourselves completely out every day and go to sleep without rocking every night. We dine out and we lunch out and we eat, drink and are happy" (47). Like Personville, it was a place where wealth came from mines, where culture was material. Its citizens wanted things, and they displayed them, as authors from Twain to Cyra McFadden have attested.

Personville is a geopolitical figure comprising elements of Butte, the Anaconda mines, San Francisco, and Prohibition Chicago, in which national anxieties are worked out. The political corruption of the East had created much of California's appeal for immigrants and natives alike, and it takes the brunt of criticism. This anxiety fueled the state's Progressive movement. But it is worth noting that Progressives governed in California and Montana, the latter having a proportionately larger Socialist Party and being the first state represented in Congress by a woman (Malone and Roeder 198–200).[5] Progressivism made political reform its focus, yet in California it was eventually assimilated by the power elite. By 1927 the unenfranchised intelligentsia, in which Hammett may be placed, viewed "reform" as the tool of a new clique. In San Francisco, no family was so identified with this manipulation as the Hearsts.

The Hearst fortune owed to George Hearst. His Homestake and Anaconda mines near Butte, Montana, acquired for thirty thousand dollars in 1882, provided the richest copper strike in history. As proprietor of Anaconda, Hearst offered a model for Personville's Old Elihu Willsson. Two years before his Anaconda discovery, Hearst found himself in possession of the *San Francisco Examiner*, a Democratic paper to which he had loaned money for promoting his political ambitions. Like young Donald Willsson, William Randolph, at nineteen, "was opposed to his father's political ambitions" (Swanberg 22). When the *Examiner* could not repay George Hearst, he took it over, but it continued to lose money.

Young Hearst became interested in journalism after a stint on the Harvard *Lampoon* and a job reporting for Pulitzer's crusading *New York World*. George Hearst pushed more important jobs at his son, and only when elected to the U.S. Senate did he leave twenty-three-year-old William to run the paper. William moved from Boston to Sausalito, bringing along his illiterate, lower-class mistress, Tessie Powers, who was as much an outsider in San Francisco as Donald Willsson's French wife was in Personville. Like Dinah Brand, Tessie was a gold-digger, having lived first with one of Hearst's friends and then moved up. She remained his mistress for eight years, leaving only when Hearst's mother reportedly gave her $150,000 (Swanberg 24–52, 68). When Hammett represented the power of Hearst in Willsson, he was only exaggerating slightly:

> For forty years old Elihu Willsson . . . had owned Personville, heart, soul, skin and guts. He was president and majority stockholder of the Personville Mining Corporation, ditto of the First National Bank, owner of the *Morning Herald* and *Evening Herald*, the city's only newspapers, and at least part owner of nearly every other enterprise of any importance. Along with these pieces of property he owned a United States Senator, a couple of representatives, the governor, the mayor, and most of the state legislature. Elihu Willsson was Personville, and he was almost the whole state. (*Red Harvest* 8–9)

No one in Butte or Anaconda or all Montana had such power. Hammett also reveals his model when the Op blackmails Elihu: "I said if he was going to talk like a sap he ought to lower his voice so that people in Los Angeles wouldn't learn what a sap he was" (*Red Harvest* 185). Los Angeles had no special significance for Montanans, but it did for San Franciscans. As home of the reform movement, Los Angeles had the upper hand in morality. What Elihu does not want revealed there are his love letters to Dinah Brand, who is also his son's mistress. This adultery motif may allude to William Randolph Hearst Jr.'s liaison with actress Marion Davies, whom he met in 1917. For Hammett such affairs revealed the hypocrisy of young Hearst's reform campaigns; hence he adopted an ironic tone in describing young Willsson's efforts: "Don starts a reform campaign in the papers. Clear the burg of vice and corruption" (10). For Hammett, Hearst was simply sensationalizing on behalf of a "reform" movement suborned by the oligarchy. Newspapers, the Op remarks, "were good for nothing except to hash things up so nobody could unhash them" (172). Newspapers were also narrative competitors of the detective magazines.

The same skepticism underlies Hammett's critique of politics. The Progressives, nominally in control of San Francisco from 1893 to 1911, had frittered away their tenure in the mayor's office. Hammett lived there during the subsequent reign of James Rolph Jr., mayor for an unprecedented twenty-one years (1911–32). The baby-kissing, flesh-pressing Rolph was a "nonpartisan" Republican, who saw the city through the Pan-Pacific Exhibition and municipal water, electric, and streetcar line construction, successes he won by ignoring corruption, gambling, and bootlegging. But the realpolitik of the battle for natural resources (anticipated by Frank Norris in *The Octopus*, 1901) Hammett ignored. *Red Harvest* doesn't even touch on the collusion of the mines, through which Willsson controls Personville, and the railroads—a fact in both California and Montana. Instead Hammett treats the Hearsts as despots of a far country, removing them to Montana. Young Willsson attacks only such paradigmatic eastern maladies as bootlegging, gambling, and police corruption, but Hearst had attacked the Southern Pacific Railroad and its flunkies in the Democratic Party. This omission of the railroads' control of natural resources is curious, not only because the S&P's stranglehold on San Francisco was a topic of California discussion but also because that grip extended to Montana's mines. But Hammett traveled the railroads and liked them. His decision to omit this scandal from his critique, and to treat reforming newspapers rather favorably, reflects a certain accommodation to late Progressivism.[6]

Progressives claimed that corruption grew from ethnic factions, such as those dominating San Francisco's labor unions, waterfront, and political parties. The city was polarized into "South of Market" (six districts), where the populace was 70 percent foreign-born (Irish, German, and Scandinavian) and largely male, due to boardinghouses and sailors, and the more affluent Pacific Heights and Western Addition areas (seven districts) that developed after the 1906 earthquake. Italians were on the increase (up from 6 percent in 1900 to 16 percent in 1930), but the Chinese, whom Hammett featured in his early stories, declined from 5 percent in 1900 to 2.6 percent in 1930 (Issel and Cherny 165–212, 56–59). But Hammett reflected the Butte and Anaconda region accurately, for Montana's older, conservative Irish and English workers were at odds with "thousands of Finnish, Slavic and Italian workers, many of them illiterate, who poured into Butte after 1900," according to historians Michael Malone and Richard Roeder (210). The later immigrants joined the IWW, which competed with other unions but never represented a majority of miners; however, these same immigrants supported the Progressive Party, Prohibition, and anticrime and anticorruption movements. In Montana, by "August, 1920, progressive candidates won the gubernatorial nominations of both parties," and one, Burton K. Wheeler, went on to become a famous reform-minded senator even as Hammett wrote (Malone and Roeder 220). It was clearly not Montana's politics that Hammett represented.

Organized labor, a power in Hammett's San Francisco, receives only brief attention in *Red Harvest*, despite the polarizing impact of the celebrated Billings-Mooney anarchist trial on the Bay City in 1917–18. The ineffectual character of the novel's Bill Quint is the fictional shadow of IWW leader Big Bill Hayward, a working-class celebrity between 1910 and 1930 who spoke on behalf of Billings and Mooney and who was known for flamboyant neckties, in which Hammett attired Quint. A more logical choice for Hammett would have been Frank Little, the IWW leader whose lynching he claimed he knew about. But by the early 1920s Malone and Roeder write, "the Wobblies were beaten and scattered" (214).

So ethnic factionalism drew Hammett's fire. In this respect he was in accord with national and California xenophobia. The plutocracy of Crockers, Stanfords, and de Youngs operated historically through Irish, German, and Jewish politicians. In Hammett's day, the Irish were in ascendancy. Former sheriff Tom Finn, Patrick McCarthy, and Peter and Thomas McDonough, who controlled saloons, bail bonds, and vice, are represented by police chief Noonan; Pete the Finn, a bootlegger; Lew Yard, pawnbroker and bail bondsman; Max Thaler, gambler; and Reno Starkey, recently released convict (Issel and Cherny 132–36). In the late 1920s Michael M. O'Shaughnessy, city engineer, became the power behind the throne, while Mayor Rolph led parades. O'Shaughnessy planned the Hetch-Hetchy water project and the Stockton Street Tunnel, where Miles Archer is killed in *The Maltese Falcon* by Brigid O'Shaughnessy (Issel and Cherny 175–76, 181–82). More important than Gaelic hegemony is ethnicity itself, since the Progressives were dominated by the Protestant, midwestern migrants who formed 60 percent of California's population by 1910. But only 15 percent of San Francisco's population was Protestant, so its power struggles became identified with ethnic corruption (Starr, *Inventing* 237–39).

The Progressives had found their bête noire in liquor. They supported the temperance movement early, and passage of the Wylie local option law in 1911 enabled them to vote county after county dry, with only San Francisco resisting reform. A turn-of-the-century census, writes Kevin Starr, "revealed an astonishing 440 saloons in the sixty-four-square-block, largely Irish Catholic working-class South of Market district" (*Inventing* 245). Hearst decided to help San Francisco: he swore off hard liquor, publicized programs for drying out, and paid the way of his key writers through them with front-page fanfare. On this one count Hammett's hard-drinking Op remained true to South of Market custom, even while breaking up Pete the Finn's bootlegging operation.

California Progressives may have justified Hammett's skepticism, mending fences with the Republicans, attending to the businesses created by their projects, and hewing to an isolationist line in foreign affairs. Hearst moved toward right-wing populism and finally left his San Francisco newspapers in the hands of John Francis Neylan, whom he ordered to break the San Francisco general strike of 1934.

The improbability of enduring reform must have struck Hammett. What the middle-class, midwestern migrant wanted was a housecleaning, as the Op tells Elihu: "I'll give you nothing except a good job of city-cleaning. That's what you bargained for, and that's what you're going to get. . . . With your son dead, you've been able to promise them that the newspapers won't dig up any more dirt" (*Red Harvest* 59). Hammett offered readers the apocalyptic destruction—via Prohibition-era gang warfare—of all the recalcitrant ethnic factions. The Op merely operates for society's health: "Now I'm going to have my fun. . . . I'm going to . . . [open] Poisonville up from Adam's apple to ankles" (60).

MEDIA COMPETITION

Red Harvest reflects an awareness of narrative competition. The dime detective novel had established a mass readership, and the enormous explosion in pulp magazines, numbering twenty thousand by 1922, continued this popularity in altered form. These magazines offered several stories, appeared weekly, and were illustrated. Book publishers responded with tonier detective novels. Writers fought for whoever was buying and hoped to move up; Hammett moved from pulp magazines to the Borzoi line of Knopf that cost two dollars a copy during the Depression. Since detective fiction was rooted in the pulps, however, its perceived challenge came from newspapers and film. Newspapers had a stronger "truth claim" than pulps, predicated on the utility of "facts," which they used to move into sensational reportage of crime and scandal, threatening the narrative sources of much detective fiction. The pulps began to search for something newspapers were not supplying. One item was cultural coherence, an explanatory myth or interpretation of modern life. They also capitalized on the backlash against the "yellow journalism" of Hearst, Frank Munsey, and others, which led the detective novel to contend that "real" reality lay behind the surfaces reported by other media.

Film posed a more difficult challenge. Economically it had the disadvantages of being expensive to produce and distribute, of requiring special halls, and of not being portable. Dime novels and pulp magazines were cheap and could be read on streetcars or surreptitiously at work. But film had the enormous kinesthetic advantage of motion, visual veracity, and, later, sound. The competition with the pulp novel is most obvious in the action comedy genre usually traced to Mack Sennett.[7] Sennett filmed his first Keystone production in Los Angeles in 1912, and he eventually hired and trained Chaplin, Keaton, and Arbuckle. He made film an industrial product, turning out 140 one-reelers his first year, and extended its reach downward, writes Louis Giannetti, "with gleeful vulgarity" into "the lowest social echelons" (*Masters* 81). Violent and unpredictable, the Keystone comedies featured chases, pie throwing, traffic pileups, and physical comedy that ranged from the roundhouse punch to slipping on the banana peel. Targets were bourgeois culture, the monied classes, and officious but ineffective police and other authorities; these traits would continue in film noir. For instant communication, Keystone comedy depended on conventions of dress and facial expression, and for much of its humor, it relied on fast motion.

By the 1920s Chaplin and Keaton overshadowed their master. Keaton structured his films so that the rising action led to a chase, "because it speeds up the tempo," he said, "generally involves the whole cast, and puts the whole outcome of the story on the block" (Giannetti, *Masters* 105). His comic genius also addressed socioeconomic change, especially the fickleness of the new machinery in American life. Fascinated by Rube Goldberg, Keaton confronted his heroes with physical problems that they analyzed with ridiculous attention, calculating hilariously illogical solutions. *One Week* (1920) detailed the difficulties of erecting a mail-order house sold by Sears Roebuck, and *Our Hospitality* (1923) burlesqued travel, particularly on trains.

At the time of *Red Harvest* the detective novel began to respond to the challenge of film. Hammett was among the first to integrate stylishly the plot and characterization of the detective novel with car chases and other typically Keystone elements such as exploding buildings. The magazine serial of "Poisonville" is sophisticated in its use of violence, as studies of its editing by William Kenney, William Nolan, and Richard Layman have detailed (Kenney; Nolan, *Casebook* 49–50; Layman, *Shadow Man* 89–99). The Op is constantly in motion, usually in a car going somewhere. Physical humor is persistent, whether Chief Noonan is blowing up Pete the Finn's cache of bootleg liquor or the Op is keeping Reno Starkey from flying off the running board of Dinah Brand's Marmon.

The other machine slowed up for us to climb aboard. It was already full. We packed it in layers, with the overflow hanging on the running boards.

We bumped over dead Hank O'Mara's legs and headed for home. We covered one block of the distance with safety if not comfort. After that we had neither.

A limousine turned into the street ahead of us, came half a block toward us, put its side to us, and stopped. Out of the side, gun-fire.

We did our best, but we were too damned amalgamated for good fighting. You can't shoot straight holding a man in your lap, another hanging on your shoulder, while a third does his shooting from an inch behind your ear. (182)

Hammett's gags range from the macabre to puns on *amalgamated*, a word used to name labor unions and streetcar lines (and a metallurgical process).

In another of Hammett's *Red Harvest* action sequences, he shows the discovery of a stylistic irony applicable to action. "The chief's car got away first, off with a jump that hammered our teeth together. We missed the garage door by half an inch, chased a couple of pedestrians diagonally across the sidewalk, bounced off the curb into the roadway, missed a truck as narrowly as we had missed the door, and dashed out King Street with our siren wide open" (112). While it owes to film, Hammett made this irony into his own literary device by the novel's end: "I kicked the pooch out of the way, made the opposite fence, untangled myself from a clothes line, crossed two more yards, got yelled at from a window, had a bottle thrown at me, and dropped into a cobblestoned back street" (183). Like an art nouveau object, the sentence is a rhythmic and repetitively patterned exterior; no "feelings" or subjective reactions intrude. Hammett vaulted into the detective fiction limelight partly because he discovered this narrative equivalent of life's new design.

The style that Hammett developed in the Op stories and *Red Harvest* is deft but muscular and "at its best, was capable of saying anything," wrote Chandler (*Simple Art* 17). It falls within Walker Gibson's well-known definition in *Tough, Sweet, and Stuffy* of *tough talk* (7), yet it has unique features. Like the prose of Hemingway or Mencken, the Op's diction is characterized by short, simple, largely Anglo-Saxon words. In a typical story, his vocabulary is 77 percent monosyllabic and only 2 percent non-Anglo-Saxon. Hammett's stress on clarity is manifest in Dick Foley, the Op's assistant, who satirizes euphemisms such as "in conference" and "a victim of foul play" (see Marling, *Dashiell Hammett* 43–46).

Hammett's prose aligns with other criteria from the functionalist era of American industry and design: it features the first-person pronoun, eschews the passive voice, and employs short clauses. In Hammett's early work, his sentences average thirteen words in length. Descriptive passages run into flab at seventeen words, and fight scenes are built of sentences averaging eight words each, some only three or four words long. In the narrow columns of the pulp format, these sentences were not only easy to read but also formed their own tiny paragraphs, leaving white space, as in art nouveau, to indicate quickened action.

The speed of this prose resides in its verbs, which are rarely passive and often run as high as 20 percent of the word count. They tend to be simple, especially when the Op describes his actions, and only compound or passive when he characterizes his opposition or fills in a case history. Parallel verb structure helps Hammett cover ground:

> We crossed an alley, were beckoned through another gate by a big man in brown, passed through a house, out into the next street, and climbed into a black automobile that stood at the curb. . . .
>
> I walked around a few blocks until I came to an unlighted electric sign that said *Hotel Continental*, climbed a flight of steps to the second-floor office, registered, left a call for ten o'clock, was shown into a shabby room, moved some of the Scotch from my flask to my stomach, and took old Elihu's ten-thousand-dollar check and my gun to bed with me. (*Red Harvest* 52–53)

Speed is dangerous, an attribute of gangsters such as Max "Whisper" Thaler, who has the Stutz touring car and a driver who "knew what speed was" (*Red Harvest* 52). The effect of speed is enhanced by skillful transitions, elisions, and periodic sentences. Time and space are compressed as we move from scene to scene. If the Op seeks information from someone windy or inarticulate, he summarizes: when Old Elihu shoots the burglar, "the explanation was profane and lengthy and given to me in a loud and blustering voice" (40). Hammett often delays the introduction of a new scene until the end of a periodic sentence, forcing us to absorb other details first: "It was close to two-thirty in the morning when I reached the hotel" (38).

This style is built on a metonymic aesthetic. The narrator may leave out feelings or decline to cultivate the good wishes of the reader because he assumes in advance much common knowledge. But other authors who tried this style found the mere intimation of a subsurface content insufficient. In his early work, Hammett's verb-rich and action-rich style never permits questions about motivation or mental processes to arise. He constantly invokes the material world, which he describes with a draftsman's precision. The implication of this smooth-surfaced physical world for the emotions that the writer presumes to share with us is addressed, in *Red Harvest*, in the embedded dream narratives. The articulation of simultaneous external and internal narratives awaited the elliptical mastery that Hammett would achieve in *The Maltese Falcon*.

By far the most interesting and exuberant character in *Red Harvest* is Dinah Brand, described by one boyfriend as "a soiled dove . . . a de luxe hustler, a big-league gold-digger" (21).[8] Originally Hammett appears to have intended her as one of those vacuous flappers from Anita Loos's *Gentlemen Prefer Blondes* (1925). Dinah is "so thoroughly mercenary, so frankly greedy, that there's nothing disagreeable about it" (26).

Parsimonious and physically unimpressive, the Op is bound to clash with Dinah. He refuses to bribe her, declines to wine and dine her, and turns down the part of gallant defender. This prodigal operative adheres to the rules of the home office, yet he becomes her favorite. But Hammett gave Dinah such precise, vital details that she outstripped her model, which was growing worn. The initial suggestions of hard living, of prematurely spent innocence, critiquing the gold-digger, are followed by cascading details of her dishabille:

She was an inch or two taller than I, which made her about five feet eight. She had a broad-shouldered, full-breasted, round-hipped body and big muscular legs. The hand she gave me was soft, warm, strong. Her face was the face of a girl of twenty-five already showing signs of wear. Little lines crossed the corners of her big ripe mouth. Fainter lines were beginning to make nets around her thick-lashed eyes. They were large eyes, blue and a bit blood-shot. . . .

Her coarse hair—brown—needed trimming and was parted crookedly. One side of her upper lip had been rouged higher than the other. Her dress was of a particularly unbecoming wine color, and it gaped here and there down one side, where she had neglected to snap the fasteners or they had popped open. There was a run down the front of her left stocking. (30)

Coming from the unsophisticated Op, this critique is all the more damning. Hammett appears on the edge of unmasking the value (and fashion) system that creates gold-diggers, especially when he writes that Dinah has "a face hard as a silver dollar" (98). But the Op cannot bend to Dinah, nor can she cleave to him, without turning the novel toward romance. Dinah threatens to usurp our interest in the criminals: "She crossed left leg over right and looked down. Her eyes focussed on the run in her stocking. 'Honest to God, I'm going to stop wearing them!' she complained. 'I'm going barefooted. I paid five bucks for these socks yesterday. Now look at the damned things. Every day—runs, runs, runs!'" (31). Scenes such as this show the struggle that Dinah makes to conform to the image of the gold-digger. But her body is not lithe and boyish. The distance between Dinah and the ideal cannot be bridged by manufactured goods, and she articulates the frustration of women who could not imitate the lacquered look of the 1920s flapper. "Your legs are too big," the Op puts in. "They put too much strain on the material" (79).

The gold-digger in dishabille is a critique of "roughness," but Hammett, striving to be a popular author, must also entertain. Part of the entertainment value in Dinah is her lack of harmony with the geometric settings and smooth characterizations the era regards as modern. Dinah lives in a house that "was disorderly, cluttered up. There were too many pieces of furniture in it, and none of them seemed to be in its proper place" (29). The difference between the socks she feels like and the stockings she desires to be is the cultural dialectic of the rough and the smooth.

Hammett's critique is finally rather conservative: he associates the gold-digger with speculation. Dinah is first seen "at a table that had a lot of papers on it. Some of the papers were financial service bulletins, stock and bond market forecasts" (29). She has already used inside information about strikes (from Bill Quint) to speculate in Anaconda stock (33). Now she and the Op bet on the fixed Kid Cooper fight, and Dinah is mesmerized by the changing odds. "Inside stuff," says the Op of the fight in an "ex-casino" (65, 69). Kid Cooper dies for refusing to cooperate with the odds, as Hammett plays with the statistical theme. The clearest identification of speculation's meaning for Hammett is Dinah's indignant rejoinder on winning despite long odds: "I can expect anything I want" (76).

The alignment of these elements with respect to the fabula of the prodigal is interesting: the Op, initially a faithful son, is reluctantly and ironically prodigal. He is *sent* to a far country by the Old Man. Not about to spend the father's money on foreign whores, he merely observes this far country where whores speculate. He adopts their methods only to destroy them, his own prodigality displaced on women and the far country. Repentance is replaced by the "results" that allow his return to the Old Man. All of the prodigal's rationales seek to deny the father's authority, but all of his actions confirm it. The fabula, however, demands that Dinah be put away, and stylistically, her dishabille seems intended to preclude sexual allure and to facilitate this. The Op, though, becomes nostalgic for rough values.

Hammett addressed interior/exterior conflict in the novel's embedded narratives, which concern alienation. Just as Keaton added dream sequences to his films, so Hammett gave his novels a "psychological" dimension by embedding "parables." The Op has two dreams: one of a vanishing woman wearing a long black veil, another of a sombrero-clad suspect whom he pursues. These also serve two pragmatic functions. They give a "coked-up" version of Dinah Brand's murder, the details of which Reno Starkey later confirms. Both dreams are also quests: the first, for a personal emotional life, ends in shame; the second, for a man (reflecting the Op's occupation), ends in death. Taken sequentially, the allegorical thrust of the dreams is that the admission of emotion leads to death. The Op has been warned, like heroes of Grail quests, by "supernatural" means after taking a potion (he is drugged with laudanum).

But the dreams play a role in the novel's ideological arbitrations as well. Dinah, romance, and the aesthetics of rough/smooth have to be disposed of. The prodigal must free himself from the "foreign whore" before returning to his father. Hammett stages the dream in his own hometown, indicating the depth of this mythopoesis: "I dreamed I was sitting on a bench, in Baltimore, facing the tumbling fountain in Harlem Park, beside a woman who wore a veil. I had come there with her. She was somebody I knew well. But I had suddenly forgotten who she was. I couldn't see her face because of the long black veil" (149).

This passage is striking in the way it allegorizes the Op's alienation (necessary for the fabula). The Op "had come there with her" but has "forgotten who she was" now that he faces home. Hammett's dreamer disposes of the roughness of a past in the far country by a smoothing craftsmanship (perhaps alluding to Hawthorne's "The Long Black Veil"). Since the Op is sleeping, auditory images are strong. The obscuring folds of the veil repeat the tumbling streams of the fountain. Tumbling water, flowing veil, and, later, the falling dreamer become parallel stylistic elements.

In the next section the Op loses the woman as a crowd shouts "Fire! Fire!" and fire engines roar. Only when he stops looking does he find her, getting off a train and beginning to kiss him. Not only the settings but also the auditory images are progressively mechanized—from fountain to fire engine to train. Machinery removes and delivers the loved one, anticipating Chandler and his "celibate machine" as well as film noir. A major difference between Hammett's and their sensory figurations is that Hammett's Op, despite his displacements, will still manifest the traditional guilt, with the necessity of repentance.

In the second dream, the Op chases a "small brown man" over church roofs: "My hand knocked his sombrero off and closed on his head. It was a smooth hard round head no larger than a large egg. My fingers went all the way around it. Squeezing his head in one hand, I tried to bring the knife out of my pocket with the other—and realized that I had gone off the edge of the roof with him." This dream turns out to be a "coked-up" version of Dinah's murder: the egg-shaped head is the bulbous handle of the ice pick with which the Op may have killed her. The sexual and kinesthetic values of this dream contrast with those of the first. The earlier emotional estrangement, with its frustrated heterosexuality, gives way to the dynamic diction of "knocked" and "closed" and "went all the way around" and "squeezing" and "realized that I had gone off," suggesting ejaculation. Unlike the woman, this man yells and laughs to get the Op's attention. Pursuit is a public spectacle rather than a private torment, and the object of desire, as he flees over smooth and slippery surfaces, is always just beyond reach. Finally the Op grasps his head as they fall "giddily down toward the millions of upturned faces in the crowd" (151). This dream suggests outcomes to the first, namely the pursuit and elimination of the "small brown" foreign self, cleaving off the prodigal or alienated in oneself. That this dreamer captures the object of his desire, in front of a churchgoing populace, without any of the former opprobrium, suggests not only homo-sexual possibilities but also broader consumerist ones—a liberation from sanctions against "self."

Two shapes dominate the second dream: the round of the egglike head and the sombrero, and the edge of the knife and roof. The Op's kinesthetic dilemma is his inability to grasp the "smooth." His man is apprehensible if the Op can wield the knife, if he can cut or edge or groove (or kill) him. But the egg thus made graspable, though it may in the sexual sense be im-pregnated, is ruined for aesthetic consumption. Its phenomenal essence is destroyed, and so the Op goes "off the edge" before he can grasp it or make his mark. Such a reading might appear overwrought were not the egg such a common aesthetic emblem of the 1920s, from Sherwood Anderson's "The Egg and I" to the East and West Eggs of *The Great Gatsby*. Vernacu-lar speech was riddled with phrases like the Op's "This Reno is a tough egg, isn't he?" (144). This egg, this ovum, this smoothness, is essentially female for Hammett, and Reno is the Op's favorite gangster, while other gangsters have "cutting" qualities: Max "Whisper" Thaler has "features as regular as if they had been cut by a die" (11).

With this dialectic of rough/smooth in mind, we can even group the characters. The rough, like Dinah, are a reservoir of soiled but precious authenticity. They include Bill Quint, the IWW radical, a "square-set man in rumpled gray clothes" (6); and Kid Cooper, the "ruddy straw-haired solid-built boy with a dented face and too much meat around the top of his lavender trunks" (71). Also rumpled or pudgy are the Op, Dinah, Chief Noonan, and Dan Rolf (Hammett's self-portrait). In contrast, criminals like Starkey and Thaler are smooth, as is Old Elihu Willsson, whose face is a geometric design that anticipates Sam Spade: "The old man's head was small and almost perfectly round under its close cut crop of white hair. His ears were too small and plastered too flat to the sides of his head to spoil the spherical effect. . . . Mouth and chin were straight lines chopping the sphere off" (13). In this cubist reduction, character is surface: smoothness equals financial and physical power.

But Hammett was still ambivalent about the smooth, as indicated by the Op's contrasting assistants. "Mickey Linehan was a big slob with sagging shoulders and a shapeless body that seemed to be coming apart at all its joints. His ears stood out like red wings, and his round red face usually wore the meaningless smirk of a half-wit. He looked like a comedian and was" (108). Like Arbuckle, Linehan is easygoing, trusting and trustworthy. In contrast, Dick Foley, who suspects that the Op murdered Dinah, is a "boy-sized Canadian with a sharp irritable face. He wore high heels to increase his height, perfumed his handkerchiefs and saved all the words he could" (108). In his self-preserving suspicion and verbal economy, Foley is the model office worker, but he is also vain and foreign. This nexus of self-styling, streamlined speech, and foreignness is not yet trustworthy. But the contrast is finally ambiguous, because Foley is also the source of a verbal compression that the Op finds amusing (and shares in action sequences) and that Hammett intends the reader to understand as a positive value:

"Spot two. Out three-thirty, office to Willsson's. Mickey. Five. Home. Busy. Kept plant. Off three, seven. Nothing yet."

That was supposed to inform me that he had picked up Lew Yard at two the previous afternoon; had shadowed him to Willsson's at three-thirty, where Mickey had tailed Pete; had followed Yard away at five, to his residence; had seen people going in and out of the house, but had not shadowed any of them; had watched the house until three this morning and had returned to the job at seven; and since then had seen nobody go in or out. (132)

Foley's report per se is a failure, because the Op has to make his elisions meaningful. That the semantics of Foley's speech are spelled out implies that an ideology of metonymy had appeared, but the suspicion in the revealed story that "helper" Foley is actually an "opponent" indicates that Hammett was not ready to capitalize on it. Hammett's leaning toward "meiosis" is clearer in lawyer Charles Proctor Dawn, whose self-infatuation recalls the story "Nelson Redline." Dawn speaks in filigree and is probably a satire on Philo Vance: "I may say this, my dear sir, without false modesty, appreciating with both fitting humility and a deep sense of true and lasting values, my responsibilities as well as my prerogatives as a—and why should I stoop to conceal the fact that there are those who feel justified in preferring to substitute the definite article for the indefinite?—recognized and accepted leader of the bar in this thriving state" (Red Harvest 163–64).

"What'll it cost?" the Op asks (164). The contrast could not be blunter.

Dawn joins the corpses, as much for his logorrhea as by plot necessity. But Hammett's attraction to verbal economy and the smooth was still in conflict with his disposition to favor characters of frumpy, old-fashioned reliability, so *Red Harvest* is caught in an internal dialectic between old and emerging styles. Until he invented a character who reflected the smoothness of his style, the genuinely new cultural product within his ability would remain beyond his grasp.

Advertising taught Hammett to consider his readers carefully and gave him the habit of creating points of identification. The quotidian characteristics of the Op are the most obvious, but we may overlook *Red Harvest's* nineteenth-century commonplace about clean collars. Op: "I bent a fresh collar around my neck and trotted over to the City Hall" (133). Reno, "collarless and in shirt-sleeves and vest, sat tilted back in a chair" (153). The bar owner was "a fat man with a dirty collar, a lot of gold teeth, and only one ear" (176).

Another commonplace in *Red Harvest* is "cards." The dominant game of the earlier era, cards figuratively encompasses the unknown situation from which the skilled player can emerge victorious. As the Op says, "I was in a good spot if I played my hand right" (137). A commonplace about spats will be relevant when Raymond Chandler occupies our attention. Until then we must file Hammett's treatment: "The punch carried MacSwain across the room until a wall stopped him. The wall creaked under the strain, and a framed photograph of Noonan and other city dignitaries welcoming somebody in spats dropped down to the floor with the hit man" (91).

Some points of reader identification were still so new as to require explanation. Among the maladies plaguing the public, according to copywriters, was "nervousness." As Tom Lutz explains in *American Nervousness*, nerves were de rigueur, a result of urbanization, mechanization, and office jobs. Cigarettes, gum, exercise, and Hammond's Brain Pills were touted as restoring "brain force" lost at work (Lutz 107). So the Op explains a good deal of nervous behavior, including his own: "I wanted a cigarette, but cigarettes were too well known as first aids to the nervous for me to take a chance on one just then" (*Red Harvest* 156). The development of nervousness into hysteria, a phenomenon detailed by Lutz, is illustrated in the Op's belief that he may have killed Dinah.

The Op goes to a far country, takes up with a "foreign whore," and destroys his own moral capital and everyone else's economic capital. He comes to a state of repentance: "This damned burg's getting me. If I don't get away soon I'll be going blood-simple like the natives" (142). He longs for the order of his father's house. He disengages himself from a foreign father he has mistakenly hired out to (after two failed reconciliation scenes), loses his foreign whore, and finds his real "father": "The Old Man was the manager of the Continental's San Francisco branch. He was also known as Pontius Pilate, because he smiled pleasantly when he sent us out to be crucified on suicidal jobs. He was a gentle, polite, elderly person with no more warmth in him than a hangman's rope. The Agency wits said he could spit icicles in July" (108–9).

This jobholder's God, like Job's God, requires daily self-mortification in the form of a report, as Mickey Linehan reminds the Op: the Old Man "said he hadn't got any reports from you for a couple of days" (109). The Op's reports will not stand the Old Man's scrutiny, so he does not send them. These reports are not a minor omission, but a key feature of the fabula as it appears in the papyri. The Op must justify his transgression by reference to the higher value of "efficiency": " 'If it works out the way I want it to, I won't have to report all the distressing details,' I said. 'It's right enough for the Agency to have rules and regulations, but when you're out on a job you've got to do it the best way you can. And anybody that brings any ethics to Poisonville is going to get them all rusty. A report is no place for the dirty details, anyway, and I don't want you birds to send any writing back to San Francisco without letting me see it first' " (109–10).

Technology provided a model in which the omission of steps equaled efficiency; here the failure to report provides satisfying opportunities for rebellion against the corporate pyramid. The narrative establishes ideological equivalents to the Op's omissions in the work environments. Sins against the paperwork regime are permitted when there are spectacular results: "I've got myself tangled up in something and as soon as the Old Man smells it—and San Francisco isn't far enough away to fool his nose—he's going to be sitting on the wire, asking for explanations. I've got to have results to hide the details under" (110). In this rebellion, a common belief in "results" sanctions fewer human steps. "I've arranged a killing or two in my time, when they were necessary," says the Op (142). They are, here. He not only achieves his object, but Old Elihu asks him to become police chief of the reconstituted town. The suggestion of this fantasy of elder brother–ism is enough. The Op "could be" elder brother in the far country, but he prefers home. "I spent most of my week in Ogden trying to fix up my reports so they would not read as if I had broken as many Agency rules, state laws and human bones as I had" (198).

The detective as letterwriter, as *fonctionnaire* in a bureaucracy, is not entirely new (François Eugène Vidocq wrote from his agents' reports), but Hammett's alignment of the fabula of prodigality, the confessional letter, and the emerging dialectic of the rough and smooth was suggestive. His mode of emplotment was still comedic—this prodigal will be received by his father, a feast awaits him, the disharmonious forces of the world are reconciled—but the mode of his argument was shifting from the integrative and organic view of synecdoche to the reductive and extrinsic explanation typical of metonymy. From the opening details of "Personville called Poisonville" and the unshaven policeman, the metaphoric style of *Red Harvest* is largely synecdochical: details represent organic qualities of the whole. Personville represents urban political corruption during Prohibition, whether San Francisco or Baltimore. Yet the emphasis on patterning in narrative elements, from Dinah to the dream sequence to the styles of speech, shows Hammett's increasing attraction to the singularity of agents, causes, and acts.

The Maltese Falcon

The Maltese Falcon (1930) is arguably America's greatest detective novel, but its status as such is the product of a continuing cultural consensus. When published it announced a new style, one adopted widely, which we, viewing it in retrospect, have come to accept as *the* style of the period. In other words, *The Maltese Falcon* is a classic not only because of its literary quality and response to its age but also because when we have looked back on it we recognized the origins of what we have become. Alternate genealogies are always available, but we do not see ourselves in *The Benson Murder Case* (1928) or *Little Caesar* (1929) or even in Hammett's other work.

Part of the *Falcon's* attraction is its plot, the distillation of two years' worth of writing. During that time Hammett claimed to have written 250,000 words—an amount equal to half of the Bible. From "The Whosis Kid" he took the claustrophobic apartment settings and character of Ines Almad, an alluring foreigner with robbery loot, on the lam from three partners. When the partners show up, the action is heightened by the confining space and their mutual suspicion. From "The Gutting of Couffignal" Hammett took the circumstantial plausibility of his detective's surrender to a beautiful woman who offers her body and has the means to support him, as well as the detective's ritual recitation of his code.

Brigid O'Shaughnessy, an exotic femme fatale with a name resonant in local politics, hires Sam Spade and Miles Archer to protect her from former partner Thursby. Archer functions as an older brother, with whose wife Spade is cavorting. When Archer and Thursby are murdered, Spade decides "to keep the family troubles in the family" (21). This prodigal becomes his elder brother. Then Brigid draws him into her plan to sell a jewel-encrusted statue to her former partners Cairo, Wilmer, and that avatar of Arbuckle, Casper Gutman. They come to San Francisco, where they are greater prodigals than ever Spade was, a vision of invasion from within that we saw earlier in Dos Passos. The foreign element is supplied by the exotic (and mostly true) history of the icon. The Knights Templar who created it were successful in their far country, Malta (see Marling, *Dashiell Hammett* 70–73; Layman, *Shadow Man* 110–11). The formerly dissolute Spade must reconstitute control over society's store of energy. Never really believing in the icon's value, he collects fees from everyone; his pragmatism contrasts with the romanticism of the crooks he plays against one another. Cairo and Wilmer (homosexuals) and Gutman (sadist) are precluded from our sympathy, but Brigid's romance with Spade deepens until the climax, when he reveals that she killed Archer (which the "objective" style precludes readers from knowing). Seeing himself as her next "sap," Spade gives an anguished recitation of his code and turns Brigid over to policemen Polhaus and Dundy. The final scene presents Spade with a choice between Effie, his secretary and a de-sexualized mother figure, and Iva, the elder brother's wife for whom he must now provide.

The Maltese Falcon is famous for its "objective" point of view: Hammett appears never to look omnisciently into the minds of his hero or other characters, but merely to describe what we would see by following along. We are not privy to motive, a potential advantage in preserving the revealed story. Hammett exploited this fully, making his stylistic elisions part of our impression of Spade's mind: if we knew the detective's thoughts, we would understand why he acts the way he does, and there would be no mystery. *Objective style* refers to passages like this:

> A telephone bell rang in darkness. When it had rung three times bed-springs creaked, fingers fumbled on wood, something small and hard thudded on a carpeted floor, the springs creaked again, and a man's voice said:
> "Hello. . . . Yes, speaking. . . . Dead?" (10)

Hammett tells us nothing of Spade's reaction to being awakened, much less his feelings about his partner's death, which becomes one of the novel's mysteries. By eliding such information, the objective style emphasizes actions and objects, forcing us to schematize the subjectivity of the character's consciousness. Our perception of the relation between actions becomes the "reaction" of the character, which film noir later constructs by technique. No passage is more famous for this than Spade's cigarette-rolling after learning of Archer's murder:

> Spade's thick fingers made a cigarette with deliberate care, sifting a measured quantity of tan flakes down into curved paper, spreading the flakes so that they lay equal at the ends with a slight depression in the middle, thumbs rolling the paper's inner edge down and up under the other edge as forefingers pressed it over, thumbs and fingers sliding to the paper cylinder's ends to hold it even while tongue licked the flap, left forefinger and thumb pinching their end while right forefinger and thumb smoothed the damp seam, right forefinger and thumb twisting their end and lifting the other to Spade's mouth. (10–11)

This sentence works on two metonymic levels: it represents Spade's interior state through elision, rendering it as a kind of mechanization; and it parodies entailment, the elaboration of a process typical of mechanization, especially on the assembly line. But what does Spade feel? We don't know.

The illusion of objectivity is established early by such passages. At the scene of Archer's death, Hammett devotes half a page to a tableau that turns out to have little narrative import but that further overdetermines this style:

> An automobile popped out of the tunnel beneath him with a roaring swish, as if it had been blown out, and ran away. Not far from the tunnel's mouth a man was hunkered on his heels before a billboard that held advertisements of a moving picture and a gasoline across the front of a gap between two store-buildings. The hunkered man's head was bent almost to the sidewalk so he could look under the billboard. A hand flat on the paving, a hand clenched on the billboard's green frame, held him, in this grotesque position. Two other men stood awkwardly together at one end of the billboard, peeping through the few inches of space between it and the building at that end. The building at the other end had a blank grey sidewall that looked down on the lot behind the billboard. Lights flickered on the sidewall, and the shadows of men moving among lights. (12)

No clue is found here, and billboards never reappear, but the objective style points to itself, like the man in the grotesque crouch connecting the advertising of the billboard to the ground, who is surely Hammett's self-portrait. We leave such passages feeling that the whole novel is told from the objective point of view.

It was advertising that had suggested to Hammett the power inherent in a style that left readers to fill in the meaning elided by objectivity. In one of his advertising book reviews of the early twenties he called it "meiosis."

> Meiosis—to give understatement of this sort its technical name—has nothing to do with modesty of moderation in speech as such, with conservative statement, with strict adherence to the truth. It is a rhetorical trick, the employment of understatement, not to deceive, but to increase

the impression made on reader or hearer. In using it the object is, not to be believed, but to be disbelieved to one's advantage. One says to his reader: "I am deliberately telling you less than the truth. Here is something you can't believe literally. You've got to believe more than this" (in Johnson 317).

To be fair, this style often suggests appropriate feelings about characters and actions, partly through its muscular verbs, without violating its rule. Take this passage: "Spade *stood* beside the girl, *put* a hand on her head and *smoothed* her hair away from its parting. 'Sorry, angel, I haven't—' He *broke off* as the inner door opened. 'Hello, Iva,' he said to the woman who had opened it" (25). The emphasized verbs describe observable actions but provide a metonymic sequence of action for evaluation. We know nothing, objectively, of Spade's subjective reaction to this intrusion. But a great deal of emotion is implied by the situation per se and by the strong parallel verbs, which give a sequence of physical motions, unguided by dialogue, thought, or reflection. Spade caresses one woman; then another comes in, and he (soon) caresses her. His motives and feelings are unknown, but his sexual empathy is broad and repeatable, like something mechanized.

It is difficult to write an entire novel in this style, however, and Hammett found ways of couching subjectivity in pseudo-objective description: "She squirmed on her end of the settee and her eyes wavered between heavy lashes, as if trying and failing to free their gaze from his. She seemed smaller, and very young and oppressed" (37). Who is the source of the simile "as if"? To whom does Brigid "seem" if not to Spade? Both sentences require another consciousness for comparative purposes; it can be only Hammett's or Spade's, and readers seem to settle on the latter. This is a (mis)cueing that increases as the novel progresses: "Spade's surprise was genuine" (53). "Anxiety looked through her smile" (60). " 'I don't give a damn about your honesty,' he told her, trying to make himself speak calmly" (64). These are miscues because they encourage us to feel we understand Spade's motives, when misunderstanding Spade is what preserves the central mystery.

Two other important devices by which Hammett evaded the limits of objectivity were dialogue and synecdochical description. Most of the characters have conversational signatures: Gutman repeats grace phrases, like "By Gad, sir" and "Well, sir." Brigid refers to Cairo as Joe when everyone else calls him Joel. She also speaks in a fragmented, reiterative style, as when she delivers her speech of repentance (which turns out to be a repeat): "I know I've no right to ask you to trust me if I won't trust you. I do trust you, but I can't tell you. I can't tell you now. Later I will, when I can. I'm afraid, Mr. Spade. I'm afraid of trusting you. I don't mean that. I do trust you, but—I trusted Floyd and—I've nobody else" (37). The ideology inculcated by the objective style argues against trusting such speech as genuine, as does the one-sided trust Brigid urges on Spade.

Hammett uses synecdoche principally to describe men and Spade's relations to them. Spade is characterized by the "steep rounded slope of his shoulder" and his "conical" shape (2), which "made his body like a bear's" (11). Being blond, he is also a "golden bear," the California state animal. When he is threatened by Dundy, Spade's "upper lip on the left side twitched over his eyetooth," a detail repeated several times (19, 79). "I'm sorry I got up on my hind legs," he apologizes (22). His comparison to a bear supplies our organic understanding of Spade later when "red rage came suddenly into his face and he began to talk in a harsh guttural voice" (93) or "his eyes burned yellowly" (101).

Recently this "objective" style has been questioned. James Guetti, in an instructive 1982 essay, examined the prose of Hammett, Chandler, and Ross Macdonald from the paired perspectives of information theory and reader response criticism. He found Hammett's style, especially his descriptions of characters, "provoking, even irritating" because the descriptions are a "collection of visual fragments."

We may know from information theory that the information present in any situation is proportional to the "resistance" of that situation. We may feel "informed" while reading Hammett's prose, then, because all these separate items, all these details, compose a resistance to our reading efforts, and our response to that resistance is to increase those efforts. We try harder and harder to smooth the story out, to break it down to something hardier and neater than this list of details, to reduce it in volume by somehow changing its state from a mixture of separate things to a more homogeneous solution. (Guetti 134)

Guetti does not ask questions about readers of 1930, their economic lives, their horizon of reading expectations, or such aesthetic issues as rough versus smooth. Given his approach, that is perfectly acceptable. He is little interested in questions of genre or the way in which emerging and declining styles mediate one another. He is a "modern reader," whose critique suggests that we no longer read Hammett in a context that makes his style meaningful. Albeit indirectly, Guetti raises the question of the function of this style and whether it has a relation to history.

The passage that most provokes and irritates Guetti is Hammett's introduction of the villain, Casper Gutman: "The fat man was flabbily fat with bulbous pink cheeks and lips and chins and neck, with a great soft egg of a belly that was all his torso, and pendant cones for arms and legs. As he advanced to meet Spade all his bulbs rose and shook and fell separately with each step, in the manner of clustered soap-bubbles not yet released from the pipe through which they had been blown. His eyes, made small by fat puffs around them, were dark and sleek. Dark ringlets thinly covered his broad scalp" (*Maltese Falcon* 118–19). Guetti's critique is out of sympathy: "It repeats itself dissonantly and insistently. . . . Its sentences lose their grammar and become lists. . . . Its concern with explanatory clarity becomes overextended and boring. . . . And it is so intent upon its variation of detail that its construction becomes gratingly unvarying" (135–36). In Guetti's estimate, this stylistic debacle exists to challenge the reader, to provide "resistance" to the aggressive drive to solve the mystery, which is "Whodunit?"

Surely this is to impute to Hammett, the copywriter, a disinclination to meet readers in their realm that would have doomed him to the same obscurity that has claimed S. S. Van Dine. Such literary lightning rods as Dorothy Parker deemed these descriptions the essence of Hammett's modernity. There is no evidence that Hammett wanted us to pit our wits against his. As Chandler noted, he wrote "for people with a sharp, aggressive attitude to life" (*Simple Art*, 16). So why is his style "resistive"? Simply put, the cultural conflict that gave *The Maltese Falcon* its stylistic power has abated. A cluster of emerging design and economic values crystallized in this novel, and we forget that the outcome could have been otherwise.

From its opening words, *The Maltese Falcon* concerns itself with the clash of the rough and the smooth in the domain of popular style. These values are illustrated by Hammett's change from the Op to an art nouveau detective: "Samuel Spade's jaw was long and bony, his chin a jutting V under the more flexible V of his mouth. His nostrils curved back to make another, smaller, V. His yellow-grey eyes were horizontal. The V-*motif* was picked up again by thickish brows rising outward from twin creases above a hooked nose, and his pale brown hair grew down—from high flat temples—in a point on his forehead. He looked rather pleasantly like a blond satan" (1). As more than one scholar has noted, this is an impossible face. If we attempt to draw it, we have a design of V's that caricatures a devil. The point of opening the book with this description is that such distinct visual emphases position the hero immediately among competing design cultures, and hence with respect to socioeconomic change. The whiplash angles of Spade's face echo the popular curvilinear motif of art nouveau. Hammett, designing a new hero for new readers in a new era, tells them by this design that Spade is no Victorian detective. Spade is modern, seemingly amoral, rather than a synecdoche for any reassuring quality, as, say, Sherlock Holmes was for reason. Spade has organic and familiar exterior features, but they mediate a new internal dynamic.

The function of representing the purely modern falls to Miss Wonderly (Brigid O'Shaughnessy), whose multiple names suggest her dispersed, variable personality and whose description makes her unique without suggesting any synecdochical type (as Dinah Brand did the gold-digger): "She was tall and pliantly slender, without angularity anywhere. Her body was erect and high-breasted, her legs long, her hands and feet narrow. She wore two shades of blue that had been selected because of her eyes. The hair curling from under her blue hat was darkly red, her full lips more brightly red. White teeth glistened in the crescent her timid smile made" (2). "Without angularity anywhere," "long," "narrow," "pliantly slender," and made up in red (hair and lips) and attired in two shades of blue—could Brigid's glistening white teeth complete a pun on the American flag? Gone is Dinah's dishabille. Brigid, modeled on a Miss O'Toole in Samuels's office, is thoroughly modern: smooth, aerodynamic, and painted in primary hues. Just as the newly designed typewriters, automobiles, and telephones were sheathed, so Brigid's emotions and motives are not visible. But her fairing will soon be stripped away to reveal the unmodern O'Shaughnessy.

The two styles, Spade and Wonderly, are opposed in the first three hundred words. Then the context of the conflict is detailed:

> The tappity-tap-tap and the thin bell and the muffled whir of Effie Perine's typewriting came through the closed door. Somewhere in a neighboring office a power-driven machine vibrated dully. On Spade's desk a limp cigarette smouldered in a brass tray filled with the remains of limp cigarettes. Ragged grey flakes of cigarette-ash dotted the yellow top of the desk and the green blotter and the papers that were there. A buff-curtained window, eight or ten inches open, let in from the court a current of air faintly scented with ammonia. The ashes on the desk twitched and crawled in the current. (2)

The modern workplace is the terrain to be contested. Its visual portrayal as mechanized and ash-dotted dates to the 1890s and ash can school painters. Its literary rendering, beginning with Stephen Crane and proceeding through the muckraking journalists, became such a convention that Fitzgerald could depend on it (the Valley of Ashes) in *The Great Gatsby*.

In Spade and Wonderly, we meet two adaptations to workplace anxiety. Wonderly, completely identified with the new and the modern, is suspect, as her stammering inarticulateness reveals. She anxiously questions her own actions: "I shouldn't have done that, should I?" "That is what he would tell me anyhow, isn't it?" (6). We cannot trust her because the ellipses in her dialogue are designed to elicit information, rather than presuming a world shared with Spade. Her exterior design may designate her as modern, but she actually expresses an amorality that is futureless. On the other hand, Spade's apparently guarded way of speaking and showing emotion, in contrast to his satanic appearance, manifests a reassuring concern for survival. But this guardedness will turn out to be an ideological sleight of hand, by which the modern implies (only) those traditional qualities it requires. Spade may not be modern, but he is more modern than the others, a realization that comes only after we have taken his side and been led to the novel's ultimate endorsement of a new style of behavior.

Spade's sub-rosa modernity is developed by the conventions of description, Guetti's "reading resistance." There is no chance that we will side with Spade's partner, Miles Archer, for he is a draft horse from the past: Archer is of "medium height, solidly built, wide in the shoulders, thick in the neck, with a jovial heavy-jawed red face and some grey in his close-trimmed hair." "His voice was heavy, coarse" (5–6). Archer is killed early by the avatar of pure modernity, Miss Wonderly, near the Stockton Street Tunnel planned by her patronymic father, Michael O'Shaughnessy. Spade's ironic "You've got brains, yes you have" at the moment he is cuckolding Archer makes it clear the latter is only Babbitt with a private badge. Sergeant Tom Polhaus and Lieutenant Dundy belong not only to the Victorian era but also to the ethnic infighting. "The Lieutenant was a compactly built man with a round head under short-cut grizzled hair and a square face behind a short-cut grizzled mustache. A five-dollar gold-piece was pinned to his neck-tie and there was a small elaborate diamond-set secret-society emblem on his lapel" (17). Dundy, Archer, Polhaus, and Shilling are variations on a type that Hammett sets up as the Sap, to contrast with Spade. The essence of this type is the absence of sheathing. They are rough, and their mental operations stand revealed like a Victorian scale's gears: Dundy's eyes fix Spade "in a peculiarly rigid stare, as if their focus were a matter of mechanics, to be changed only by pulling a lever or pressing a button" (18).

On Miss Wonderly's side, the crooks appear, one by one, as progressively more slippery versions of the smooth. Like Max Thaler of *Red Harvest*, they are too cut, too tight:

Mr. Joel Cairo was a small-boned dark man of medium height. His hair was black and smooth and very glossy. His features were Levantine. A square-cut ruby, its sides paralleled by four baguette diamonds, gleamed against the deep green of his cravat. His black coat, cut tight to narrow shoulders, flared a little over slightly plump hips. His trousers fitted his round legs more snugly than was the current fashion. The uppers of his patent-leather shoes were hidden by fawn spats. He held a black derby hat in a chamois-gloved hand and came towards Spade with short, mincing, bobbing steps. The fragrance of *chypre* came with him. (*Maltese Falcon* 46)

Like Miss Wonderly (and Dick Foley of *Red Harvest*), Cairo is fashion-conscious and "glossy," but like Gutman, he is plump and "bobs," intimating some covered-up flaw in the smooth. In holding Spade at gunpoint to search his office, Cairo is more overtly hostile than Wonderly. His stylistic threat does not become clear until the appearance of Gutman, who is Fatty Arbuckle refined figuratively. Here is the quintessential "too smooth" character: his smooth surface has been subdivided—into bubbles, ringlets, eggs, pearls, and patent leather—until it becomes rough and inefficient. By reticulating and dispersing smoothness, Hammett found a phenomenal way of making it rough and repulsive, a sensory warning that we turn against Cairo and Wonderly. "Too smooth" is not to be trusted. Thus do conventions of description bracket the appropriate smoothness for Spade.

Of the remaining characters, less description is given. The aptly named Effie (short for Euphemia, meaning "fair speech" and "abstinence from foul speech," hence "constancy" [Partridge 72, 82]) is a "lanky sunburned girl whose tan dress of thin woolen stuff clung to her with an effect of dampness. Her eyes were brown and playful in a shiny boyish face" (*Maltese Falcon* 1). Her visual style, like Spade's, suggests the mediation of the modern by hints of organic familiarity: her exterior is not completely smooth, but smooth enough, with a self-preserving, guarded emotional demeanor.

These descriptions are not a devilish obstacle to solving the mystery, but the ideological bracketing of meiosis. Such repeated details as the patent-leather shoes of Cairo and Gutman are markers in the "fashion rhetoric" of larger social forces. As Roland Barthes noted, "the fashion text represents as it were the authoritative voice of some one who knows all there is behind the jumbled or incomplete appearance of the visible forms" (14). That such signs should be perceived as "resistance," rather than as a path to solution, simply means that the older conflict, now that we live in its outcome, has lost its immediacy.

THE SAP

The climax of *The Maltese Falcon* is not the unmasking of the falcon as a fake, but Spade's revelation that he is turning his client and ostensible romantic interest, Brigid, over to the police.

"You didn't—don't—l-love me?"
"I think I do," Spade said. "What of it?" The muscles holding his smile in place stood out like wales. "I'm not Thursby. I'm not Jacobi. I won't play the sap for you." (250)

This response suddenly clarifies stylistic and emotional elements in the novel, crystallizing them in *sap*. Among other things, Spade's response subordinates romance to self-discipline, professionalism, and class interest. It opens a view of Spade's character, now seen to accommodate feigning both love and hate. It reveals what is modern about him, which is his interior.

Spade's reasons for not being a sap may strike us today as hypocritical, but in 1930 this list explained his curious behavior throughout the novel and illuminated in retrospect his actions, for a good deal of the mystery was why Spade acted as he did. He begins with an appeal to the traditional social bonds that typified a nineteenth-century community: "When a man's partner is killed he's supposed to do something about it." But neither partnership nor community have roles in Spade's life: he is a loner, without wife or coeval. Spade, rather, suggests homologous elements in the emerging structure of society, which Hammett quickly lists: "Then it happens we were in the detective *business*. Well when one of *your organization* gets killed, it's *bad business* to let the killer get away with it. It's bad all around—bad for that one *organization*, bad for *every detective everywhere*" (252, emphasis added). This argument reflects a narrow allegiance to a specific profession and the perception by its members of the world as it affects their interests: Spade is a small businessman. The third reason tightens this focus on profession: "I'm a detective and expecting me to run criminals down and then let them go free is like asking a dog to catch a rabbit and let it go" (252). But earlier detectives did just that when larger interests dictated: Philo Vance did it, Trent did it, and so did the Continental Op. The new standards imposed by getting a living in a narrow trade, however, preclude the acknowledgment of traditional community ties and emotional bonds.

The fourth and fifth reasons explain the preclusion of emotion as self-preservation: "No matter what I wanted to do now it would be absolutely impossible for me to let you go without having myself dragged to the gallows," and "I couldn't be sure you wouldn't decide to shoot a hole in *me* some day" (253). There are even notes of competition and survival of the fittest here, as the emerging ideology seizes useful elements of the preceding system. Hammett strips from the Victorian social model some useful affective aspects while retaining its laissez-faire economic freedom and self-interest. The latter becoming primary, Spade finally turns them on Brigid's championing of affection: "All we've got is the fact that maybe you love me and maybe I love you." She encouraged his affection in order to reap economic gain, he says, as though he were an unwary consumer: "I won't because all of me wants to—wants to say to hell with the consequences and do it—and because—God damn you—you've counted on that with me the same as you counted on that with the others" (254). These lines perform important ideological work. The serialization of sexuality was ostensibly taboo under the old system, because commerce in it undermined the family; under the new system, such commodification is possible but seems to threaten the illusion of individual uniqueness necessary to synchronous isolated work. Yet the discovery that sexuality can be managed in serialization by denying it an affective content is implicit in Spade's behavior, for he sleeps with Brigid in order to search her apartment.

No, Spade is not a sap, which is slang for "saphead," connoting a fool or dupe. Tom Sawyer applied the word to Huck Finn in 1884. In the 1910s *sap* was short for "homo sapiens," but the traditional use soon returned, as Keaton showed in *The Sap-head* (1920). The figure is worth examining. On being sapped, "the circulating fluid of a plant or animal" runs out: what should be inside comes outside (Wentworth and Flexner 442). A sap is one whose inner essence has leaked in unseemly fashion to the exterior. The implied norm against which the figure works is a contained inner essence and a hard, smooth exterior (the egg). It is a figure that does not deny fluid inner emotions—anxiety, depression, love—but that emphasizes their management.

The first character identified as a sap is Miles Archer. Both his cuckold-ing by Spade and his death at Brigid's hands can be traced to insufficient self-management. Archer can't see beyond the quick hundred dollars and her trim figure: he's for the immediate, visceral reward. Not accidentally is he married and that "partnership" undermined. Archer's petty venality represents the passing economic phase. Spade has his name taken off the door, for if he were Archer he'd be dead, just as Thursby is dead. Lieu-tenant Dundy, the Irish cop who is Spade's nemesis, is a lesser sap. Spade defines himself against Dundy, who can't see where his real interests lie. He tries to provoke Spade with heavy-handed interrogation, unfounded accusations, and late-night visits, when Spade has instrumental value to him, and vice versa. Such details as the gold-piece tie clasp and the "small elaborate diamond-set secret-society emblem" identify Dundy as a lodge member at a time when Robert and Helen Lynd tell us that such geo-graphically based organizations had given way to professional associations (304). Dundy even says, "I've warned you your foot was going to slip one of these days," echoing the religious imagery of Jonathan Edwards. "Don't be a sap, Dundy," says Spade (*Maltese Falcon* 19, 90). Dundy hits him; he understands the charge and responds in the old mode. Unlike Polhaus, who takes a professional interest in Spade and passes him information in-formally, Dundy subscribes to the conspiracy theories of district attorney Bryan. Hammett parodies this worldview, which would link the falcon to "Dixie Monahan" and Chicago gamblers (on Valentine's Day, 1929, Al Capone had eliminated the O'Banion gang). The reverse was true in *Red Harvest*, where the Op's invocation of "Chi" unnerved Bill Quint. Ham-mett was keeping up with Progressive thought, in which eastern gangsters no longer explained California's problems, as Technocracy and EPIC had recognized.

All of Gutman's gang are saps: Wilmer is undersized, homosexual, and profane; Cairo is a dandy and a homosexual; Gutman is bulbous and abusive to his daughter; Brigid is a serial seductress and economic ad-venturess. Their common pursuit of the falcon, emblem of speculation, defines them as anachronisms, just as the basic plot, deriving from Arthur Conan Doyle's "The Sign of Four" and its pursuit of lost Indian treasure, owes to colonial romance.[9] They represent a prodigality and refusal to "fall" that once astonished Hammett in Arbuckle. So the rotund Gutman is their leader. They live well and dress lavishly, without jobs, without explained funding. After they have the falcon, they propose to leave their "legal difficulties" to Spade, who knows legalities too well. Hammett's personal fondness for prodigality glints along Gutman's "cherub" smile when the latter proposes to pursue the falcon to Constantinople, but Hammett enforces thematic closure by having the betrayed, younger Wilmer—whom Gutman "always considered as a son"—kill his "father." "He ought to have expected that," remarks Spade (255).

Spade, with his efficiency apartment, Murphy bed, store-bought products, office, and secretary, embodies the emerging economy. His lack of heterogeneous social contact is clear. In *Red Harvest*, the Op had partners, met Bill Quint and Dinah Brand, and achieved camaraderie with the crooks. When Sam Spade walks down the street, he is likely to be shadowed. He trusts no one, yet he knows at least as many people as the Op and has more useful professional contacts—acquaintances of instrumental value like hotel detectives, cabbies, policemen, and lawyers. But there is no geographic or community relation among these economic islets, no sense of polity. The same technology that provides Murphy beds and billboards requires that detective work be narrowly and efficiently organized. Like the urban office worker of the late 1920s, Spade focuses on self-preservation and work, which for him are synonymous. He has no church, no lodge, no hobbies, no affective ties, no neighbors.

This lack does not glare because it is depicted as an admirable self-sufficiency: it is emotional smoothness. But when Effie Perine sees Spade perplexed by Brigid, Iva, and Dundy, she cues the reader to this life's demands: "You always think you know what you're doing, but you're too slick for your own good" (31). This slickness—mental and emotional "smoothness"—and its cost are the center of the novel's ideological innovations. Even the most alluring models of exterior smoothness, such as Brigid, may be simply examples of sheathing that disguise the anachronistic values of the old economy. True smoothness must be interior as well as exterior: its manifestations are coolness, skepticism, feigned comprehension, suspension of judgment, a sense of humor. Smoothness is not intuitive or organic but a dispersed attention that allows each elision to remain blank until the whole meaning crystallizes.

The smooth is not easy. Hammett's descriptions of Spade's "growl," the "wales" that stand out in his cheeks, his "harsh guttural voice," and his "dreamy" quality when he is about to hit someone—these testify to its difficulty and offer the reader a model sufficiently complex to be worthy of emulation. One suspects that Dorothy Parker, among others, took Sam Spade to heart because he embodied not only the new behavior of the emergent economy but also its cost.

As Hammett indicated by titling an important chapter "Three Women," Brigid O'Shaughnessy, Effie Perine, and Iva Archer serve, in the mythic sense, as the Fates. They ask questions, represent mysteries, and possess occult powers: Brigid can solve the mystery of the falcon, Iva can implicate or exonerate Spade in her husband's murder, and Spade consults Effie's "female intuition." They are among the more prominent manifestations of the Grail motif in the detective novel. Hammett folded in a number of psychological and socioeconomic features, the logic of which led Cain and Chandler to embody the emerging economy in a female foil. Hammett had not known how to resolve Dinah Brand, so he fragmented her.

Psychoanalytic analyses point out that Spade comes into "possession" of two women formerly attached to other men and postulate that he is subject to a "fear of Oedipal victory" with regard to Effie Perine, his "desexualized day-time mother" (Bauer, Balter, and Hunt 282). But the imperative of ideology to manage sexuality consumes relentlessly just such shibboleths and taboos. Effie is purposely just like Mom; sublimated oedipal victories were old news in popular narrative, not to mention advertising, by 1930. All the ideological hints in the novel point to Effie as Spade's appropriate partner. Only her disappointment that he apparently does not believe in romance, a regret that signals the emergence of metonymy, keeps them apart in the final scene.

As potential partners the three women represent the choices faced by Hammett's male readership. Effie is the girl next door: lanky, sunburned, playful, boyish, earthy, and candid—a "spunky" type much admired in narrative. Leora Tozer of Sinclair Lewis's *Arrowsmith* might be her model. Her "desexualization" must be understood against the convention of the 1920s that a woman serving a man in the workplace would be emotionally, if not sexually, exploited; for examples we need only refer to Dreiser's novels. In this respect, Hammett actually empowers Effie, who becomes a kind of office wife, an economic partner who is competent, efficient, and honest, as well as a team player. Spade's physical intimacies with her may seem as uncharged as a small child's bedtime hug, but when the falcon comes into their possession, they are not mesmerized like Gutman but quickly secure it. The only male-female partners in the novel, they function as the nuclear family, the die on which all Perry Masons and Della Streets were stamped.[10]

The falcon must be declared a fake before Brigid, to show that she is not appropriate. Her profligacy, addiction to speculation, and bad-girl sexual liberality must be exposed as a threat. Brigid's name implies a foreignness, and she early on calls herself Miss Le Blanc, suggesting Blanchfleur, who nearly diverted Sir Galahad from his quest for the Grail. "Can I buy you with my body?" she asks, thus conveying her role as whore in the fabula of prodigality (64).

Iva Archer falls between Effie and Brigid, though closer to the latter. Iva cheats on her husband and, like Myrtle Jennison of *Red Harvest*, serves as a cautionary example: both characters seem to be inspired by the spectral "pig woman" of the 1926 Hall-Mills murder case. Spade's inclination is to pull up the covers over Iva and to say "thank you" when he is done. But Iva controls central narrative information—where she was the night of her husband's murder—and she seems Spade's lot when the novel ends. So shallow is she that Spade shivers, as if having Iva was to become Archer, to cuckold himself. This is, however, one of the oldest variants of the fabula—having the elder brother's wife.

When the rogue male in Spade refuses the logic that implies Ida, Hammett dangles the possibility of sexual consumerism before us. Only Effie can speak to Spade candidly about his business or a woman's "shape." She uses his chair when he is absent; she massages his temples in a scene that by its isolation and physical contact is provocative. But do they have to get married? She offers Spade no knowledge about himself, none of the allure of death that Brigid represents, nor is she his Genevieve. Can't they be playmates? According to the fabula, the passionate and clairvoyant aspects of woman are an illusion well lost. But Mrs. Effie Spade would be the economic truth about marriage: mundanity and the sacrifice of romance to expediency and money-getting. The companionate possibility dangles, but the fabula weighs heavily. That Effie should reprimand Spade for his unromantic behavior is not only a brilliant final concession but also a recognition that women transmit the core beliefs of society. Men adjust, bear new tensions, and fit themselves to a changing social grid, but the affective tradition in 1930 was still passed down through mothers.

RETROSPECT AND ALLEGORY

The most influential interpretation of *The Maltese Falcon* is Robert Edenbaum's perception that "in the last pages of the novel . . . the reader (and Brigid O'Shaughnessy) discovers that he (and she) has been duped all along." Spade, says Edenbaum, has known from the moment he saw Archer's body that Brigid was the murderer. "Spade himself then is the one person who holds the central piece of information . . . he is the one person who knows everything, for Brigid does not know that he knows. And though Spade is no murderer, Brigid O'Shaughnessy is his victim" (in Madden, *Tough Guy Writers* 82). Edenbaum concludes that "Brigid . . . is the manipulated, the deceived, the unpredictable, finally, in a very real sense, the victim." The key to this interpretation is Edenbaum's notion that Spade is a kind of "daemonic agent," that is, a vehicle of allegorical impulse. Those who try to redeem the sentimental level of the action have missed the point, says Edenbaum. They say "You're right, you're right, but couldn't you better have been wrong?" The point is that allegorically Spade could not have been wrong: neither the form of allegory nor the revelation of his knowledge in the climactic scene permits the reassumption of values that have been sloughed off. Edenbaum's feat of reading the novel against the grain of sentiment (and the 1941 film) also focuses revealing light on Brigid. Untouched by affection, she counts on Spade's responses to her vulnerability. She "falls back on a set of conventions that she has discarded in her own life, but which she naively assumes still hold for others," writes

Edenbaum (84). Seen in retrospect from the finale, Spade reveals how a "modern" self-interest identifies sentiment, contains it, and reveals it to be manipulation for economic ends.

This retrospective understanding of the novel's action may finally be more important than alleged allegorical impulse. In allegory, by and large, meaning accrues concurrently with reading; nothing is withheld from the reader. If we know with Spade in chapter 2 who killed Miles Archer, then we are reading allegory. If we do not, if we fill in Spade's growls and Brigid's stammerings with affective meaning, then retrospect shows we have been insufficiently suspicious of the motives of others, less than comprehensive in our canvassing of data. And details do not fully support Edenbaum. Spade, for example, does not know how Brigid got a gun until he learns from district attorney Bryan of Thursby's weakness for femmes fatales, nor can he see the planning in Brigid's murder of Archer until he finds the rent receipt indicating her intent to move. And if Spade does not know, and the objective or meiotic technique prevents us from knowing, then it is not allegory.

Like the economic ideology it endorses, this narrative is an instance of "instrumentality," exactly in the sense popularized by John Dewey and pragmatism in the second and third decades of the twentieth century: the truth of ideas or forms is determined by their success in solving actual problems. Retrospection has great instrumental value for ideological suggestion in narrative. Doesn't the ideological reorientation at the novel's end, which gives Edenbaum his hint, lead us to understand that our interpretation of data was wrong? We prefigured Spade, but he had another model of understanding to which he fitted events, eluding our genre-based assumptions. That doesn't make him "daemonic," however, or change the emplotment to allegory. Rather, like the inside/outside, rough/smooth dialectics that create so much of the characterization, it suggests that Spade holds a proleptic ideology in tension with the apparent romance. And that ideology is the instrumentalism by which the meaning of *The Maltese Falcon* is completed.

No better example of this instrumentalism exists than the "Flitcraft parable." Just before he sleeps with Brigid, Spade tells her a long story about a real estate agent (read "speculator") who left his office for lunch one noon and never returned. He passed a construction site, and "a beam or something fell eight or ten stories down and smacked the sidewalk alongside him" (*Maltese Falcon* 70–71). Suddenly Flitcraft's eyes opened: "He felt like somebody had taken the lid off life and let him look at the works." Life was not a "clean orderly sane responsible affair"; rather, he saw that "men died at haphazard like that, and lived only while blind chance spared them." According to Spade, "What disturbed him was the discovery that in sensibly ordering his affairs he had got out of step and not into step, with life. He said he knew before he had gone twenty feet from the fallen beam that he would never know peace again until he had adjusted himself to this new glimpse of life. . . . Life could be ended for him at random by a falling beam: he would change his life at random by simply going away" (71).

This naturalistic conception of the universe leads Flitcraft to wander for several years, marrying a woman similar to his first wife and replicating his old circumstances, except that he calls himself Charles Pierce (a twist on the name of Charles Sanders Peirce, the pragmatist). Spade "always liked" this part of the story: "I don't think he even knew he had settled back naturally into the same groove he had jumped out of in Tacoma. . . . He adjusted himself to beams falling, and then no more of them fell, and he adjusted himself to them not falling" (72).

In Edenbaum's reading, Spade subscribes to the "Dreiserian" nature of Flitcraft's insight (in Madden, *Tough Guy Writers* 83).[11] Beams do not continue to fall in Flitcraft's world, but they do in Spade's. Edenbaum turns to the analogue between Spade recounting her husband's sea change to the first Mrs. Flitcraft and Spade telling this story to Brigid. "If Brigid were acute enough . . . she would see in the long, apparently pointless story that her appeals to Spade's sense of honor, his nobility, his integrity . . . will not and cannot work" (84).

Edenbaum halts here. Since in his view Spade is a demonic agent, the stories he tells can only be comprehended allegorically. Yet two objections are obvious. Spade, Brigid, Gutman, Cairo, and Bryan all tell stories: there is a lot of dialogic jostling for primacy. Second, Spade's appreciation of Flitcraft's naturalism is ironic, just as in the earlier "Seven Pages" and "An Inch and a Half of Glory." Those characters resembled Hammett's first version of Flitcraft, the Englishman Norman Ashcraft in "The

Golden Horseshoe" (1924). A genealogy suggests that Hammett's impulse remained unchanged. Ashcraft, resenting his wife's wealth and desiring to prove his independence, migrates to America, leads a scruffy life, despairs, and commits suicide. To this point it's a prodigal son story. But Ashcraft's identity is assumed by criminal Ed Bohannon, who lives on the former's money and is hanged for Ashcraft's "murder." Bohannon is a fantasy about an enjoyably disreputable life available beyond the family confines, which the Op shares, a kind of doubling of the prodigal son theme that fascinated Hammett. In *The Maltese Falcon* Flitcraft walks out on two hundred thousand dollars, "a new Packard, and the rest of the appurtenances of successful American living," just as prototype Ashcraft shed his wife's stultifying fortune (69). Flitcraft re-creates what he left and thinks he has done better, with "no feeling of guilt" (70). For Hammett the romantic sanction for prodigality remains unwithered under the sun of experience in the "far country" if guilt can be vanquished. In neither story does the detective find a repentance that would facilitate the prodigal's reintegration. Once you've been prodigal, Hammett now avers, you die, you re-create home, but you don't go home again.

The urban setting of the Flitcraft parable, overlooked in an allegorical reading, is also important. Cities were perceived by recently urbanized readers as straitened by greater organization. The threat of death by falling beams is a kind of post hoc displacement and justification of their departures from farms, small towns, and traditional families, just as Flitcraft's second family is an idealized compensation. In fact, beams do not continue to fall in Flitcraft's, the reader's, or Spade's worlds, but some people, like Flitcraft and Brigid, are disposed to organize life as if such an excuse existed.

Here is the instrumental lesson of the Flitcraft parable for Spade. The universe may not be rational—random events like falling beams do occur —but rationality is still the best instrument with which to go hunting. The chance event drives people away from cover, from adaptive or habitual responses, but only reveals motive for a short time. Prodigal sons never think about returning until they are walking on their uppers. Hammett's irony is seen in the actantial genealogy: Spade (a prodigal turned elder brother) tells Brigid (an apparent prodigal) about Flitcraft (a prodigal who adapts and "succeeds"), who is based on Ashcraft (a prodigal who adapts and fails).

So each time Spade asks Brigid for an "adaptation" and she equivocates, his certainty about her motive grows, but he withholds it until he can most emphatically endorse the pragmatic value of the narrow self-interest and professional class consciousness of the elder brother. The elder brother always comes last. His retrospect, unlike allegory, induces a shift in the mode of understanding from formism to mechanism: there was a rule guiding events after all! There are no ends, no romantic self-transformations, only the acts of agents. This shift also serves to distinguish the "useful" instrumentality of Spade from the pragmatic "duplicity" of Brigid. Instrumentalism provides a way of assessing—What results does this produce?— that precludes the misevaluation of unalloyed romanticism, which had led Americans to speculate in stocks or to invest in Ponzi pyramids, not to mention questing after Maltese falcons. If we can say that Brigid represents the speculative attitude, we may add that Spade functions as a prudent creditor, collecting his fees from everyone, feigning interest in their projects, but foreclosing when losses loom.[12]

It is not a question of what kind of mothers will flappers make or where is bobbed hair leading us. This is about something that is already finished. For whatever is going to happen to this generation of which I am part has already happened.

—Ernest Hemingway, draft of *The Sun Also Rises*

James M. Cain,
Journalist

When Ruth Snyder and Henry Judd Gray were tried in 1927 for murdering Snyder's husband, James M. Cain was among those following the story, and like Hemingway, he had opinions on flappers as mothers. An editorial writer at the *New York World*, Cain specialized in light, humorous editorials, writing two or three a day. But this was the minor face of a major talent, for Cain had an unusual ability to figure social change in narrative. The Snyder-Gray case, his own philandering, and the Depression gave him a singular chance to use this talent.

Ruth Snyder, age thirty-one, a striking blond with "a gaze of Scandinavian iciness," was accused of murdering her husband, Albert (Hoopes

233).[1] She had supposedly persuaded Gray, her lover, to bludgeon Albert with a sash weight, then strangle him with picture wire. But Gray, a traveling salesman for Bien Jolie Corset Company, was so short and so dejected during the trial, reported the New York Times, that spectators thought him a dupe and began to compare him to Chaplin's Little Tramp. This interpretation, suggested by reporters battling to win circulation, was the first in a case that would dominate America's front pages for eight months. Magazine and editorial writers also assayed the flapper mom and her beau: Gray was a "salesman," Ruth his "bloody blonde," and Albert the "Type G-6 cuckold."

All figures floundered until Gray broke down on the stand and confessed that Snyder was a "Tiger Woman" in bed. That phrase assigned dramatic roles, implying a sexual melodrama, and guaranteed the trial its huge audience. The figure of the Tiger Woman explained how Snyder made Gray an accomplice, and it allowed the press to focus widespread anxieties about changing sexual mores. After sex, said Gray, Snyder always claimed her husband was humiliating, punishing, or beating her. "I'd like to kill the beast," Gray would respond heroically. Snyder would prop herself up on an elbow. "Do you really mean that?" she would ask meaningfully (New York Times, May 3, 1927: 1). There was clearly a Tiger Woman under her marcelled surface. This was an old-fashioned, newspaper way of organizing changing gender roles for ideological intelligibility. It explained the contrast between cool exterior appearances and primitive interior emotions in a synecdoche that dates at least from Shakespeare: "O tiger's heart wrapp'd in a woman's hide" (Henry VI, Part 3 I.iv.137). This figure quickly triumphed over competing ones.[2]

Among the 130 reporters holding assigned seats were some with famous names: Damon Runyon, Peggy Joyce, Fannie Hurst, and Heywood Broun. Will Durant produced a daily commentary for twenty-five Scripps-Howard papers, and Aimee Semple McPherson, the Los Angeles evangelist, reported for the revivalist press. Producer D. W. Griffith sized up the possibilities (DeMille had already used the imposing Queens County Courthouse as background for scenes in Manslaughter in 1922). Thousands of spectators vied daily for entrance, including millionaires and the marquis of Queensbury. Homemakers took the five-cent subway ride to

Long Island City, bringing picnic lunches so they wouldn't have to give up their seats. Counterfeit tickets proliferated, and lapel pins with miniature sash weights were sold. Those denied seats heard the testimony in the halls, where loudspeakers boomed out confessions only whispered by witnesses. Western Union built a 108-line telephone room to aid the outpouring coverage. Damon Runyon said that if Gray and Snyder "explained" anything, it was stupidity, so he called the affair "The Dumbbell Murder."

But few crimes tapped so deeply the widespread suspicion about the debilitating effect of the 1920s on American character; by 1927 there was a search for causes, and not only by Hemingway. If he thought the flappers-as-mothers debate a canard, Cain had an opposed explanation. Hemingway found the key in the past, but Cain faulted the present, siding with his friend Alexander Woollcott, who wrote that "Ruth Snyder was so like the woman across the street that many an American husband was haunted by the realization that she also bore an embarrassing resemblance to the woman across the breakfast table" (in Kobler 261). This suspicion of violence in the woman across the table was linked to the buoyant economy, which somehow influenced sexuality.

Some interpreters, such as those who wrote for *Outlook*, located blame in the past and in the present: "It is not because they were so different from their neighbors, but so much like them, or at least like many of them, that their story has been read with absorption by the multitude. . . . It was a crime of that moral degeneration that is the inevitable product of long-continued self-indulgence" (May 18, 1927: 13). The more sophisticated, such as John Kobler, who edited a book on the trial, almost grasped the socioeconomic schizophrenia about women through which men read the trial. That task is easier now, more than sixty-five years later, in part because the trial's most celebrated by-product—Cain's *The Postman Always Rings Twice* (1934)—crystallized the era's anxieties. If women were to assume economic power and freedom, they would have to pay a price for it. They might, in the figuration Cain proposed, acquire economic power, but they must cede to men the right to serialize desire, its discourse, and its relation to the new economy.

"All the essential facts and a multitude of unessential details in the case are publicly as well known as if the crime itself with its vile preliminaries had been committed in full view of all the world," asserted the editors of *Outlook* (May 18, 1927: 13). What shocked *Outlook* and the general public was that there appeared to be two Ruth Snyders. On the one hand, her Queen's Village neighbors called her Tommie because she bobbed her blond hair in flapper style. Even after her arrest, they said she was "spunky" and "a good fellow," noting that she sewed her clothes, her daughter's dresses, and the drapes and curtains in their new bungalow and filled the cellar with preserves. She had been a sickly child, and she had worked hard as a switchboard operator and typist before meeting Snyder. Economically independent, she nonetheless dreamed of being provided for, like the heroines of the romance novels she consumed. She had borne Albert a child even though he was still in love with a dead childhood sweetheart, after whom he named his boat and pets. Ruth was a good cook and supervised her daughter's prayers every night, and the police testified that she cried on "discovering" her husband dead.

The second Ruth Snyder was hated by other women on her block. She lived in a new $19,500 house, ignored her neighbors, and refused to join local clubs, caring only for booze, gambling, Broadway shows, movies, and men. Tight with money, she was always looking for freebies. She was getting her comeuppance, her neighbors thought, believing without question that she and Gray sapped, suffocated, chloroformed, and garroted Albert the evening of March 20, 1927.

About Judd Gray, age thirty-four, opinions were more uniform. A descendant of Plymouth Puritans, he took the stand and said he had "a very fine little wife and a wonderful little daughter" (*New York Times*, April 3, 1927: 1). His marriage of fourteen years, as unhappy as that of the Snyders, it turned out, was not scrutinized as a source of "motive." Neighbors testified that he was a "live wire" and a "peppy fellow," while his employer regarded him as a model salesman and had given him the best eastern territory. He was small and curly-haired, with a cleft chin and horn-rimmed glasses, a dapper product of the age of Bruce Barton and Dale Carnegie: "Sixteen years of salesmanship made itself apparent in the ingratiating manner which he assumed toward Justice Scudder," wrote the *Times*, insinuating something about salesmen that readers of H. L. Mencken and Sinclair Lewis would recognize. Indeed, Gray felt he was "just one of those Americans Mencken loves to laugh at," reported Kobler (14). Gray's lawyers counseled him to adopt bland mannerisms, because reporters suspected him of a hidden "animal magnetism" corresponding to Snyder's tigerishness. They told the press of Gray's multiple church memberships and of his attempts to convert Ruth to Protestantism. "Evidently the initiative throughout was with the woman," concluded *Outlook* (May 18, 1927: 13).

The deceased, Albert Snyder, had been art editor of Hearst's *Motor Boating* magazine, had belonged to a bowling league, and was friendly and engaging. He was "more of a favorite because of his ready laugh at other men's jokes than because of any talent for entertainment of his own," wrote the *Times* (April 3, 1927: 4). Before moving to their new, cream yellow house, the Snyders had lived in Bay Ridge (Brooklyn), but Albert had felt they traveled with "too fast a set." Ruth gambled a little, was fond of Prohibition booze, and liked to stay out late. He wanted her to remain the innocent twenty-year-old he had married when she was a typist at his magazine. Her courtroom confession that Albert took her to only one Broadway show in eleven married years brought a sympathetic murmur from the Manhattan dilettantes. When she claimed in court that she didn't drink or smoke, however, the judge had to silence the snickering. But the squirmy perception the literati increasingly shared with the press was that Gray and Snyder were not "criminals" but representative products of the Jazz Age. The future had been imaginable to them only as a vantage on lost opportunities for pleasure. So there seemed a certain logic to murdering your husband. "We all do strange things at times," wrote Peggy Joyce in the *Daily Mirror* (Kobler 54).

Like many young men on the eve of World War I, Gray had married and begun a family before shipping off to Europe. Innocence ended in fields at Verdun, in trenches at Belleau Wood, but also with the taste of Europe, experience with sex and alcohol. Like Hemingway's Krebs, Gray returned to a world of contradictions: war had made the nation prosperous, but millions of men were looking for work; people drank prodigiously, but Prohibition was in force; girls wore rouge and smoked and talked about free love, but Mother said he wasn't to marry that type. When he married the woman his parents liked, she bored him.

By 1925 Gray must have felt that life was passing him by again. He was good at talking to women, but the corsets he sold were not for the lithe, boyish-looking women his eye followed in the street. Corsets had come back to help women over thirty, women with children, women never imagined by high fashion, to achieve the flapper's sheathed look. On his sales trips he cultivated a homely girl in Buffalo from whom he borrowed money. Then a friend in the stocking business introduced him to Ruth in Henry's Restaurant on Thirty-fourth Street, and he saw a chance to make up for lost time. He explained how to get corsets free by writing to manufacturers: Could he get her one? She didn't wear corsets, she said, but she liked something for nothing. In fact, the trial revealed, she already knew a nylon salesman and a heater salesman and didn't need to buy those items. They went to his office, deserted on Saturday, where she said she was too sunburned to squeeze into a corset, and he volunteered to rub lotion on her.

Their affair was like that, with bad dialogue, an excuse for not missing what the age offered, and an imitation of style, from the love letters in which they addressed each other as "Momsie" and "Snookums" to the copy of Loos's *Gentlemen Prefer Blondes* they kept in their permanent suitcase at the Waldorf. (Originally their trysts were at the Imperial Hotel, but they decided it wasn't good enough.) The sex was apparently a revelation, for they stepped up their meetings to three times a week. Afterward she shopped at Macy's, or they went dancing at nightclubs. They weren't missing "life," but it was a throwaway relationship, a pretense for consumption, a veneer of Jazz Age.

What stood out in the trial was not this companionable consumption, but something harder, a ruthless drive to sell short the future that Gray and Snyder absorbed from the speculative economy of the 1920s. Its essence came in testimony that Snyder had taken out personal injury insurance on her husband for fifty thousand dollars and double indemnity in case of death. To do that she had to trick him into signing three blank policies. With the terms filled in, she hid them in a safe deposit box under the name Ruth Brown and instructed the postman to deliver payment coupons only to her. She paid the $895 in premiums from personal savings. In the courtroom spectators joked about the postman's signal (he was supposed to ring twice) and "double indemnity," making the phrases into commonplaces for duplicity.

Gray had gotten his flapper, but he called her Mommy, and her hard-boiled economic behavior brought the schizophrenia into focus. Some interpreters, like Bruce Bliven of New Republic, had fought a rearguard action for flapperism, arguing that it was an admirable feminism. "Flapper Jane," he wrote, was enjoying "a victory so nearly complete that we have even forgotten the fierce challenge which once inhered in the very word. . . . They don't mean to have any more unwanted children. They don't intend to be debarred from any profession" ("Flapper Jane" 67). But Bliven was overwhelmed by legions like Charles Pabst, author of a widely reprinted article titled "Doctor's Warning to Flappers." He warned that starvation dieting was injurious, that Prohibition booze caused eczema and acne, that bobbed hair promoted folliculitis ("flapper's rash"), and that black hair dyes caused kidney disease. The flapper, Pabst intimated, endangered her future offspring (21–22).

The trial peeled away such layers of interpretation. First to go were commentators certain the trial showed the extent of "moral decadence." Next were those who saw a conflict between Victorian repression and Freudian sexuality and examined the lovers for signs of the "animal magnetism" that each attributed to the other. Gray's confession ignited this bonfire: "With some veiled threats and intensive lovemaking she got me in such a whirl that I didn't know where I was at," he said. "I have been in a literal hell" (New York Times, May 3, 1927: 1). Gradually reporters found the economic substrate. Most, like the editors of Outlook, divided criminals into two categories: "One consists of those who are criminals by profession. . . . They have a philosophy that is more or less conscious. . . . the law is not of their making, and therefore places them under no obligation. Property rights are, in their eyes, simply the privileges acquired by classes of society to which they do not belong. Wealth is his who can get it. . . . Even human life may be sacrificed to accomplish their ends." Gray and Snyder were not this type, gangsters who refused the contract that Rousseau said society extended to everyone. On the other hand, there were criminals of impulse: "In a moment of passion or of weakness, under stress of great temptation or through the relaxation of the will, they commit some act condemned alike by the law and by their own conscience. Such are likely to be criminals but once" (*Outlook*, May 18, 1927: 13). The possibility of redemption was open to criminals of this type, according to Christian doctrine and the editors of *Outlook*, if they had not hardened their hearts against God's grace. Trouble was, court testimony made it appear unlikely that Snyder and Gray had hearts (soul). They seemed something new, entirely "self." It was singular, wrote the *Times*, that "Mrs. Snyder and Gray were persons of good standing, with no glaring blemishes on their reputations; both married for years, apparently happily" (May 10, 1927: 20).

Yet this singularity evaporated during the trial, as the sum of Snyder and Gray's socially sanctioned deceits added up to a widely seen citizen who lived within and appeared to accept the social contract but secretly resented and undermined it, extending the rapacious economic drive of the era to every human activity. The reading public learned that Judd borrowed money from Ruth too, hundreds of dollars he never repaid; that she bought bootleg liquor by the case, though she claimed not to drink; that she tried to cheat the insurance company when she lost a fur coat; that she told her husband she was visiting a pregnant girlfriend, then went on a ten-day sales trip with Gray. As for the murder, they planned to blame "a colored man," then saw an Italian newspaper and decided that bits of it at the scene would suggest the Mafia (*New York Times*, May 10, 1927: 1). They coolly worked out how to get Albert drunk and drug him and where to buy the sash weight. There was a pint of whiskey stashed to give Gray courage. After the murder, they tossed the house and stole Ruth's jewels and Albert's money, simulating a robbery. Then Gray gagged and bound Snyder (her idea) and left her to be found by her daughter in the morning. This was no "crime of passion" but an ordinary one, in the sense that it had something in common with buying on margin and selling short. A lot of people did that, and a lot of people were flappers: Ruth Snyder showed where flapping and speculation led.

Both were convicted; appeals came to naught. Despite a protest by clergy on behalf of the repentant Gray (Snyder remained a stone-faced atheist), the two were sentenced to death at Sing-Sing by electrocution, a "humane"

Average net paid circulation of THE NEWS, Dec., 1927:
Sunday, 1,357,556
Daily, 1,193,297

DAILY ✦ NEWS

PINK EDITION

NEW YORK'S ✦ PICTURE NEWSPAPER

Vol. 9. No. 173 56 Pages

New York, Friday, January 13, 1928

2 Cents

BOTH MUST DIE

Story on page 3

Scene in Justice Aaron J. Levy's court during argument which resulted in vacating stay of execution granted Ruth Wednesday night. Photo shows (A) Justice Levy listening to argument of (B) Edgar F. Hazleton and (C) Robert P. Beyer, deputy attorney general.

Henry Judd Gray, whose appeal to federal law failed. LOST LAST DESPERATE BATTLE TO ESCAPE DEATH!—Shortly after 11 o'clock last night the closing scene was scheduled to be enacted in one of greatest dramas in criminal history, with Judd Gray and Ruth

Ruth Brown Snyder, who lost last desperate gamble for life. Snyder giving their lives for brutal murder of the woman's husband, Albert Snyder. After granting a last-minute stay of execution for Ruth, Justice Levy vacated it yesterday.—Story, p. 3; other pics. back page.

Descriptions of Executions in Later Editions of THE NEWS

Ruth Snyder, the "Tiger Woman" who inspired James M. Cain's *The Postman Always Rings Twice*, and her beau, Judd Gray, were the subjects of tabloid journalism from coast to coast right up to the moment of their executions in 1928. (©Daily News, L.P. Reprinted with the permission of Daily News, L.P.)

method pioneered by New York State in 1888. Gray went first, and Snyder followed. She was among the first women ever electrocuted.[3]

Among the millions following the trial was thirty-four-year-old James M. Cain. He had an infallible sense of what tickled the public. His pieces on food and on hog calling (which he practically invented), in favor of man-eating sharks and jazz in church, and against bluestocking censors or federal regulation of baseball were the best-read items on the *World* editorial page. These "light editorials" earlier brought Cain to the attention of H. L. Mencken, who encouraged him to attack the "boobery"—politicians, preachers, union leaders—and used his work in *American Mercury*. Cain was flattered, since Mencken represented the intelligentsia as he knew it, and he took up curmudgeonly iconoclasm. With Mencken's help, Cain began to write freelance fiction too, first an unsuccessful play about a messiah of the coalfields, then short stories. He recognized that he was not the skeptic that Mencken was, nor a pathologist of the world's metabolism, like Walter Lippmann. And his personal life was chaotic: the same age as Judd Gray, he had just divorced a woman on whom he cheated, and he was seeing a married woman.

The trial held Cain's interest in part because he thought he understood Gray and Snyder, but they had committed murder, and he couldn't sort out his sympathies, his passions, from the essentially conservative function that he as an editorial writer fulfilled. Coached by Felix Frankfurter, he had just gone as far left as he could in an editorial protesting the planned execution of Sacco and Vanzetti. Now came Gray and Snyder, who had bought a version of the 1920s sold by the media. This fascinated Cain as much as it horrified his elders and seemed to reveal the conflict behind flappers as mothers: sex as a style, a consumable, versus sex for procreation.

Cain was peculiarly fitted to become his era's melodramatist of this conflict. Born in 1892 to a large Irish family in tidewater Maryland, he was raised in an atmosphere that he described to biographer Roy Hoopes as "Feinschmecker Catholicism," meaning that the Cains were "gourmets of religious ritual" (20). They attended mass regularly, said Cain, because "the services were mounted in a manner worthy of Ziegfeld." By thirteen, Cain did not believe a word of the "whole mumbo-jumbo, especially the

A friend of H. L. Mencken, the crusty Cain talked a tough-guy lingo from the side of his mouth but saw his own philandering in Ruth Snyder's lover, Judd Gray.

confessional, where I was faking and suddenly knew that the priest knew it" (20). Not surprisingly, Cain's narrative forte was to be the faked confession. In later life he would regard the Church as "one of the most destructive forces in history" (413), but at the time of the trial, he inhabited a more artistically productive middle ground on which skepticism mixed with an intimate knowledge of religious ritual.

The son of a college president, Cain as a boy skipped several grades and spent much time trying to look older, styling himself as a pool shark and playing the iconoclast. Admitted to his father's college at fifteen, he investigated the founder, the Reverend William B. Smith, and discovered "the most celebrated drunk of his time" (Hoopes 16). Unfortunately, his father imitated the founder. This frailty inclined Cain to regard human nature skeptically, when he later failed at singing opera (his lifelong passion) and at jobs as a clerk, a roads surveyor, a high school principal, and an insurance salesman.

Despairing, Cain decided to become a writer, and he found a job with the *Baltimore American*. His first real success came during World War I, when he was editor of the *Lorraine Cross*. Cain left for World War I "pledged" to Mary Clough, a mother figure whom he later said he had kissed no more than a dozen times (Hoopes 85). After the armistice, he and Mary took vows, living unhappily together for three years: he offended her by dressing sloppily, treating Prohibition as a joke, and speaking a tough-guy lingo out of the side of his mouth. Mary tried to civilize him, but Cain bragged of his affairs with other women in front of their friends. When a fellow reporter put his own wife and children in a boardinghouse and went to New York to live the bohemian life, Cain applauded. In 1924 he deserted Mary for Greenwich Village himself (104–5).

Through his *Baltimore American* connections Cain got an introduction to editors of the *World* and the job writing for Lippmann. He lived in New York mostly with Elina Tyszecka, a Finn whose spouse, like Cain's, was elsewhere, but he dated five or six women. According to one reporter, Cain "was almost aggressive about wanting you to know he was living in sin." When Elina went on a long trip, he moved in with yet another woman, a reporter at his paper (Hoopes 126–27). Cain drank prodigiously with Mencken when he was in town, and otherwise with the *World, New*

Yorker, or Algonquin Round Table crowds. They all had a cynical view of relations between the sexes. "Love is the illusion that one woman differs from another," Mencken thundered. Cain thought himself romantic when he countered, "Love is the discovery that one woman *does* differ from another" (527).

In 1925 he began to write increasingly antireligious pieces for *American Mercury.* He attacked those who led altruistic lives in "The Pathology of Service," finding them insufferably dull and uncommonly prominent among the ranks of backsliders. In "Servants of the People" Cain ridiculed Seventh Day Adventists, and in "The Pastor" he wrote that "the typical American man of God in these our days is so loathsome, such a low, greasy buffo, so utterly beneath ridicule, so fit only for contempt" (Hoopes 129).

In 1926 Mencken introduced Cain to Philip Goodman, a pioneer of modern advertising and a devotee of the theater, who persuaded Cain to write a play titled *Crashing the Pearly Gates.* Based on Cain's reporting of strikes in the coalfields, the play depicts domestic tensions between a coal miner, his fanatically religious wife, and their crippled son. The wife takes up with a confidence man who masquerades as the Messiah. Faced with coincidental opportunities to "cure" the son and to give the miners victory in their strike, the messiah barely resists temptation. It was a bold idea for 1926 (Sinclair Lewis wouldn't shock readers with *Elmer Gantry* until 1927) but an awkward mix of religious iconoclasm and economic drama. The play closed after a week, but it laid out Cain's major themes: economic hardship, sexual temptation, and the prodigal stranger who disrupts a weakened nuclear family. The meeting of confidence man (prodigal) and cripple (elder brother) was an interesting variation, but the play seems to have failed because it never focalized redemption.

When the Snyder-Gray trial started, Cain and his affairs were in characteristic dishabille. Elina returned to New York divorced, expecting to marry Cain, but he was still married to Mary and seeing yet another woman. So Cain divorced Mary and married Elina, adopting her children, but their passion waned. He resumed his affairs. He was never to have children of his own.

There were problems at work. Lippmann, having trouble with *World* publisher Bayard Swope, killed Cain's editorial on Sacco and Vanzetti's innocence and substituted one approving of their execution. He did not tell Cain, who exploded when he saw the paper. Like the Algonquin Round Table writers, Cain followed that trial accompanied by a vague guilt about Sacco and Vanzetti's dying in the midst of America's gaudiest decade. By 1928 Cain saw that his job was precarious. Then the market crashed, and Swope sold the paper to Scripps-Howard.

Cain had wanted to write in "deeper waters," as he put it, for several years. His friend Morris Markey had gone to the *New Yorker* in 1925, and Cain followed in 1931, taking the position of managing editor, a job so thankless that its holder was called "the Jesus." Personality conflicts between editor Harold Ross and James Thurber, E. B. White, John O'Hara, and Ring Lardner made Cain's life tense, but he was more dispirited because the *New Yorker's* first generation—Dorothy Parker, Franklin P. Adams, Heywood Broun—departed after the executions of Sacco and Vanzetti, dedicating themselves to "serious" writing. Something like a repudiation of the 1920s was brewing, and Cain detested remaining among the naive scraps of gaiety. When Elina left on a European trip, Cain told his agent that he wanted to move to Los Angeles. At 3:00 P.M. that day, Paramount telephoned to offer him four hundred dollars a week.

Cain was to work in Hollywood with modest success for twenty years. He was clairvoyant about audience taste and wrote exceptional dialogue, but he did not think visually: early on he seems to have realized that movies were not his métier. He turned to short stories in lean times and found that when he "confessed" for a character, he achieved commercial success. To sharpen his senses initially, he had the contrast of New York and California, of the Roaring Twenties and the Depression thirties. His first hit was "The Baby in the Icebox" in 1933, based on a visit to a lion farm near Ventura (Hoopes 225).[4]

The Postman Always Rings Twice

Such oddities of California life fascinated Cain, and when his next film contract ran out in February 1933, he began to work on a novel that he called *Bar-B-Que*. This was California as seen by a New

Yorker. The basic plot came from the Snyder-Gray case, which Cain discussed with Vincent Lawrence, a veteran Hollywood screenwriter to whom *The Postman Always Rings Twice* (1934) would be dedicated. Lawrence addressed everyone as "buddy," wore forty-five-dollar suits and left twenty-dollar tips. His principles of plot construction were legendary: "Once you start rolling that snowball, buddy, you got to roll it. You go off and leave it, when you come back, it'll just be a wet spot on the lawn" (Hoopes 231). Lawrence said the audience had to care about the characters and thus the most effective plot was a love story, which depended on a device he called the love rack: one of the lovers had to be a "losing lover." He reminded Cain of an anecdote about Snyder and Gray that provided the "love rack" for *Postman*: "I heard that when Ruth Snyder packed Gray off to Syracuse where he was to stay the night she murdered her husband, she gave him a bottle of wine, which he desperately wanted on the train. But he had no corkscrew with him and dared not ask the porter for one, for fear it would be the one thing they'd remember him by. When the police lab analyzed it, they found enough arsenic to kill a regiment" (Hoopes 233).

This was untrue. The *New York Times* (May 3, 1927: 4–5) reported that Snyder left Gray a pint of untainted whiskey under a pillow to bolster his courage; on the train he carried another pint of whiskey laced with mercuric chloride, with which Ruth had tried to poison her husband previously. Gray said in court that he was just removing the whiskey from the murder scene, testifying that Ruth had told him the liquor was poisoned. For Cain, though, the apocryphal incident was more important. The poisoned wine took the "love rack" beyond romance to gothic, to mutual betrayal, and it indicated the perfidy of flappers as mothers. It could be grafted to the "fanatically religious wife" Cain used in *Crashing the Pearly Gates*, whose apparently passionate character would turn out to be motivated by economic factors.

It happened that a nearby lion farm in El Monte had been the scene of a tragedy a while before Cain wrote "The Baby in the Icebox." The manager, John Rosnan, was clawed to death by one of three escaping lions before his chief guide, Joe Hoffman, could fetch a rifle and kill the animals. Gossip circulated about the circumstances of the accident (*Los Angeles Times*, Oct. 1, 1928: 23). It also happened that, on the road to the lion farm, there was a filling station: "Always this bosomy-looking thing comes out—commonplace, but sexy, the kind you have ideas about. We always talked while she filled up my tank. One day I read in the paper where a woman who runs a filling station knocks off her husband. Can it be this bosomy thing? I go by and sure enough, the place is closed. I inquire. Yes, she's the one—this appetizing but utterly commonplace woman" (Hoopes 225). She would be Cain's Ruth Snyder, the Tiger Woman.

Crisp and pastel, California seemed the perfect setting for a retelling of the Snyder-Gray murder, one in which the lovers' mutual betrayal would be a figure for the social and economic "guilt" that Cain sensed in his own and the nation's disgust with the hedonism of the 1920s. Since he was most comfortable "confessing" a character, he would adopt a first-person point of view and tell the story from a vantage he understood. He would "confess" for Judd Gray. Newspapers had suggested Chaplin's Little Tramp. Gray could be a hobo, folding in social anxieties about the unemployed.

It took Cain six months to write the story of Frank Chambers, a drifter who finds work at the roadside sandwich joint of Greek immigrant Nick Papadakis and his sultry wife, Cora. The account of Frank and Cora's steamy sex, their decision to murder Nick, the initial botched attempt, their success in a faked auto accident, and her confession under pressure follows the sequence of the Snyder-Gray case. Cain got his characters arrested and confessed, but once they were "racked" he stopped. Lawrence diagnosed the problem. The love element stalled with Cora in jail: "Get her out of there. . . . Your story doesn't move until she's free and they start up their lives again" (Hoopes 233).

Cain struggled with the second half of the story for months before remembering either the insurance job he held briefly or the "double indemnity" details of the trial. He saw that the insurance worldview made an ironic economic contrast with the initial world of sexual temptation: a figure for the kind of economy emerging in the Depression. He invented a defense lawyer named Katz whose rivalry with the district attorney leads him to trick the prosecution into a squeeze play between three insurance companies. As plotting, this may remind us of O. Henry's devices, but ideologically it shows that justice is purely economic efficiency. Since it is cheaper for the companies, they reverse their testimony, an economy of

Charles Gay, of Gay's Lion Farm in El Monte, near where James M. Cain lived. Not always docile, three lions killed his manager in 1928 before an assistant shot them. His delay caused gossip and provided Cain with the plot for *The Baby in the Ice-Box* and the motif of "cats" for *The Postman Always Rings Twice*. (Daily News Photographic Morgue, Department of Special Collections, University Research Library, UCLA)

scale. Hence Nick and Cora are thrown back together after having betrayed one another. The power that each thought to have attained really resides in the apparatus of the law, insurance companies, and police. They become two "losing lovers," growling in one cage.

Cora becomes pregnant, and Nick reticently proposes to marry her, but in an accidental repetition of the original crime, he kills her in an auto accident. This time he is convicted and sent to death row, where he discovers God and writes the confession readers have been reading. Many people find this ending, indeed, the whole relationship after Frank and Cora's release, unsatisfactory. For them, the melodrama of lust and crime breaks; there is a narrative rift, after which the characters show a cynicism and suspicion at odds with the speed and eroticism of the novel's first part.

The late revelation of the confessional form especially imparts a more conventional morality to the closure than anticipated, as Joyce Carol Oates noted in comparing the novel to Dostoyevsky's *Crime and Punishment* and Camus's *L'Etranger* (in Madden, *Tough Guy Writers* 111–12). But in the context of its day, this constrictive, punitive second part explained the way life was going to be. For us the discontinuity between the parts, and the religious motifs retrospectively revealed, bare the ideological structure that popular appetite craved.

Unlike Hammett, Cain was able to imagine the prodigal's unrepentant return to what had been his family. He need only murder his brother or father and possess that man's wife. It is the plot that Lieutenant Dundy imagined in *The Maltese Falcon*: Spade kills Archer to get his wife and the partnership. The objective point of view that made this plot a possibility had also shown how attractive such a corrupted hero could be. And Dundy's plot superimposed the "far" and "native" countries, allowing a figurative comparison of the 1920s with the 1930s.

Frank Chambers's "far country" is south of wherever he happens to be. When the story opens he is returning from Mexico. After he fails to persuade Cora to take up his hobo life, he flees south to Los Angeles and gambles away his savings. Frank and Cora murder Nick on the road leading south over the Santa Monica Mountains, and later Frank flees to Central America with Madge Allen, the lion tamer. He always leaves the North with his pockets full of patrimony, the result of someone else's planning and capital investment. Cain uses "South" as a metafigure, what Julia Kristeva and Fredric Jameson have termed an *ideologeme*.[5] Frank's function, however, remains unchanged when he returns north, so that his spending can be contrasted with stay-at-home saving.

Arriving with nothing, Frank is animated by a program of general consumption. He's hungry. When fed, he will want something else—to seduce Cora. He is an actantial representation of desire, sexual and material. Nick Papadakis, who feeds him, has worked and saved and wants a son, someone to whom he can give. Since his young, American wife resists his program, Nick begins to adopt Frank into his family as his "son." Beyond food and shelter, he gives Frank responsibility for his auto repair business, money to purchase staples, and technological hegemony in the garage. He urges his wife to dance with Frank and invites him on family picnics. Cora's program, despite her apparent bitterness, is grander than Nick's or Frank's: she wants to be socially, economically, and genetically respectable. There is no elder brother per se, but Cora's program makes her the preeminent saver.

The actors' differing competences to carry out their programs are what moves the story. Frank's function—consumption—is totally dependent on gifts, so that his will and skill to consume usually do not overwhelm the other actors. Nick's giving has ample opportunities, but his will wavers, and his skills (amatory and technological) are minimal. Cora seems only to have will, but she has it in such amounts that, as events present possibilities, new skills emerge to match her program.

Frank's narrow program is achieved after the murder; he wanted to consume the father's substance and to have Cora. Oedipally, he has killed his father and married his mother, so he is temporarily without a new object. But Nick's death gives Cora new possibilities, halted only by the appearance of the police/legal structure in district attorney Sackett and defense lawyer Katz. Their function is represented by their hundred-dollar bet: they are a figure for the competition of the market. Katz and Sackett halt Frank's program, and he falls under the greater program of Cora, whose possibilities are expanded by the limits the police/legal function places on Frank. She develops skills and begins to act on her lack of a child and a "respectable" husband.

In the second half of the story, Frank's and Cora's narratives diverge, for they are alienated. Frank's new object is security, and his opponent is Cora, for she can turn him in. When she leaves to visit her sick mother, he feels free and reverts to his program of prodigality, going to Honduras with Madge. Returning home, he meets Cora in mourning black and Kennedy, a former employee of Katz who tries to blackmail them. Now Frank has a realization: he wants to depart penniless, merely to be secure. But when Madge stops by and reveals the trip south, he can't even do that: Cora can turn him over to the police/law, but that would defeat her greater program, since she has become pregnant (unknown to Frank). Frank is then triply trapped, because Cora's pregnancy obviates his sexual skills, while she controls the economic and police/legal possibilities. Cora is then the only one who can give Frank security or allow him to consume, and by doing so she incorporates him into her program of having a family. There is not only a reconciliation scene between them but also a marriage. The oedipal echo is obvious, but in the economic fabula Cora becomes Frank's father.

The second narrative cycle ends in Frank's death (he has killed two givers) and the revelation of a hidden elder brother, who is "chance" in Hammett's Flitcraftian sense—rationality within the matrix of probability. Spending and giving are for naught without his saving, so the illusion that they can result in well-being is dispelled by the novel's end.

To achieve this Cain changed the reader's relation to the fabula by shifting the function of father often (from Nick to Cora to the emerging economy to a traditional deity), so that there does not appear to be any dependable giver. This dissociation of function from actor makes unconvincing narrative but is consistent with the shift from father to the name-of-the-father, to use Jacques Lacan's formulation, that Raymond Chandler will achieve. In Cain the function of father is almost immanentized, so the traditional theology of the ending seems mere cant in Frank's mouth and distances us from a repentant prodigal who asserts the provenient grace of a divine father.

Frank's values are more clearly identified by the contrast between *gypsy*, associated with him, and *sucker* or *sap*, which he applies to other men. Frank wants to be a gypsy, not a sap, in contrast to Nick, who wants to be a family man. In her economic self-aggrandizement and resistance to Frank's daydream of "the road," Cora is not-gypsy and not-sap. But what is she? Unveiling her value is the enterprise of the text's second part, but it must first fill in the gypsy/sap conflict. Frank offers us many candidates, from Nick to those drifters he cheats of $250 playing pool, after which he "beat it out of town quick" (Cain, *Postman* 29). But since he differs from them only in being stabilized temporarily by desire, there is reason to suspect that these transients and Frank himself represent the same ideological pole. Drifters, hobos, and the unemployed formed a volatile cohort that concerned employed Americans, especially Californians, during the Depression. We can see the values better if we arrange them on the kind of semiotic grid devised by A.-J. Greimas to clarify such conflicts (see figure 3).[6]

Most readers, as Garraty reminded us, were employed. The hobo was

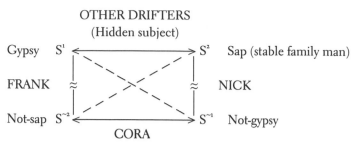

Figure 3

thus a pointed ideological vehicle. The values of this appealing traditional figure opposed the emerging technologies of consumption after the Crash, as well as the massive legalization of the New Deal. Readers are little different from the "saps" noted by Cora, who envisions them holding "a lousy parking lot job, where you wear a smock" (*Postman* 14).

A dictum of analysis in popular culture has it that "dangerous" impulses must be aroused before they can be managed and defused with substitute gratifications. Cain's arousal links copious sex, male violence, and a rebellion against job-holding—a difficult mix to manage in the terms of an emerging system that needed women as well as men as skilled workers and as independent-minded consumers. Cain had to revalorize male-female relationships in his second narrative cycle in three steps: by making women a locus of potential counterviolence (Cora can send Frank to jail), by changing the basis of male-female relationships from sex (desire) to family (reproduction), and by making death the penalty for failing to manage lust or to become a stable worker. Violence is a constant in these stages, but it is extracted from personal relations to become a monopoly of the state. Frank's violence in sex and in killing Nick is dwarfed by the power of the state that executes him.

The emerging values cluster around Cora, whose narrative is an economic melodrama:

> I won a high school beauty contest, in Des Moines. . . . The prize was a trip to Hollywood. I got off the Chief with fifteen guys taking my picture, and two weeks later I was in the hash house. . . .
>
> Then two years of guys pinching your leg and leaving nickel tips

and asking how about a little party tonight. I went on some of them parties. . . . You know what I mean about them parties? . . .

Then he came along. I took him, and so help me, I meant to stick by him. But I can't stand it any more. . . .

That road, it don't lead anywhere but to the hash house. That hash house for me, and some job like it for you. A lousy parking lot job, where you wear a smock. I'd cry if I saw you in a smock. . . .

I'm not what you think I am, Frank. I want to work and be something. (12–14)

Cora changes from an economic speculator, who believes that something called Hollywood will provide for her without her labor, into the realist that Depression capitalism required. Her Iowa origin was itself an *ideologeme*, signifying a rural migrant who believed in the advertising about California. Cora is educated when she tries out for the movies: "They gave me a screen test. It was all right in the face. But they talk now. The pictures, I mean. And when I began to talk, up there on the screen, they knew me for what I was, and so did I. A cheap Des Moines trollop, that had as much chance in pictures as a monkey has" (12). Cora begins to understand the totalizing nature of the new technology—picture and voice—and she accepts it as truer than preceding systems, in part because it shows her the minor role she has, just as the Depression deflated the personal expectations of millions. Cora is the character who adopts the emerging system, while Frank says, "Whole goddam country lives selling hot dogs to each other" (96).

As Cora adapts, the question of the design values of the new technology enters. Cora had based her expectation of success in film on appearance alone. When technology added sound, the logic of design required a seamless extension of image. A smooth shiny girl, she notes, cannot sound like a Des Moines trollop. Cora gathers that she failed because her skills were one-dimensional; in fact they recall Arbuckle: "I went on some of them parties." This is a lesson about the sexual control required by the emerging system for workers and consumers, which the course of Cora's development shows her to heed. Desire is not a "party" but a system.

Cora rejects the "gypsy" overtures of Frank, urging him to root himself, to help her operate and expand the gas station and diner, and to begin a family. Her desire to "make something" of the Greek's economic legacy may seem morbid, and we may find Frank's desire to flee after the murder more attractive, but Cora's plan is the more realistic. Cain blocks Frank with the six-month suspended sentence that prevents them from leaving, but this sentence is also to an economic world: to the diner and the difficulties of wresting a living from it. That Cora learns her lesson is evident from her plans to expand the diner outside, to have refrigerated draft beer coils, Tivoli lights, and "radio music" under the trees. Her "beer garden" appeals to sight, hearing, and taste; it applies as much technology as possible within a consistent design. It is totalized, entirely "outside," its exteriority uniform in a way that her screen test was not. During her new success, no customer enters the old diner, nor do we find Frank in the garage.[7] Cora and Frank face the world as an economic unit for the first time.

But Cain needed to keep his lovers "on the rack." Cora can no longer be prosecuted for Nick's murder because of double jeopardy laws. But when Madge Allen drops by, Frank is trapped. The requirement that men face the necessity of gaining a stable living, giving up their dreams of hunting and gathering, transforms the "love rack" into a male psychodrama of marriage. The only resolution is killing the wife, which is legally prohibited. But of course if they regarded one another as speculative vehicles, as Snyder and Gray showed, she could be "consumed" or "broken" and discarded.

Frank feels most trapped when Cora announces that she is pregnant. "Family" as ideological value was introduced earlier, when Cora was horrified by the idea of having a "greasy Greek child" (37). But there it functioned in a racial context rather than in an economic one. "Family" is revalorized when Cora receives a telegram saying that her mother is ill; the existence of her parents, much less their condition, was hitherto unmentioned. Cora goes home to visit, and Frank goes off philandering with Madge. When Cora returns in mourning, Frank is surprised that she has taken the death hard. She dwells on "family" to the point of asking Frank if he saw his family on his putative trip to San Francisco. "What for?" he asks. Her motive in returning, in opting for Frank, turns out to be "family": "I couldn't have this baby, and then have it find out I let its father hang for murder" (112). It is significant in the male psychodrama that she voices the legal threat she poses to Frank at the moment she confronts him with his paternity. For Frank the imaginary solution to this conflict is Cora's "accidental death," a substitute gratification that Cain lays before men audaciously.[8]

This is the moment when the prodigal conceives and rehearses his speech to his father: "I was all ready to start out with her again clean," Frank says (115). He does not drown Cora in the ocean. She "strains" herself, and his fantasy comes true when their car hits a culvert during their dash to the hospital. That he is convicted of killing Cora (not Nick) is apt, for the fabula pairs savings and genetic descent, in this narrative Cora and her child.

Despite its misogynism, Cain's novel seems to have attracted female readers by folding in elements of the popular romance and gothic novels. Joyce Carol Oates testified to the interesting "inscrutability" of Frank's motives, and Tania Modleski has shown that this element is crucial to Harlequins, where it combines with retrospect to reassure women that the contemptuous hero is really a good guy. In *Postman* we see Cora literally dying to believe this. Modleski explains in *Loving with a Vengeance*,

> Since the reader knows the formula, she is superior in wisdom to the heroine and thus detached from her. The reader, then, achieves a very close emotional identification with the heroine partly because she is intellectually *distanced* from her and does not have to suffer the heroine's confusion. . . . Since readers are prepared to understand the hero's behavior in terms of the novel's ending, some of the serious doubts women have about men can be confronted and dispelled. Many likely explanations for the contempt men show towards women, explanations which might be plausible enough in real life, come to seem like narrative snares. (40)

Oates touched on something similar in remarking on the alienation she felt in Cain's stripped-down style.

If the Harlequin romance is a "hysterical" text, in which "the reader finds herself, in hysterical fashion, desiring the subversion of the heroine's attempts at self-assertion," then its basic premise is "that a good man is hard to detect; the solution usually involves the discovery that the man who had seemed most suspicious and unreliable is the real hero all along, and the man who had seemed above suspicion . . . is the villain" (Modleski 39). Is this not Frank in the first half of *Postman,* the apparently evil but secretly good male, replacing the apparently lovable but actually evil Nick? But after the "love rack," Cora's suspicion turns to paranoia. "Women in Gothics are persecuted, to be sure, but the persecution is not, as in romances, experienced as half-pleasurable," writes Modleski. "The Gothic heroine, unlike the romantic heroine, is not destined to turn her victimization into a triumph" (83). Cora falls from love into fear, hatching a "paranoid" plot to kill Frank. But this is justifiable, as it turns out: he is plotting to kill her too.

Gothics are also supposed by critics to show women that they are not their mothers. Cora knows she is not her mother after the funeral, but she only learns that she is not the "hell-cat" she repeatedly calls herself after she meets Madge. Madge was the Tiger Woman, and Madge has been left. Cora sheds the Tiger Woman, the Flapper Jane role, for the economic mother that she discovers herself to be.

Cain's novel ultimately endorses not only a restricted sexual and economic agenda but also a racial one. "Nick the Greek" is a seme for blacks, for Mexicans, for Italians, for eastern Europeans, for all immigrants. For Frank, Nick is "economic man" and also a "sap." Frank sizes him up as the source of a free meal, which Nick provides after harder "Americans" throw Frank off the hay truck. Nick's generosity proves he is a sap, because he doesn't see Frank for what Frank admits to being. Nick believes in an immigrant version of the American dream, represented by his neon sign of Greek and American hands shaking and the scrapbook showing his naturalization papers. Like Hammett's Poisonville and Chandler's Moose Malloy, he is "economic man" in the old sense. His superannuation is reflected by his technological ineptitude: Frank repairs the autos and the screen door and conceives of the new neon sign.

Clearly Cain knew that in 1934 immigrants were not an economic problem, not even to the jobless like Frank. Their values, like Nick's guitar and wine, are even depicted as communal, historic, devoid of technology. Nick requires no defusing, no management, so why is he "Nick the Greek"? Because immigrants were still an enormous problem socially in the 1930s.

In the 1946 film of *The Postman Always Rings Twice*, starring John Garfield (Frank) and Lana Turner (Cora), strong shadow and metonymic patterning emphasize the increasing organization of society and the isolation its legal apparatus can impose on transgressors. (©1946 Turner Entertainment Co. All rights reserved.)

Disproportionately numerous in cities, lacking English, suspicious of public officials, they remained unassimilated. Southern Europeans were the commonest scapegoats. This had been the liberals' point about Sacco and Vanzetti in 1927.

Cain exploited this tension fiendishly, making race a potential disruption of traditional kinship systems and white male sexual privilege. Frank sizes up Cora as a woman who has married outside her tribe: the Greek has no legitimate right to her, according to rules both Frank and Cora acknowledge, unless she also is a foreigner. Cora is anxious about her white heritage, for it offers economic entrée.

"You think I'm Mex."
"Nothing like it."

"Yes you do. You're not the first one. Well, get this. I'm just as white as you are, see? I may have dark hair and look a little that way, but I'm just as white as you are. . . . My name was Smith before I was married. That doesn't sound much like a Mex, does it?" (4–5)

Cora's economic anxiety is linked to this racial ambiguity. Frank, familiar with California, knows that Mexicans rank below Greeks. "I knew for certain, then. . . . It wasn't those enchiladas that she had to cook, and it wasn't having black hair. It was being married to that Greek that made her feel she wasn't white, and she was even afraid I would begin calling her Mrs. Papadakis" (5).

In the racial scheme that Frank invokes, Cora has traded herself to a foreigner for economic security, which in the fabula positions her as "foreign whore." Frank, a muscular, tall Aryan, implies his superiority. "How come you married this Greek, anyway?" he asks. When Cora asks if it's his business, he replies, "Yeah. Plenty" (7). He asserts the primordial right of the males of the tribe to "give" women in marriage. Cora's tacit belief in the tribe is evident in her remarks about Nick's smell, his greasiness, his bay rum hair oil, and her refusal to have his child. Tribalism then combines with misogynism and motifs from racy novels to condone Frank's sexual sadism: "Her lips stuck out in a way that made me want to mash them in for her" (4). "I sunk my teeth into her lips so deep I could feel the blood spurt into my mouth" (11). "[I] swung my fist up against her leg so hard it nearly knocked her over" (13). "I hauled off and hit her in the eye as hard as I could" (46). Misogynism is "sanctioned" by Cora's adventurism outside the tribe.

The initial resolution of *Postman*'s multiple and contradictory appeals is simply a misogynist fantasy: woman and family are killed. The inadequacy of this is apparent even to Frank, for in prison he is prey to questions and powers larger than himself. Among them are the truths produced by the priest and by the crude Freudianism of a fellow inmate. Frank rejects both in favor of the "family" conception he had previously attacked, for it is the rogue male in himself that Frank, that society, has to execute. The emerging system must not quash desire, but must channel it, so that gratification by things can be accurately predicted. Adventures in prodigality may be had only at the price Frank pays, hence only vicariously.

Double Indemnity

Later, when Cain wrote *Double Indemnity* (1936), he stayed even closer to the Snyder-Gray case, making his protagonist an insurance salesman. Walter Huff meets Phyllis Nirdlinger just as Ruth Snyder met her beaux, when he comes to her door selling insurance. She asks questions that make him suspicious, but her intentions complement his desire to dupe his employers, and he joins her in a plot to murder her husband. Huff explains his plan to collect on the double indemnity feature offered in case of death on a railroad journey. But after the two commit the perfect murder, a faked suicide, they are estranged, because Huff's employers—led by Keyes, the claims chief—shadow Phyllis's every move. Like Chambers, Huff loses interest in the "foreign whore" after killing her husband. But his program is still to consume, to seduce (someone). He falls for Phyllis's stepdaughter, Lola, just as Frank pursued Madge. But Lola reveals Phyllis's complicity in a series of grisly murders and that Phyllis is dating Lola's former boyfriend Nino Sachetti. Since he is now the "father," Huff grows appropriately paranoid: have Phyllis and Nino duped him into committing murder? Will Nino, the new prodigal, kill him? Has he been a sap? He plots to murder Phyllis, but she ambushes him. Waking in a hospital with police about to blame Lola, Huff confesses, then commits suicide with Phyllis.

For *Double Indemnity* Cain scaled back his religious motifs, but the central features of confession remain. Huff begins on the word *I* and addresses the reader directly a dozen times in the first forty pages. His references to "this House of Death, that you've been reading about in the papers" establish a degree of anteriority, and his asides—"Getting in is the tough part of my job, and you don't tip what you came for till you get where it counts"—give his account retrospection and the moral weight of confession (Cain, *Double Indemnity* 29). The final pages reveal it to be just that—a notarized testament he has traded for temporary freedom.

Huff is closer to Judd Gray than Chambers was. He has "ethics," related as much to capitalism as to Christianity, and he resists what he feels happening to him. As in *Postman*, lust in *Double Indemnity* is the crack by which other sins gain admission: sexual desire persuades him to stay and draw out Phyllis's proposition of murder. But Huff's program changes constantly: he wants to seduce Phyllis, to outwit the system, to have Lola, to kill Phyllis, to save himself, and to save Lola. His desire is metonymic. Whereas Chambers's program was limited by will and skill, Huff's is continually renewed. This consumptive capacity seems to be what made Huff an appealing film noir hero: he's an existential rebel in a consumer economy. The trend of his program places sexual lust behind a more abstract desire to outwit the statistical system of the insurance industry: "I'm going to put it through, straight down the line, and there won't be any slips" (23). Unlike Chambers, Huff already works in the system of probability.

Cain's use of insurance made statistics an overt subject, personified in the obnoxious Keyes. With an intimate knowledge of Keyes's skepticism about "accidents," Huff watches him close in on truth. Much of Huff's narration concerns his airtight alibis, a perfectionist mania that here supplies the same rational appeal that intricacies of the legal system did in *Postman*. Phone calls are made, movies attended, memories jogged, evidence dispersed, distances and time calculated—yet Keyes refutes everything with actuarial tables.

> Here's suicide by race, by color, by occupation, by sex, by locality, by seasons of the year, by time of day when committed. Here's suicide by method of accomplishment. . . . Here's method of accomplishment subdivided by poisons, by firearms, by gas, by drowning, by leaps. Here's suicides by poisons subdivided by sex, by race, by age, by time of day. Here's suicide by poisons subdivided by cyanide, by mercury, by strychnine . . . *But there's not one case here out of all these millions of cases of a leap from the rear end of a moving train.* (*Double Indemnity* 67)

Huff understands probability and accommodates it, he thinks, in his own "roulette" concept of statistics:

> I'm a croupier in that game. I know all their tricks, I lie awake nights thinking up tricks, so I'll be ready for them when they come at me. And then one night I think up a trick, and get to thinking I could crook the wheel myself if I could only put a plant out there to put down my bet. That's all. When I met Phyllis I met my plant. If that seems funny to you, that I would kill a man just to pick up a stack of chips, it might not seem so funny if you were back of that wheel, instead of out front.

I had seen so many houses burned down, so many cars wrecked, so many corpses with blue holes in their temples, so many awful things that people pulled to crook the wheel, that that stuff didn't seem real to me any more. If you don't understand that, go to Monte Carlo or some other place where there's a big casino, sit at a table, and watch the face of the man that spins the little ivory ball. After you've watched it a while, ask yourself how much he would care if you went out and plugged yourself in the head. (29–30)

For Huff it's a purely statistical, metonymic world, in which "tragedy" no longer has any teleological meaning. But the emerging economy needed to limit this aggressive rationality rather than to have insiders use what usually did not happen against it. Huff's error is Flitcraft's error in *The Maltese Falcon*, founding a plan on an exception. That Huff works in one of the growth industries of the Depression may have offended intellectuals, for reviewers of 1936 treated him as we might have a Wall Street broker of the 1980s. But popular audiences seem to have sympathized, and we need only glance at the issues of *Liberty* magazine in which the novel was serialized to understand how widespread was the embrace of the system that Huff problematizes. Each article in *Liberty* has a "suggested reading time"! The mechanical icons of the novel—the train, the cars, the ship—are celebrated in advertisements and articles, anticipating American entry into World War II, and statistics pepper the magazine as filler and as content.

Religious imagery still contributes to Cain's theme, notably in Huff's early confession that he stands fascinated at the edge of a precipice: "I was standing right on the deep end, looking over the edge, and I kept telling myself to get out of there. . . . What I was doing was peeping over that edge, and all the time I was trying to pull away from it, there was something in me that kept edging a little closer, trying to get a better look" (18). Jonathan Edwards used the same image 195 years earlier. Pride in reason precedes the murder, but religious motifs predominate after. Huff returns home so rattled that he cannot think: "I had to have something to mumble. I thought of the Lord's Prayer. I mumbled that, a couple of times. I tried to mumble it another time, and couldn't remember how it went" (61). A few nights later, discovering his fear of Phyllis, Huff relates, "I did something I hadn't done in years. I prayed" (79).

Like Chambers, Huff moves from the initial desire system to one in which he is alienated: "I had put myself in her power, so that there was one person in the world that could point a finger at me, and I would have to die" (62). Discovery of his error opens Huff to the experience of grace, which is identified as the pure love that he feels for Lola: "I got to laughing, a hysterical cackle, there in the dark" (90). Then comes a revelation that makes him sit up and turn on the light. "It was just a *sweet peace* that came over me as soon as I was with her, like when we would drive along for an hour without saying a word" (95).

It turns out to be a false peace, for Huff proceeds with plans to murder Phyllis, thus conflating alienation and grace. Lola is an iteration of the serial sexuality that is Huff's program: having had Phyllis, having killed her husband (Lola's father), he now has a right to kill Phyllis and to have Lola. As in *Postman*, here Cain blends misogyny and religious imagery: Huff, confined to his hospital bed, imagines "Lola, a lot of cops around her, maybe beating her up, trying to make her spill something that she knew no more about than the man in the moon. Her face jumped in front of me and all of a sudden something hit it in the mouth, and it started to bleed" (111).

This vision of innocence crucified leads Huff to confess to Keyes, this novel's elder brother: "While I was telling him, I hoped for some kind of peace when I got done. It had been bottled up in me a long time. I had been sleeping with it, dreaming about it, breathing with it. I didn't get any peace" (112). Peace comes only when Huff recognizes the proper economic "families": Lola and Nino, Phyllis and himself. "Some kind of peace came to me then at last. I knew I couldn't have her and never could have had her. I couldn't kiss the girl whose father I killed" (121).

This is an ideological step beyond *Postman*, for Frank wanted only to seduce. Huff has serial desires but realizes that some degree of self-discipline is necessary in order to consume. He respects Keyes, the elder brother, who has made the enforcement of statistical truth his program. Keyes takes it "on his own personal responsibility" to cut a deal for Huff with the company and Old Norton (the superannuated father figure), thereby uniting the foci of consumption within the statistical norm and the elder brother's point of view.

As in *Postman*, in this novel the final pages establish the retrospective confessional framework. Huff agrees to leave a notarized confession for Keyes in return for freedom. This is the document we have read. When Huff speaks to us from his "chair" beside Phyllis, he conjures the image of Gray and Snyder in the electric chair (California used the gas chamber), but he ends his account by performing his own execution, a suicide pact with Phyllis. There is no maudlin discussion of heaven's reality this time. Faced with that popular hell of other people, Huff chooses suicide, a much figured alternative in the 1930s (John O'Hara's *Appointment in Samarra*, 1934; Horace McCoy's *They Shoot Horses, Don't They?* 1935). The sin to be guarded against in the deepest hours of the Depression was the temptation, as McCoy wrote, to "pinch-hit for God."

Edmund Wilson thought Cain was one of the "poets of the tabloid murder," whose theme was "class war." They were, he believed, "carrying on the tradition of Frank Norris, Jack London and Upton Sinclair" (21). But class warfare is difficult to see in *Double Indemnity*. Naive about California, Wilson sensed correctly that Cain, McCoy, and the others formed a regional group. In *Double Indemnity* Cain merits this recognition, for he had acclimated. He made Phyllis a native, overthrowing the scheme that blamed the East. Huff mentions the La Crescenta flood of 1934 and tells us that "in California February looks like any other month" (14, 19, 40). The man Huff kills is "an oil pioneer" at Signal Hill, who looks and sounds a lot like Raymond Chandler. Huff shows a familiarity with the oil business when talking to Phyllis: "You mean that down in the oil fields, some rainy night, a crown block is going to fall on him?" Such a blunder would be committed by "some punk up near San Francisco" (20, 26). Huff knows about bonding vintners and cozying up to Hollywood actors. He is Cain's first protagonist who operates in a California context rather than in a national one.

Part of this context is a new racial hierarchy, with Greeks no longer at the bottom. Huff patronizes the Chinese—"They got me out of the American way of drinking tea"—and employs a Filipino houseboy who "beats Clark Gable" when it comes to clothes (15, 46). European Americans, even Beniamino Sachetti, rank over Asian immigrants. Sachetti's name appears to be an elision of Sacco and Vanzetti, his story a compensatory retelling of their plight. As in the narrative by Eugene Lyons, "Sachetti" is the son of noble parents (his father is a physician), as well as an intellectual (he's finishing his doctorate) who is misunderstood by Americans (Phyllis, Huff, and Keyes) and wrongly arrested by police (who suspect him of shooting Huff).

Both of Cain's novels take the form of confession. Confessions are "taken," we say, by those who handle the legal and political arrangements of society, whether elders of Israel, Spanish Inquisitors, or Puritan witch hunters. "One confesses—or is forced to confess," Michel Foucault writes. "The confession is a ritual of discourse in which the speaking subject is also the subject of the statement; it is also a ritual that unfolds within a power relationship, for one does not confess without the presence (or virtual presence) of a partner who is not simply the interlocutor but the authority who requires the confession, prescribes and appreciates it, and intervenes in order to judge, punish, forgive, console" (61).

Confession is doubly potent when sex is its subject. "From the Christian penance to the present day," remarks Foucault, "sex was a privileged theme of confession" (61). As this discourse developed, he argues, "it is no longer a question of simply saying what was done—the sexual act—and how it was done; but of reconstructing, in and around the act, the thoughts that recapitulated it, the obsession that accompanied it, the images, desires, modulations, and quality of the pleasure that animated it" (63). The agency of domination in this relationship "does not reside in the one who speaks, but in the one who listens and says nothing . . . in the one who questions and is not supposed to know" (62). This entity reconstructed "in and around the act" is the ideology constituted by any given era, what Foucault calls the "discourse of science," to which we, if we are to wrest meaning from Chambers's or Huff's confessions, must adjust ourselves. Thus an apparently lascivious narrative has an essentially didactic function.

This dominance of listening only was noted earlier, in different words, by Joyce Carol Oates. She wrote that "coming to [Cain] from the great psychological realists, Joyce and Mann, one understands how barren, how stripped and bizarre this Western landscape has become. It is as if the world extends no further than the radius of one's desire. . . . To be successful, such narrowly-conceived art must blot out what landscape it cannot cover; hence the blurred surrealistic backgrounds of the successful Cain novels" (in Madden, *Tough Guy Writers* 111–12). Of course, we hardly have any choice, after the "great realists," but to apprehend Cain's melodramatic plots as ironic reductions; but Oates also identifies the phenomenological attraction of consuming Cain's confessions.

Oates, whose critique bothered Cain, described in effect the visual and literary design of speed; it is "narrowly conceived" against a "blurred" background. A narrative limited by the narrator's desire is streamlined. It presents events as a metonymic-desiring pattern. These events are "acts" of "agents" inhabiting the field that the narrator's desire perceives, and as White noted, such mechanist accounts "are open to charges of lack of scope and a tendency toward abstraction" (17). As Huff says of Keyes, whose worldview organizes the novel, "He's a theorist" (*Double Indemnity* 63). In noting the "iron-hard pattern of necessity," in which "everything is 'past,' finished, when the narrator begins," Oates emphasized the importance of confession's retrospection: "accidental encounters have the force of destiny behind them," and "the improbable machinations of fate . . . operate with a relentlessness out of all proportion to the people involved" (in Madden, *Tough Guy Writers* 112). Her comparison to *L'Etranger* is productive too, because even as we recognize in both confessions what Oates terms "the tale of the man under sentence of death, writing to us from his prison cell" (111), we sense that the "confession" of Camus's hero is ultimately unrelated to the individual as locus of exchange, social or economic. Cain's use of confession is. Meursault is not a consumer, but Chambers and Huff are. They position us likewise, as potential recipients, novitiates in an emerging discourse on power, sex, and economics.

There is a specifically American homiletic tradition that contributes to the reception of Cain's confessions. Incorporation of a "realistic narrative" into the sermon was a technique of the great Anglican dons, receiving its fullest development in the American colonies at the hands of Puritan preachers such as Increase Mather. In the eighteenth century, the American homiletic tradition was popularized and lent structural elements to the nineteenth-century development of melodrama. Oates's observation that "everything is past, finished, when the narrator begins" provides a lens on

Cain's use (in Madden, *Tough Guy Writers* 111). Cain narrates in the first person, and all is done. His narrators possess the resolution at the beginning. They can draw on the sedimented hermeneutic habits developed by the Puritan tradition, particularly narratives of captivity among the Indians, such as those of Mary Rowlandson and John Williams. It was Cotton Mather who ushered Williams's testimony into print, then interpreted its account of the captivity of Hannah Dustin in a series of sermons that anticipated Cain's substitution of ideological gratifications for troublesome realities in American popular narrative.

The homiletic tradition had a structure of text, doctrine, reasons, and application. The text was the Word of God, a biblical passage exfoliated. The doctrine consisted of the major principles contained in the text, often numbered and forming the skeleton of the sermon. In the reasons, a series of examples, often drawn from everyday life, developed the doctrine. Here Mather and others offered narratives of the Indian wars, captivity, witchcraft, or other ways in which Satan threatened the New Jerusalem. The process by which "realistic" narratives replaced the reasons, implying that they were a discourse on the doctrine, has been admirably detailed by Richard Slotkin in *Regeneration Through Violence*. The homiletic form concluded with the uses, or application, which instructed the audience on the lesson it should have drawn. The importance of this form to American narrative can hardly be overestimated. "Sermon-form narratives, replacing the metaphorically shapeless 'reports' of early days," writes Slotkin, "became the Puritan establishment's first line of intellectual defense against the unruliness and atomism of their people" (67). These sermons gave shaping structure to American experience that persevered, as Slotkin shows in Daniel Boone and James Fenimore Cooper, long after the homiletic apparatus had become less visible.

The confession as regeneration, through the telling of violence, became a culturally resonant form. It moved from the narration of trials of bravery leading to sainthood to what Foucault called a "literature ordered according to the infinite task of extracting from the depths of oneself, in between the words, a truth which the very form of confession holds out like a shimmering image" (59). The role of the auditor of confession also changed, from a process in which the confessing party empowered himself or herself to an erotics of production on behalf of the auditor.[9] Auditors moved away from identification with actors (trials of bravery) to a focus on personal production of desire. The power of confession to continue producing the narrative frisson, as Northrop Frye has hinted, became greater after mercantilism, with readers in a passive but consuming position (*Great Code* xx). Because all confession is incomplete, readers can demand "details in and around the act," moltings, until the context of their desire appears. This production disperses importance from the central act to the ephemera, which can be constantly reorganized for an audience endlessly hungry.

Repositioning the audience eventually changed the efficacy of the sermon. But the form was by that time pregnant with sedimented meaning and widely understood as truth production by invocation of the diabolic appeal of the senses. In succeeding decades popular narrative was able to call on homiletic conventions apart from their original intentions. Cain relied on such sedimented cues, so much so that we may discern a narrative gap like that between the original homiletic reasons and uses. Cain's narrator prepares us for this shift by functioning both as subject of the narrative and interpreter of his experience. He "authenticates" himself, as Foucault says, by the "discourse of truth he was able or obliged to pronounce concerning himself" (58). He speaks from a position after the facts he recounts, in which he has received God's grace, embodying an authority not only with regard to the point toward which he leads us but also in the means by which he moves us.

The first parts of the novels cover in a swift and visceral manner the story of a single man who seduces a married woman. With her he plans to kill her husband, does so, and apparently outsmarts the law, avoiding punishment. This is the "realistic" narrative of the reasons. Then, in place of the initial sign system of desire, for which we supply our own meanings, Cain substitutes a system representing the forces of techno-economic production, highly mechanical and logical: the legal system, the insurance industry, or business economics. Trying to reason out his behavior or that of his female accomplice via the new rule system, the narrator draws us into a web of rationalization that grows sticky: "They brought me orange juice and I lay there trying to figure that out. You think I fell for it do you?" (*Double Indemnity* 108).

Reason shows itself inadequate to the task of mediating between the two systems. The narrator grows frustrated, then desperate, arriving at a moment of fear or anger preceding that of grace. Cain's narrators suffer some event (the love rack, the double cross), after which all that remains is to give up, to acknowledge the inscrutable nature of God's will. But God is dead, and the emerging techno-economic system looms in his place. We have been moved hermeneutically, as in Puritan homiletics, but the suggestion of substitute gratifications for desire in the second, initially unperceived economic matrix casts a shadow over our original desire, suggesting we discipline our expectations.

Cain's narrators, as they pass through the moment of doubt, experience metaphoric or actual equivalents of baptism and rebirth. Frank Chambers, swimming with pregnant Cora, says, "All the devilment, and meanness, and shiftlessness, and no-account stuff in my life had been pressed out and washed off, and I was all ready to start out with her again clean, and do like she said, and have a new life" (*Postman* 114). Intellectuals, however, have thought that Cain fumbled closure, ending with punishments that recur to the text and the doctrine. Frank Chambers accidentally kills his wife and child; circumstances disclose the first murder, and he is sentenced to death. Walter Huff is sentenced to death in life with serial murderer Phyllis and decides that death itself is preferable. The final paragraphs of both novels reveal that the narrative comes from death row, from a death ship, entrusted to a priest or other emissary. For the mass readership, however, the text appears to come from the grave, from a self-commodified narrator, representing the highest authentication of the confessional homiletic form.

Technique and Technology

What Oates cites as the "blurring" of the apparent surface detail in Cain shares a quality with the elimination of the redundant "he said" and "she said" that endears Cain to teachers of creative writing. This focus is cogently argued by David Madden, who said that Cain's ability to sell the most sordid plots revealed his primary talent to be construction of "the pure novel," that is, a narrative in which the author by technical finesse seems never to be present, never to be omniscient, never to judge (*James M. Cain* 153–61). These are all appreciations of that metonymic representation of speed that Cain achieved.

The basis of this speed is partially technique but also, as Oates observed, "the radius of one's desire" (in Madden, *Tough Guy Writers* 111). Frank Chambers is no highbrow, but he expresses the half-cynical objectivity of the common man: he doesn't describe settings or bother with self-analysis but defines himself by his desires for food, drink, sex, sleep, or things. If we weren't running to keep up with his astonishingly primitive worldview, Cain's narrator would be funny. Considered out of context, his "thoughts" are often non sequiturs: "I kissed her. Her eyes were shining up at me like two blue stars. It was like being in church" (*Postman* 15). Such sentences are usually followed by plot twists, new scenes or chapters, and we pursue frantically. So the "speed" often originates in the narrator's estimate of himself as nakedly animalistic. In a few pages we learn to accept abutments of desire and smithereens of cynicism as a coherent personality. Everything in this world must be related to food, sex, money, shelter, cars, gambling, envy, or laziness.

But the narrator only implies so. As Cain remarked, "The reader has the illusion he is reading about sex" (Hoopes 380). Technique does play some part, however, not only in the kinds of elisions that Madden cites but also in compressions that establish "desire" through commonplaces—details, exchanges, thoughts—that function as signs in a system of desiring. The most obvious of these are the cats, hellcats, pumas, and "Katz" that populate the narrative and invoke the Tiger Woman of the Snyder-Gray trial. But many of the signs are metonymic placeholders. The word *shape*, for example, has no referent as Cain uses it. It is an empty vessel that we must fill with meaning: "Except for the shape, she really wasn't any raving beauty" (*Postman* 2); "Under those blue pajamas was a shape to set a man nuts" (*Double Indemnity* 10); "I wasn't the only one who knew about that shape" (*Double Indemnity* 14). *Shape* could be read a number of ways, as "buxom" or as "slender." Mae West and Mary Astor were both available for substitution. In the emerging fashion system of the 1920s, this "shape" had been filled with the boyish and slender, as Ursula Parrott testified, but in the 1930s fashion retrenched. The point is that *shape* is an open metonymic slot in a system of desire that we fill with our definitions in order to gain meaning from the narrative. So seductive is this game, the myriad commonplaces prompting the production of desire, common or forbidden, that we do not notice the confessional design accruing power until the narrative "gap." Across the gap, we see that Cain set up an ideological pattern.

Emblems of technology appear early in each of Cain's narratives. In *Postman* there is the sign that Frank convinces Nick to buy: "It had a Greek flag and an American flag, and hands shaking hands, and Satisfaction Guaranteed. It was all in red, white and blue Neon letters and I waited until dark to turn on the juice. When I snapped the switch, it lit up like a Christmas tree" (10). Frank's introduction of this technology changes Nick's fortunes, increasing his trade, allowing trysts for Frank and Cora, and nearly causing Nick's death. That Nick then dies in a car is no more an accident than that Frank should seduce Cora in one. As we saw, Cora thinks happiness is "a big airplane engine. . . . But when you put it in a Ford, it just shakes it to pieces (88). Cain's characters are completely adapted to and unself-conscious about technology. Huff of *Double Indemnity* lives by an intricate grid of autos and telephones, plans a murder using a train, and can set up Sachetti as a fall guy because "he didn't even have a phone" (104).

But Cain gave precise meaning to technology, unlike desire, by his use of the insurance industry, with its technique of applied mathematics known as statistics. Cain had worked for the General Accident Company in 1914 selling insurance to brokers, and he took pains to get the details correct. *Postman* reveals that insurance is the power behind the legal system. Apparent authorities, like Sackett, with his "intuitions," turn out to be illusory. Katz knows how the crime occurred, for his worldview is framed by insurance companies. Statistics replace Old Testament justice with a system of mathematically derived rules of human behavior and norms, defending against the sort of capricious consumer that Alfred Sloan feared.

Insurance tables will reveal that Huff acted not from passion, but from

more predictable motives that were economic. We know that by the conclusion of *Double Indemnity* Keyes will have caught Huff, and we are
disposed to concede credibility to a "scientific" justice system that is but-
tressed by the insurance industry's resources. "They'll spend five times as
much as Los Angeles County will let me put into a case," Sackett tells
Chambers in *Postman*. "They've got detectives five times as good as any
I'll be able to hire. They know their stuff A to izzard, and they're right on
your tail now. It means money to them. That's where you and she made
your big mistake" (61).

Minor features of Cain's plots try to reassure us about the reliability of
this system. Statistics may be wrong in some cases, but they will be correct about the majority. The release of Frank and Cora is unlikely to be
repeated, as Frank's recapture shows. After inviting us to outfox the legal
system with him, Frank fails to evade its statistical truth, and we can judge
our abilities against his. Could we have done better? Huff too seems clever,
but his tough-guy act is reduced to a pathetic sentimentality. Better to
avoid his fate and find pleasure within the norms.

The legal arrangements of society were shifting from the personal and
ethical to the institutional and statistical, and a new technology of justice
was emerging even as the old system sputtered along. The ability to invest
the shift with value was Cain's genius, though it may appear a retrograde
one. It is well to remember that the year in which *Double Indemnity* appeared (1936) capped an unprecedented period of law-passing under the
New Deal: thousands of new regulations dictated everything from the hours
of work and location of picketing to the frequency of radio waves and com-
position of highway surfaces. There were new social security and personal
income taxes, and Roosevelt had packed the Supreme Court to make sure
his legislation stayed in place. Cain figured this legalization of American
life forcefully, using the Snyder-Gray trial to show the price of a failure
to adapt.

It seemed a little too pat. It had the austere simplicity of fiction
rather than the tangled woof of fact.
—Raymond Chandler, *The Big Sleep* (158)

Raymond Chandler,
Oil Executive

At the least, Raymond Chandler read in the newspapers that
the Los Angeles Stock Exchange halted trading in Julian Petroleum stock
on May 4, 1927. It was the scandal of the year in the oil industry he
worked for. Squadrons of police had to restrain rioting investors, forty-two
thousand of whom, mostly small-time Los Angeleans, were wiped out at
a stroke. Vanished was a company with a paper value of $150 million. A
group of wealthy investors including Louis B. Mayer, Cecil B. DeMille,
and Harry Haldeman had formed a pool to manipulate the price of "Pete"
stock with company president Sheridan C. Lewis. They had faced down

an investor panic in early 1927 in return for cash "bonus payments," but these constituted illegal "interest," so the state called a halt.[1]

The average "Pete" investor saw only that the rich got richer while he lost a lot. But from his office at South Basin Oil Company, Chandler saw a lot more; he had watched oil pitchman Chauncey C. Julian manipulate the stock for years. Earlier in 1927 nearly a million shares of "Pete" were traded a month, when only 230,000 shares existed. When Julian was forced out, new owners Sheridan Lewis and Jacob Berman bought a stock brokerage to take advantage of the credibility that Julian had established, then printed and sold even more bogus shares, using the proceeds to pay bonuses to the Mayer pool. When finally the pyramid collapsed, four million bogus shares existed, the bribes reached ten million dollars, and fifty-five prominent Los Angeleans were named in a grand jury indictment for a fraud of one hundred million dollars. Over at Chandler's office, there was self-righteous approval.

But a curious thing happened in court. "Even the judge was forced to comment on the laggard manner in which the prosecution conducted its case," notes Bruce Henstell (42). District attorney Asa Keyes, the avenging angel of Los Angeles justice for twenty-five years, left the case to assistants, then sat by as they stumbled over the rules of evidence. When the jury decided on May 23, 1928, that none of the fifty-five were guilty, it was "the most stunning verdict ever uttered in a Los Angeles courtroom" (Henstell 42). Would this brazen exploitation of the Folks by an alliance of bankers, brokers, and swindlers go unpunished? The *Los Angeles Examiner* said the verdict "makes robbery easy in Los Angeles," while the *Los Angeles Times* complained of "the incompetent and bungling manner in which the case was presented" (in Henstell 43).

It was not until Bert Ramsey, a self-styled "investigator" for the County Efficiency Bureau, presented his dossier on district attorney Keyes to a grand jury in the wee hours of November 1, 1928, that the full story emerged.[2] Ramsey, described by Keyes as a "discharged and disgruntled" employee, showed that Keyes had taken $140,000 in bribes from Berman. The deals had been cut in the shabby Spring Street tailor shop of Ben Getzoff. One of the tailor's helpers had taken notes on business cards, recording the dates and names of the individuals. Ramsey knew how to tap the helper's resentment and to overthrow both their bosses. "It took me just one year," said Ramsey. "Here is the district attorney under arrest. I kept my word" (*Los Angeles Times*, Nov. 2, 1928: 1).

The day that Bert Ramsey became a hero, Raymond Chandler, age thirty-nine, could look out the window and see a pillar of black smoke rising from a fire on one of the first Los Angeles oil properties, that of G. Allen Hancock. Hancock had purchased the historic Rancho Rodeo de las Aguas in 1860 and had discovered the La Brea oil field in 1892. By 1928 it was largely abandoned, and there was talk that the Hancock estate would be given to the city for a park.[3] On the day of Ramsey's revenge, clouds of dense black smoke rolled over the Wilshire and Hollywood districts all day, as city and county each presumed that the fire lay in the other's territory and ignored it (*Los Angeles Times*, Nov. 1, 1928: 2).

Chandler was auditor and vice president of South Basin Oil, a holding company for dozens of small outfits that operated near Long Beach on Signal Hill, the world's richest oil field. It was a stone's throw from "Julian Pete" in Santa Fe Springs. Chandler made a princely thousand dollars a month, drove a company Hupmobile, and kept a Chrysler roadster for personal use. He lived west of downtown out toward the smoke, at 2315 West Twelfth Street, in a "solid" neighborhood, but he moved almost yearly and soon would be near Beverly Hills and the Wilshire Country Club, right by the homes of Hancock, E. L. Doheny, and other oil pioneers.

By all accounts Chandler was an efficient, unusually aggressive young executive. Less than a year after joining South Basin as a clerk in 1922, he learned of a scandal in the accounting department. The auditor was arrested for embezzling thirty thousand dollars and was tried, convicted, and replaced by John Ballantine, a scrupulous Scot. He chose Chandler to help straighten out the books, and they had apparently just done so when Ballantine fell dead at his desk of a heart attack. The police came and questioned Chandler, who accompanied them to the morgue and saw the autopsy. When he returned to work, he was the auditor of the Los Angeles office.

In addition to managing the staff, Chandler handled all contracts and purchases and served as an executive in the paper companies that typi-

Chauncey C. Julian, oil promoter extraordinaire and business nemesis of young Raymond Chandler, swindled thousands of Californians. (Daily News Photographic Morgue, Department of Special Collections, University Research Library, UCLA)

Attempts to prosecute Chauncey Julian failed until a disgruntled "efficiency investigator" showed that the district attorney Asa Keyes (second man on the elevator) was on the take. Here Keyes is being led away to San Quentin. (Daily News Photographic Morgue, Department of Special Collections, University Research Library, UCLA)

fied the industry. Joseph B. Dabney, South Basin's founder, had acquired trucking, drilling, and mining companies in imitation of Shell, the only larger company at Signal Hill. Chandler handled the legal details and later described himself as "a director of eight companies and a president of three, although actually I was simply a high-priced employee. They were small companies, but very rich." He said he had the best office staff in Los Angeles and paid them higher salaries than they could have got anywhere else. "My office door was never closed, everyone called me by my Christian name, and there was never any dissention, because I made it my business to see that there was no cause for it" (MacShane, *Selected Letters* 443–44).

If Chandler's tone hints of noblesse oblige, it may owe to his lifelong anxiety about his Americanness. A foreigner who penetrated the heart of American business, he held to an immigrant's conception of economic democracy, and then, when disabused, to a residual idealism. Chandler liked to say that he "was conceived in Laramie, Wyoming, and if they had asked me, I should have preferred to be born there." In fact, he was born in Chicago on July 23, 1888, but that was "not a place where an Anglophile would choose to be born" (MacShane, *Life* 3). Chicago was the eastern terminus of a stretch of railroad maintained by his father, Maurice Benjamin Chandler. His mother, Florence Dart Thornton, emigrated in 1885 from Ireland to Nebraska, where she had relatives. She returned to Europe ten years later with seven-year-old Raymond when her alcoholic husband abandoned them.

The melodrama did not stop there. Chandler's uncle, a solicitor in Waterford, had bought a house in London for his mother and sisters to live in after his father's death. It was there that Florence fled, the unfortunate beauty returned in disgrace and made to feel her ignominy. The women ran a matriarchy but treated little Ray, the only male, as the man of the house. He developed his own standards, which placed great value on women and on loyalty to them, while resenting the treatment his grandmother accorded his mother: old women would not fare well in his fiction. In London he learned that he was Irish and somehow outside polite society, that class distinctions mattered. But every summer the Chandlers visited Ireland, where Raymond's uncle practiced law (while hating it) to support his mother's social pretensions. In Waterford the Thorntons, who were Protestants, looked down on Catholics and practiced all the subtle discriminations they had learned in London. "What a strange sense of values we had," Chandler wrote. "My grandmother referred to one of the nicest families we knew as 'very respectable people' because there were two sons, five golden haired but unmarriageable daughters and no servant. They were driven to the utter humiliation of opening their own front door" (MacShane, *Selected Letters* 367). But Chandler absorbed this value system, as other incidents he recounts in his letters make clear.

After a brilliant private school career, Chandler took the civil service exams and placed first on the classics section and third overall out of six hundred candidates. The prize was a clerkship in the British Admiralty, a job that was supposed to let him develop the literary career he coveted on the side. But the eighteen-year-old Chandler was unsuited to the position and quit after six months: "I had too much Irish in my blood to stand being pushed around by suburban nobodies. The idea of being expected to tip my hat to the head of the department struck me as verging on obscene. What to do? I had grown up in England and all my relatives were either English or Colonial. And yet I was not English. I had no feeling of identity with the United States, and yet I resented the kind of ignorant and snobbish criticism of Americans that was current at that time" (MacShane, *Selected Letters* 250). Three years later, with a sheaf of book reviews and romantic poetry under his arm, Chandler boarded a steamer bound for the United States. En route he met Mr. and Mrs. Warren Lloyd, a Los Angeles family (via Iowa) with oil money and Ivy League educations, just returning from a year in Germany. They shared with Chandler the exile's sense of homecoming, and they invited him to visit if he got to the West Coast.

Chandler worked his way across the country, finding St. Louis too hot and his relatives in Nebraska too crude. He arrived in Los Angeles in 1912. Within a year he was a permanent member of the Lloyds' circle, using their home for his address as he moved between rented rooms and appearing punctually at their Friday night salons, where the guests talked of parapsychology and Madame Blavatsky and listened to West Indian concert pianist Julian Pascal. The Lloyds were part of "Arroyo culture," an upper-crust Los Angeles version of late Progressivism focused on the canyons around Pasadena, where architects Greene and Greene had built spacious homes of redwood or shingle that seemed to merge with the chaparral, gardens, and sunlight. Arroyo culture, Kevin Starr writes, "gloried in local circumstances: in Indians and Mexicans" (*Inventing* 107). These indigenous elements combined with imported aspects of the genteel tradition to produce a local literature that was pastel and pagan, illustrated by the novels of Mary Austin (*The Land of Little Rain*, 1903; *The Ford*, 1917) and the poetry of wayward son Robinson Jeffers. But Arroyo culture was only emblematically genteel. Its adherents cultivated a taste for fine wines while helping to outlaw saloons in Pasadena. Immersed in this culture for a decade, Chandler later judged it harshly, but at first it fit with the romantic attitude of his earlier poetry. Besides, he owed his first job as a bookkeeper in a creamery to Warren Lloyd, an archetypal Arroyan who served as the creamery's lawyer when not busy prospecting for oil on land he owned along Ventura Avenue.

Oil was only one of several manias in Los Angeles in 1912, as the city became the embodiment of several American dreams. The citrus industry and real estate's "subdivision" of vast domains into lots created a vision of Los Angeles as a middle-class health utopia. Tourism fed on this and on the new motion picture industry. The whole community shared a boosterism, an openness to advertising and promotion. Los Angeles had the "bounce and liveliness" that Chandler had remarked of Americans in Europe, and Bruce Bliven's description of the middle-class Los Angelean could have been of Chandler: "[He] is the big, beaming man, with clipped military mustaches, whose golf is in the nineties, motor speed in the sixties, waist-line in the forties, wife in the thirties, and sweetheart in the (early) twenties. . . . He makes plenty of money, spends most of it, drives a snappy car, dresses in snappy clothes" ("Los Angeles" 199).

Chandler's youth was cut short by World War I. Still feeling British, he joined the Canadian army and was sent to the front. He was the sole shell-shocked survivor of a German artillery barrage on Vimy Ridge in 1918. Demobilized in British Columbia, he went to San Francisco, where he worked briefly in an English bank, quitting because he disliked his countrymen. In 1919 he returned to Los Angeles, an uncertain thirty-one year old.

It turned out that he was in love with pianist Julian Pascal's wife, Cissy, who was forty-eight, blond, bohemian, and theatrical. It has been argued that Chandler saw a mother in her, but Cissy was well educated, well read, opinionated. She did not look her age and concealed it from him for years. In the Arroyo culture of the Lloyds and Pascals, such affairs were handled civilly. Cissy got a divorce in 1920 but did not marry Chandler until 1924 because of the objections of his mother, who had come to live with him. The crisis and union became the central facts of Chandler's life: he had taken another man's wife, against his mother's wishes. The love triangle played against a background of prodigal guilt and chivalric fidelity would haunt his fiction.

Chandler lived with his mother until her death, while renting an apartment for Cissy. This was an expensive arrangement. Fortunately, the skills he honed at the creamery attracted the interest of Lloyd's partner, Joseph B. Dabney. Lloyd had joined Dabney, a fellow Iowan, to develop oil fields (MacShane, *Life* 34). But Dabney grew restless. Ever since Standard Oil had brought in a well at Huntington Beach in 1920, exploration had focused on hills and ridges south of Los Angeles. When Shell struck oil at Signal Hill on June 21, 1921, Dabney sold out to the Lloyds and formed South Basin Oil Company.

The only problem was that Signal Hill had been subdivided, providing an unparalleled vehicle for oil speculation by small investors. People rushed from Los Angeles in buses and taxis upon hearing news of the Shell strike, buying lots and forming syndicates on the spot. Nor was their greed unfounded, for Signal Hill and two neighboring fields produced one-fifth of the world's oil for a time. Dabney, buying up lots and operating one hundred wells, produced sixteen thousand barrels a day, second only to Shell.

Chandler went to work for Dabney and got a chance to watch the rise of an industry that was rife with speculation, conflict, and self-promotion. It was certainly a contrast to Arroyo culture. Why, just over Signal Hill in Santa Fe Springs, an extraordinary oil field had been discovered on the farm of Alonzo Bell in 1922, who then purchased two thousand acres of land and created Bel-Air. There he lived safe from the threats of kidnapping and violence that sprouted with the bars, brothels, and speculators of once rural Santa Fe Springs.

No character there was more famous than Chauncey C. Julian. In 1922 Julian had obtained a small lease in Santa Fe Springs with thirty thousand dollars of borrowed money. To raise drilling capital, he sold shares through newspaper ads:

> 11 Days More Folks! Have You Got Your Ticket on Me to Win at Santa Fe Springs? DON'T OVERLOOK ME! The odds are 1000 to one in my favor of drilling in a big one and when I do your ticket will pay $30 for every $1 you shoot. And what I mean, you collect from the Bank.
>
> Drive down to the field today and take a peek at my location. I'll promise you see SOME ACTION. And if you have a "hunch" that I am right, "for the love of Mike" don't keep putting it off, make a noise like a check, for I am already $100,000.00 subscribed.
>
> My offices will be open all day. Run in and meet me personally. C. C. Julian. (in Henstell 37)

Julian raised $220,000—more than needed—and realized he should begin a second campaign. What he didn't say was that his second syndicate was located on his existing lease. He raised another $220,000, following it with third, fourth, and fifth syndications—making $688,000 over cost while working in the comfort of his office.

By coincidence, in 1923, the year that started Chandler's rise, Julian launched an extraordinary scheme to acquire pipelines, tanks, refineries, and gas stations, just as Chandler's company was doing. As legal ombudsman for his company, Chandler was in competition with Julian for these resources. So he constantly traveled from the "civilization" downtown to the frontier of Signal Hill, southwest on the ocean, a circuit he would endow with geopolitical meaning in his fiction.

But while Chandler struggled for equipment and supplies, Julian mounted another fund-raising campaign. This offering sold out in fifty-five days, oversubscribed by two million dollars. When the state forbade the expansion, Julian moved to Nevada, where the law understood him. The Los Angeles oilmen, Arroyans included, then recruited *Times* publisher Harry

Chandler to campaign against Julian, and in 1924 they persuaded J. Edgar Hoover to assign the first in a series of FBI agents to audit Julian's books (Henstell 38). One agent after another disappeared into what Chandler later called "the nastiness," bribed or bought off or convinced that debts were assets.[4]

Beginning in 1925 Raymond Chandler was also involved with the law, but he fancied himself a champion of justice: "I always somehow seemed to have a fight on my hands. At one time I employed six lawyers; some were good at one thing, some at another. Their bills always exasperated the Chairman; he said they were too high. I always paid them as rendered because they were not too high, in the circumstances. Business is very tough and I hate it. But whatever you set out to do, you have to do as well as you know how" (MacShane, *Selected Letters* 444). Rather than proceed with what was customary in the oil fields, Chandler liked to stand up for "what was right."

> I remember one time when we had a truck carrying pipe in Signal Hill (just north of Long Beach) and the pipe stuck out quite a long way, but there was a red lantern on it, according to law. A car with two drunken sailors and two girls crashed into it and filed actions for $1,000 apiece. . . . The insurance company said, "Oh well, it costs a lot of money to defend these suits, and we'd rather settle." I said, "That's all very well. It doesn't cost you anything to settle. You simply put the rates up. If you don't want to fight this case, and fight it competently, my company will fight it." "At your own expense?" "Of course not. We'll sue you for what it costs us, unless you pay without that necessity." (MacShane, *Selected Letters* 445)

Chandler hired the best lawyer he knew, showed that the truck had been lit properly, then recruited three barmen from Long Beach to testify that they had thrown the sailors out for drunkenness. "We won hands down," Chandler wrote, "and the insurance company paid up immediately about a third of what they would have settled for, and as soon as they did this I cancelled the policy, and had it rewritten with another company" (MacShane, *Selected Letters* 445).

Chandler fancied himself an astute judge of human nature. The board of directors hired a staff lawyer after this incident, and Chandler recollected that he "found out just how to use his brain, and he said often and publicly that I was the best office manager in Los Angeles and probably one of the best in the world" (MacShane, *Selected Letters* 444). His objection was that the man drank and was unreliable, habits that would soon characterize Chandler. His heroes could always hold their drink and had that entrepreneurial pragmatism Chandler admired in Monroe Stahr of *The Last Tycoon:* "He knows how to use other people's brains," Fitzgerald wrote (58).

Chandler ran a superb office at first, impressing the secretaries by dictating clear four-page letters that were grammatically flawless, writing succinct reports and direct recommendations, closing deals, and resolving details. But gradually his behavior became erratic, in part because of his marriage. As Cissy grew older, she avoided situations that exposed her age, so Chandler went solo or with friends to UCLA football games, to play tennis, his favorite pastime, or to fly in rented airplanes with professional pilots. He seems to have felt trapped, and his drinking after football or tennis began to get out of control. One Saturday morning he went to play tennis with a friend but ended up trying to roust the friend's sick wife from bed. Reprimanded and ordered to leave, Chandler walked into a closet, where he found a pistol and pointed it at his head.

"He was a loner," said Dabney executive John Abrams. "At the annual oil and gas banquets of 1,000 rollicking oil men at the Biltmore, Chandler was a shadowy figure, stinko drunk and hovering in the wings with a bevy of showgirls, a nuisance." To Abrams, Chandler was a "martinet" who sought to "protect" Dabney and "interfered with field operations and employees" (MacShane, *Life* 35–36, 39, 36). Chandler began to disappear from work, drinking for days and then calling the office to say that he was about to jump from a hotel window. He had affairs with secretaries; for one he rented an apartment, where they had such roaring drunks on Friday that she could not rise until Tuesday and he until Wednesday. Chandler saved her job and otherwise misused his power, but friends covered for him until he became sarcastic with them too.

It was Abrams who went to Dabney and asked him to fire Chandler. Dabney let him off with a warning, and Chandler threatened to sue

Abrams. Even forewarned, he let everything slip through his fingers, and Dabney fired him in 1932, as the Depression deepened, when he was forty-four years old. "My services cost them too much," Chandler said later, "always a good reason for letting a man go" (MacShane, *Life* 40). He had been "thrown in the gutter," like Bert Ramsey. The interpretation that Chandler preferred was "insubordination," a figure he had used in his resignation from the Admiralty: his bosses had not been able to cope with a talented subordinate, who took things into his own hands and got them done. It was a figure that comprehended his Irishness in England and his Englishness in America. Experience had formed him to be an "outsider," had made him unassimilable in the large social and business structures of which he sought to be part. But the insubordinate could be a secret knight, a bedraggled aristocrat, just like investigator Ramsey, battling the cheats, the Asa Keyeses, the C. C. Julians.

Chandler fled to Seattle, where he stayed with friends and thought through his options. In his absence, Cissy, who had no choices, caught pneumonia and was hospitalized. He returned immediately, a motion toward his childhood loyalty to women, idealism in the face of tawdry personal defeat, that set his course. During this period he wrote a poem, "Nocturne from Nowhere," that describes an unobtainable woman with "cornflower-blue eyes" and a context of chivalric celibacy that would dominate his major novels. Two key passages are:

> There are no countries as beautiful
> As the England I picture in the night hours
> Of this bright and dismal land
> Of my exile and dismay.
> There are no women as tender as this woman
> Whose cornflower-blue eyes look at me
> With the magic of frustration
> And the promise of an impossible paradise.
>
> . . . .
>
> I do not think I shall touch her hair,
> Nor lay grouping fingers on her unforgotten eyes.
> Perhaps I shall not even speak to her,

But presently turn away, choked with an awful longing,
And go off under the grave English trees,
Through the gentle dusk
Into the land called Death.

(in MacShane, *Life* 21–22)

Chandler was aided in his recovery by a practical vindictiveness. The Lloyds, it turned out, sued Dabney for misappropriation of profits from their venture, and they turned to Chandler for help. He was glad to give them everything he could remember, and they gave him one hundred dollars a month, apparently for an extended period (MacShane, *Life* 42). On this sum Chandler and his wife lived while he learned short-story writing from a correspondence school. A year later, after spending five months on it, he sent his first short story, "Blackmailers Don't Shoot," to *Black Mask*. He began to visit Stanley Rose's book shops on Hollywood Boulevard, where a group of hard-boiled Los Angeles novelists hung out in the back room. He was launched, but it would take him several years to write *The Big Sleep*.

The Big Sleep

The Big Sleep begins as a "wandering daughter job" and ends as a prodigal son story. The first half concerns the attempt to blackmail General Sternwood through his daughter Carmen's gambling IOUs and nude photos. Detective Philip Marlowe finds the original culprit early on, a homosexual pornographer named Arthur Geiger. He has been bludgeoned to death, but his body, his books, and the negatives of Carmen disappear. Marlowe chases down all those who might exploit the items, chiefly Carmen's former lovers Owen Taylor and Joe Brody. Carmen's sister, Vivian, attempts to waylay Marlowe, because he may reveal her own debts to gambler Eddie Mars. These narrative elements alternate, as Marlowe works to improve the family's fortunes while the alienated Vivian undercuts his efforts. Marlowe uncovers a social structure of indebtedness, in which money flows up while a crude sexuality flows down. The paradigm of the pornographic flow is credit. Ultimately Marlowe locates moral responsibility in sleek, gray gangster Eddie Mars, whose credit ensnares Vivian, though the actual murders owe to Brody and Geiger's gay boyfriend, Carol Lundgren (modeled on Wilmer in *The Maltese Falcon*), whom Marlowe turns over to Lieutenant Bernie Ohls and district attorney Taggart Wilde. Geographically, most of these events take place in the private but "inauthentic" Bel-Air hills: Mars's influence extends there, but his base is west, in Palos Verdes.

The spaces of the Los Angeles Basin in the novel's second half help Chandler to complete the geopolitical vista that he has created. Philip Durham has shown how Chandler rewrote "The Curtain," the second source story, adding descriptions and geographic details (in Chandler, *Killer in the Rain* viii–xi). These changes take Marlowe back to the places he visited and defined metaphorically earlier, creating a spatial renesting. We watch Marlowe leave Wilde's house for his own; then he interviews Captain Gregory of Missing Persons about Rusty Regan, the General's prodigal son-in-law who has disappeared. A former IRA commander, Regan is said to resemble the detective. Marlowe next visits Eddie Mars's gambling club, where he rescues Vivian from a mugger. Then he returns to his apartment to find Carmen in his bed. He rousts her. The next day he goes to Bay City (Santa Monica) to meet Harry Jones but finds Lash Canino killing Jones. Marlowe learns that Mona Mars, with whom Regan has supposedly run off, is ensconced in the high desert mining hamlet of Realito. Half in love with Mona himself, Marlowe kills Canino and takes Mona back to Wilde's house. The next day finds him at the Sternwoods, where he sees the General, Carmen, and Vivian in scenes that close the novel. Carmen shot Regan, who has been in an oil sump all along, giving the novel what Dennis Porter has described as the ironic form of an unnecessary journey.

This geopolitical figure is established after Marlowe first visits the Sternwoods.

> Beyond the fence the hill sloped for several miles. On this lower level faint and far off I could just barely see some of the old wooden derricks of the oil-field from which the Sternwoods had made their money. Most of the field was public park now, cleaned up and donated to the city by

General Sternwood. But a little of it was still producing in groups of wells pumping five or six barrels a day. The Sternwoods, having moved up the hill, could no longer smell the stale sump water or the oil, but they could still look out of their front windows and see what had made them rich. If they wanted to. I didn't suppose they would want to. (Chandler, *Big Sleep* 18)

Chandler prepares us to understand the Sternwood family as a composite of Los Angeles oil pioneers by three figurative settings. He led Marlowe to this vista so that among those distant derricks Marlowe could clear up the mystery three days later, with his two views of the oil field bracketing the narrative.

After the exuberant detective introduces himself, the first setting described is the home of his employer: "The main hallway of the Sternwood place was two stories high. Over the entrance doors, which would have let in a troop of Indian elephants, there was a broad, stained-glass panel showing a knight in dark armor rescuing a lady who was tied to a tree and didn't have any clothes on but some very long and convenient hair. The knight had pushed the vizor of his helmet back to be sociable, and he was fiddling with the knots on the ropes that tied the lady to the tree and not getting anywhere" (1). Scholars have made much of the irony in this tableau, its invocation of Arthurian tradition, and the way it forecasts Marlowe's relations with the two Sternwood daughters. The hyperbolic dimensions of the hall also comment on their wealth, and the tableau helps us to understand that "nymphomaniacal" Carmen presumes, figuratively, a sexuality that circulates. But chivalric Marlowe will not aid her.

But two equally important settings follow, and they also emphasize the disharmony between the Sternwoods and their surroundings. Marlowe passes from this hall to sweeping vistas of green grass and "a large green house with a domed roof," where General Sternwood sits amid his orchids: "The air was thick, wet, steamy and larded with the cloying smell of tropical orchids in bloom. The glass walls and roof were heavily misted and big drops of moisture splashed down on the plants. The light had an unreal greenish color, like light filtered through an aquarium tank. The plants filled the place, a forest of them, with nasty meaty leaves and stalks like the newly washed fingers of dead men. They smelled as overpowering as boiling alcohol under a blanket" (5). The General remarks of the orchids, "They are nasty things. Their flesh is too much like the flesh of men. And their perfume has the rotten sweetness of a prostitute" (7). Why is the General in this extraordinary setting? Not to absorb the heat, but to utter the tropes Chandler assigned him. Chandler permits only a few characters besides Marlowe to speak in tropes, and since Marlowe also tells us about the General metaphorically, the interplay of their figurative voices is important. Typically an encounter between two speakers of metaphor in Chandler results in dialogic conflict, or "tough talk," with Marlowe's opponent using stale or inauthentic tropes. Here, however, Marlowe's metaphors are supposed to render "actuality," while those uttered by the General figure an idealization of it. That the General is startlingly original and that Marlowe likes him call attention to a local, political subtext.

The greenhouse and its moribund beauty allude to the "subtropical" conception of southern California. This was a long-standing notion popularized by Major Benjamin Truman, a Los Angeles journalist, who had sought a civilizing figure for the "Southland" by amassing data to show that it was a sun society, luxuriant, fertile, radiant with light and heat, where "one could grow bananas, pineapples, orchids and guavas" (Starr, *Inventing* 45). Truman's metaphor failed to win Anglo-American assent, explains Kevin Starr, because "it made the sun too hot . . . or, more frighteningly, a sun that would sap the Northern European sources of the American will, turning industrious immigrants into loafers" (*Inventing* 45). Like G. Allen Hancock, the General embodies Anglo-pioneer stock, but in his subtropical cocoon he is a long way from the presuppositions he invokes when he speaks longingly of "champagne as cold as Valley Forge" (Chandler, *Big Sleep* 6). The cold climate, self-denial, suffering, and patriotism evoked by this simile conflict with the values of the subtropical. Chandler's recognition that the General is the victim of conflicting climatic metanarratives is shown by Marlowe's counterpoint of local figures: the General's hair is "like wild flowers fighting for life on a bare rock," and he uses "his strength as carefully as an out-of-work show-girl uses her last good pair of stockings" (6). In Chandler's calculus, the most important common denominator is always the physical, local actuality, which always subverts whatever would idealize it romantically. We will later see how this "layman's physics" is the basis of many of his metaphors.

From the "subtropical" greenhouse Marlowe goes to Vivian Regan's room, where the echoes of Daisy Buchanan's living room remind us that *The Great Gatsby* was one of Chandler's favorite novels: "This room was too big, the ceiling was too high, the doors were too tall, and the white carpet that went from wall to wall looked like a fresh fall of snow at Lake Arrowhead. There were full length mirrors and crystal doodads all over the place. The ivory furniture had chromium on it, and the enormous ivory drapes lay tumbled on the white carpet a yard from the windows. The white made the ivory look dirty and the ivory made the white look bled out" (14). Again we see the lack of scale, the mismatch of individual and surrounding, the inability to design an appropriate response to environment, and the counterpointing snow. Vivian's room is the "Mediterranean" or "Italian" figure that succeeded the subtropical. If we sense, even vaguely, a figurative intent behind these three out-of-sync settings, we understand why, in this room, Marlowe responds so hostilely to Vivian's questions. Marlowe revisits these settings at the novel's end, so that the narrative between is nested in a series of figurative parentheses.

At the very center, usually unnoticed, is the legal dispensation that Marlowe has from Taggart Wilde, the district attorney, a "middle-aged, plump man" with "the frank, daring smile of an Irishman" who resembles Asa Keyes a little and Chandler a lot (64, 70). An old friend of Sternwood's, Wilde lives in Hancock Park in an Arroyo-ish house, filled with wood, leather, and exotic plants. He is the only admirable representative of the oligarchy and an impartial figure of justice in a society dominated by indebtedness. Taggart was the sort of Celtic name favored by Arroyans when naming children. Yet Wilde, as Marlowe tells the General, originally fired him as an investigator (as Keyes fired Ramsey) because "I test very high on insubordination" (8). This dismissal is the emblem of his persona, by which Marlowe wins a job from the General. The content of the central scene, aside from details of the first plot's denouement, consists of Marlowe's recitation of his code, his vows of financial parsimony, and his insistence on the identity of public and private justice.

Marlowe assumes Wilde's function gradually. Chandler's innovation on the fabula was his insight that the detective could become the elder brother, that his refusal to "enter into his father's house" could be his narrative capital. He must go to look for the prodigal.[5] Only Wilde concurs, and he speaks with Marlowe "man to man" about the General, his daughters, and the second case, which is the search for Rusty Regan, Marlowe's phantom prodigal brother. The key evidence presented by Marlowe to Wilde consists of a pornographic book and a notebook containing the names of its "borrowers." Wilde keeps the notebook and data (to give to the grand jury) but returns the porn to Marlowe, in the manner of the *des ut Dei* principle. It is a reconciliatory exchange and a figure for this actant's control of sexuality and genetic descent.

The formal structure of *The Big Sleep* also has broader parallels leading readers to the fabula. Carmen takes Marlowe to the abandoned sumps and attempts to kill him for his refusal to sleep with her. From this Marlowe deduces a pattern: Rusty Regan, whom the General says resembles Marlowe, also refused her advances but allowed himself to be drawn there and killed. Marlowe is his "brother," so he may recognize and avoid this fate even while detailing the temptations of "nastiness." His fidelity to the values of working/saving allows him to clear up questions of genetic descent (Regan is irretrievably lost, Carmen must be sequestered) and to achieve favor in his father's eyes.

The parenthetic settings close when Marlowe, having killed Lash Canino, reappears before Wilde, who now has "a tight hard face" and "bitter smile." "This is the last time, Marlowe," he says. "The next fast one you pull I'll throw you to the lions, no matter whose heart it breaks" (194–95). Now he may reenter the father's house. The allusions continue at the Sternwood mansion: "With each step the house seemed to grow larger and more silent. We reached a massive old door that looked as if it had come out of a church. . . . I went . . . across what seemed to be about a quarter of a mile of carpet to a huge canopied bed like the one Henry the Eighth died in" (196).[6]

The tenor of this unscaling suggests the failure of the Sternwoods to address the duties that their status entails, and the scene itself refocalizes power from the dying father (Sternwood) to the elder brother (Marlowe), for Marlowe offers to return the General's fee, convinced the initial assignment was a test of worthiness. He wins the General's assent to his bid to find Regan, a quest that underlines the extent to which Marlowe has functioned as Regan's brother all along. Presenting us vicariously with the experiences of the prodigal, while remonstrating on behalf of his own hidden conserving ethos, Marlowe functions as both younger and elder brother. Only the General's dying wish to see his "lost" child makes necessary Marlowe's short, ironic journey in search of an actual corpse.

The path runs, of course, through Carmen, the archetypal "foreign whore," whom Marlowe finds "bored" in the gardens "with her head between her hands, looking forlorn and alone" (202). He returns her gun, which she tucks "quickly inside her slacks." Then she gives it back "with a secret naughty air, as if she was giving me a key to her room," so that Marlowe can teach her how to shoot (203). In a fabular sunshine as bright and "empty as a headwaiter's smile," Marlowe identifies Carmen with the traditional death's head of the succubus amid the abandoned oil rigs that produced the Sternwood wealth. The confrontation is set

> not in the city at all, but far away in a daydream land. Then the oil-stained, motionless walking-beam of a squat wooden derrick stuck up over a branch. I could see the rusty old steel cable that connected this walking-beam with a half a dozen others. The beams didn't move, probably hadn't moved for a year. The wells were no longer pumping. There was a pile of rusted pipe, a loading platform that sagged at one end, half a dozen empty oil drums lying in a ragged pile. There was the stagnant, oil-scummed water of an old sump iridescent in the sunlight. (204)

This scene, drawn from Chandler's experience, depicts the decay at the heart of the Sternwood fortune. Carmen has a "scraped bone look. Aged, deteriorated, become animal, and not a nice animal" (205). But she is without power to unman the detective, who foresees all her actions. He allows her to aim her gun at him, knowing he has filled it with blanks. He controls her autoeroticism: no consumption is possible, because nothing circulates here, not oil, not Carmen's sexuality, not stock in manipulated pools. Chandler may even be forgiven a pun when Carmen has an epileptic fit and moans with "sudden sick speculation" on regaining consciousness (206).

Only Vivian Regan need be revisited, and Chandler cannot resist another figurative portrait of her room:

> A screen star's boudoir, a place of charm and seduction, artificial as a wooden leg. It was empty at the moment. The door closed behind me with the unnatural softness of a hospital door. . . .
> She was in oyster-white lounging pajamas trimmed with white fur, cut as flowingly as a summer sea frothing on the beach of some small and exclusive island. (207)

Vivian is now unmasked: the "tone poem" of her leg earlier has been replaced by the "wooden leg" of her boudoir. Just as Carmen's "whole face went to pieces" when Marlowe confronted her, Vivian's "face seemed to come to pieces" (206, 211). The door to the room, formerly huge and baronial, is now "unnatural" and hospital-like. When Vivian offers Marlowe a bribe, he responds with a lecture, ostensibly about the detective code but actually about the conflict between the parsimony of the elder brother and the money-sexuality flow:

> I am so money greedy that for twenty-five bucks a day and expenses, mostly gasoline and whiskey, I do my thinking myself, what there is of it; I risk my whole future, the hatred of cops and of Eddie Mars and his pals, I dodge bullets and eat saps. . . . With fifteen grand I could own a home and a new car and four suits of clothes. I might even take a vacation without worrying about losing a case. That's fine. What are you offering it to me for? Can I go on being a son of a bitch, or do I have to become a gentleman, like that lush that passed out in his car the other night? (213–14)

That lush, who becomes Terry Lennox in *The Long Goodbye* (1950), is the prodigal that Marlowe would be if he subscribed to the "Mediterranean" and its debilitating influence. The cautionary example of the Sternwoods distances Marlowe from the Arroyo, on behalf of whose values he had worked. He recognizes that they represent "flow" instead of law. But economically he is still their dependent, as he admits: "Me, I was a part of the nastiness, now" (215). This quandary marks the beginning of his increased sympathy for Los Angeles's Folks.

CHANDLER'S METAPHORS

The tendency of Chandler's metaphors is to posit a mechanistic, post-Einsteinian world, a world of time, space, mass, motion, and inertia. This "layman's physics" is so often the presupposition of his metaphors that it has political and economic implications, as Peter Rabinowitz has pointed out. We learn Chandler's landscape through comparisons by size, speed, impact, balance—the physical relations of matter. The General "nodded, as if his neck was afraid of the weight of his head" (7). Geiger will "think a bridge fell on him" (12). Norris has a "back as straight as an ironing board" (13). Agnes's "smile was now hanging by its teeth and eyebrows and wondering what it would hit when it dropped" (20). An "army of sluggish minutes dragged by" Marlowe (29). Newspaper stories are as close to the truth "as Mars is to Saturn" (110). A minute sound is "like a small icicle breaking" (160). Marlowe's "brain ticked like a clock" (193). Somebody, he says on waking, "built a filling station on my jaw" (178). The presuppositions of these metaphors build an ideological base. Consider one figure that characterizes the inauthentic "public" world. Several times Chandler compares small-time gangster Harry Jones to birds and Lash Canino, who has "a purring voice," to "a small dynamo behind a wall." When Canino kills Jones with a glass of cyanide, Marlowe guesses what is happening because "the purring voice had an edge, like sand in the bearing," as Canino utters the fatal pun, "Let's dip the bill" (160, 161). The physics stands out, but metonymy supplants synecdoche in this progression.

Carmen Sternwood is fixed in the first four pages of the novel by metonymic tropes that suggest her unreality: "walked as if she were floating," "teeth . . . as shiny as porcelain," "lowered her lashes like . . . a theatre curtain" (2–4). We understand that Carmen is a kind of puppet, with "artificial lips" who "had to be manipulated with springs," as is Vivian: "Her hand went up slowly like an artificial hand worked by wires" (147, 212). Such "inauthenticity" is created contextually, drawing on physical comparison, and may have suggested the rubrics of "authentic" and "inauthentic" that Fredric Jameson saw as the controlling *ideologemes* of the novel (public and private spaces). But the text is quite complex.

Marlowe's world abounds in Los Angeles comparisons. The harbor has "a loud fish-smell which one night's hard rain hadn't even dented" (41). His cabinets are "full of California climate" (51). The muzzle of a gun looks "like the mouth of the Second Street tunnel" (67). There are the "flawless lines of the orange trees wheeling away like endless spokes" as Marlowe drives and young girls' "eyes as large as mammoth prunes" (170, 51). More accessible to non-Californians and providing a similar grasp of the lived world are Chandler's domestic tropes, particularly those about the kitchen. The greenhouse is as warm as a "slow oven," and Marlowe is "trussed like a turkey ready for the oven" (5, 178). Someone's face "fell apart like a bride's pie crust," while another's is "as hard and white as cold mutton fat" (47, 97). "You're no English muffin yourself," says Marlowe (139).

In such metaphors, Chandler's political worldview is actually most acute. But the speed of the repartee prevents us from apprehending the kinds of elisions that such figures require us to make. Fortunately a revolution in understanding metaphor since 1962 allows us to unpack such tropes.[7] For example, in Marlowe's first talk with Vivian, he explodes, "I don't mind your ritzing me." Chandler's use of *ritzing* may not appear to be a conundrum, but what does it mean? *Ritzing* is marked grammatically for metaphoric and ideological investment. It functions as a metaphor, a case of what Dorothy Mack has identified as agent promotion.[8] *Your* is endowed with the qualities of *ritzing* in relation to *me*. That turns out to be helpful in parsing it. The semantic structure of ideologization supplies "acting like a rich person," when the common knowledge of the 1920s, "typical of the Ritz hotels founded by Caesar Ritz in Geneva," has vanished.

But when the historic context is restored, another more focused level of ideological work appears. The phrase "puttin' on the Ritz" gained currency around 1910 and became famous in Irving Berlin's 1929 song "Puttin' on the Ritz." Movie adaptations in 1930 and 1946 (*Blue Skies* with Fred Astaire) helped to create a commonplace, the gist of which was a bemused view of Harlem women who presumed to gain status and allure by dressing several social classes higher to resemble the white women at the Ritz. The racial and sexual salient in Berlin's use makes the figure particularly cutting if readers perceive Marlowe invoking it. On the semantic level, this is a good example of how figures of deletion (metonomy) impel readers to seek global contexts established previously.

I don't mind (your ← ritzing) + me
or (your ← drinking) + your lunch out of a bottle

By casting *ritz* as a gerund, Chandler transforms it into an act and aligns it with *drinking*. The motion implicit in the gerund is one way of invoking the context of "physics." He makes *me* parallel to *bottle*, an object whose salient quality could be emptiness, hollowness, drunkenness, or even constraint. This parallelism, its implications delayed, changes the final meaning, reversing the "I don't mind." Marlowe does mind; the register is irony. At the same time Chandler has retrospectively prefaced the entire trope with the logical operator *not*. In this negation "that which points to itself by refusing definition" (the $S^{\sim 2}$ of the Greimas grid) is Marlowe's self-empowerment, his unspoken credo. The semantic and contextual systems work together to tell us that Marlowe perceives the wealthy Vivian to be calling on a presumed, almost physical class boundary: the distinction of master and servant. The playful rejoinder that Chandler provides Vivian—"I ought to throw a Buick at you" (16)—amplifies the double entendre of physics, for it repeats ironically her presumption that she can call on greater physical forces than Marlowe. Only Chandler can throw Buicks around, and by his creation of dialogue that shows the disparity between the pretension to and the possession of power, he implodes all that appears by virtue of his style to have escaped his common denominator of a "layman's physics."

Given the wounds capitalism inflicted, why did Chandler express his politics so indirectly? The short answer is that despite his fall he retained a patrician view of the system that once supported him so comfortably. Dabney may have fired him, but the Lloyds gave him a stipend. Chandler had a private school sense of honor. Then again, his sense of narrative was basically romantic: the fabulae of his novels begin with the promise of improvement (Carmen will be protected, Rusty found, the General made happy) and gradually reveal that the actors have undermined the possibility of improvement by their alienation.

It will not surprise anyone who has apprehended Chandler's domesticity that houses function as stops on commodification. As Jameson noted, at the core of Chandler's major novels are the private, domestic, authentic spaces of Marlowe and those he respects. Like islands in a sea of invention, these are marked off by the absence of trope. They are described objectively, apart from the recurrent networks of presupposition that declare the laws of "physics," and are located in the Basin of Los Angeles, in the geography of the Folks.

The houses of the rich are different. They *sheath* from public view their victimization of the Folks. While the Hancock estate was in its original state, for example, the human cost of oil fortunes—represented by Regan's corpse—remained in the public eye. That's why they want to convert it to a park. This ability of wealth to "pull down the curtain" is one of the key differences between the private, inauthentic arrangements of prodigality and the unmasking that Marlowe insists on. This difference is visible in Marlowe's geopolitical movement. He travels to the Sternwoods' house in the hills, to the porn shop in Hollywood, to Geiger's house in the hills, and back to the Sternwoods' again. This circuit, moving from the private hills to the public Basin and back, ends by returning the unsheathed (an image of Carmen nude) to the sheathed world. Leaving the Sternwoods, Marlowe walks down the road past "big houses in ghostly enormous grounds, vague clusters of eaves and gables and lighted windows high on the hillside, remote and inaccessible, like witch houses in a forest" (36). Their residents can "pull down the curtain," police argot for anyone who deliberately vanishes without leaving a clue, as Rusty Regan is suspected of doing.

But the absence of a shade to pull down is no virtue. After visiting the Sternwoods, Marlowe emerges in the public Basin at "a service station glaring with wasted light, where a bored attendant in a white cap and a dark blue windbreaker sat hunched on a stool, inside the steamed glass, reading a paper" (36). This bored man, so reminiscent of paintings by Edward Hopper, is the alienated worker that Cora feared Frank would become in *Postman*. The Basin is democracy, level and leveling. It is populated by shoddy imitations, the Ben Getzoffs who, like Joe Brody, speak in the "elaborately casual voice of the tough guy in pictures," with "no more inflection than the voice of a faro dealer" (71, 72).

Marlowe works in the Basin, and his office has the "usual" stuff and reeks of public anonymity. "You don't put on much of a front," Vivian complains (51). In all *The Big Sleep* there are two special places. One is Marlowe's sanctum sanctorum, his rented room: "It was all I had in the way of a home. In it was everything that was mine, that had any association for me, any past, anything that took the place of a family. Not much; a few books, pictures, radio, chessmen, old letters, stuff like that. Nothing. Such as they were they had all my memories" (147). The other place stands at the center of the book, in the Basin: Taggart Wilde, patriarch of the law, lives "at the corner of Fourth and Lafayette Park, in a white frame house the size of a car-barn, with a red sandstone porte-cochere built on to one side and a couple of acres of soft rolling lawn in front. It was one of those solid old-fashioned houses which it used to be the thing to move bodily to new locations as the city grew westward. Wilde came of an old Los Angeles family and had probably been born in the house when it was on West Adams or Figueroa or St. James Park" (97). Wilde, whether modeled on Keyes or Lloyd or, most likely, Republican district attorney Burton Fitts, is the only other character whose abode fits him. Adams and Figueroa, however, was the site of oil millionaire E. L. Doheny's "Spanish gothic" mansion (Starr, *Inventing* 67–68). The address (8 Chester Place) links the two houses in a diptych of Arroyan values threatened by urban impermanence.

The most famous edifice in *The Big Sleep* is the Fulwider Building, which Marlowe described in language that has attracted much critical interest. It is in Bay City (Santa Monica), which stands politically for San Francisco.

A single drop light burned far back, beyond an open, once gilt elevator. There was a tarnished and well-missed spittoon on a gnawed rubber mat. A case of false teeth hung on the mustard colored wall like a fuse box in a screen porch. I shook the rain off my hat and looked at the building directory beside the case of teeth. Numbers with names and numbers without names. Plenty of vacancies or plenty of tenants who wished to remain anonymous. Painless dentists, shyster detective agencies, small sick businesses that had crawled there to die, mail order schools that would teach you how to become a railroad clerk or a radio technician or a screen writer—if the postal inspectors didn't catch up with them first. A nasty building. A building in which the smell of stale cigar butts would be the cleanest odor. . . .

The fire stairs hadn't been swept in a month. Bums had slept on them, eaten on them, left crusts and fragments of greasy newspaper, matches, a gutted imitation leather pocketbook. In a shadowy angle against the scribbled wall a pouched ring of pale rubber had fallen and had not been disturbed. A very nice building. (159–60)

Much has been made of this as a representation of vagina dentata, putatively the substrata of Chandler's repressed homosexuality, by Gershon Legmon and Peter Wolfe (Legmon 70; Wolfe, *Something More* 117, 131). Though undeniably present, this emphasis slights the geographic context and the larger "desire" that extends through the bracketings that close the novel. These substrata also complicate the dichotomy between the sordid local and the ideal constitutional that Jameson noted, for Chandler mapped the political and sexual on the geographic. In fact, a kind of spatially plotted "frenzy" begins in the Fulwider Building that will not be resolved until Marlowe flees the Basin for the purity of Realito in the high desert. The concept that unifies these elements is, to borrow a term from Michel Carrouges, a "celibate machine" (in Deleuze and Guattari 15). Whether or not homosexual, Chandler created a figure of autoerotic desire that is the logical culmination of public, inauthentic consumption. This preoccupation, we will find, guides film noir.

The "celibate machine" is described by Gilles Deleuze and Félix Guattari as the superstructure of "a much older paranoiac machine, with its tortures, its dark shadows, its ancient Law" (16). The machines that Carrouges identifies—Duchamp's "Large Glass," Kafka's "Penal Colony"—contain an inner script (for example, Duchamp's box of notes). The Fulwider has its "scribbled wall" and "fragments of greasy newspaper." The function of these inner scripts is to allude to patriarchal law, which Lacan called the name-of-the-father and which post-Lacanians Deleuze and Guattari call the name-of-the-despot.[9] Their contention is that the preeminence given consumption had undermined, indeed retired, the patriarchal function and with it the Lacanian notion that the unconscious is structured like a language. "Under capitalism," explains Eugene Holland, "there is no fixed center of this kind, no transcendental signified, no established authority-figure; rather exchange value and the market ruthlessly undermine and eliminate all traditional meanings and pre-existing social codes" (296). This explains why the fathers (Wilde, Sternwood) become metonymic variations in Chandler's remodeling of the fabula of prodigality.

Celibate machines "achieve a genuine consummation," write Deleuze and Guattari, "that can rightly be called autoerotic . . . as though the eroticism of the machine liberated other unlimited forces" (18). The "machine" is both a mechanization of experience and, schizophrenically, an embodiment of pure intensities, a duality that Chandler provides in his building and the overheard murder of Harry Jones. Such potential intensities slumber everywhere on the ground of public, economic decoding: there are numbers without names, plenty of vacancies, and small sick businesses. This would seem anticapitalistic, except that the Fulwider Building is described as home to insurance offices and a front for bookies: it is actually a figure for "betting," or speculative frenzy. The "painless dentists" and mail-order frauds are icons of paranoid pleasure/pain, like the elevator operator whom Marlowe sees "waiting for a customer." Everywhere are sites of potential intensity: the single drop light, the false teeth like a fuse box, the elevator, and the prophylactic.

But the intensity of Chandler's "machine" lies especially in the accelerating narrative that the building activates. Deleuze and Guattari define the machine as producing repulsion and attraction in a "matter [that] has no empty spaces" (21), and Marlowe notes "the clandestine air of the building prompting me" from the lobby to the stairs to an office, where he overhears, in helpless, delicious guilt, the murder of innocuous Harry Jones by Lash Canino, which will sanction Marlowe's murder of Canino (Chandler, *Big Sleep* 160). A store of repressed energy is created before a frenzy, in Chandler's case heightened by tropes. When Marlowe, the celibate knight, makes himself vulnerable to Canino and then finally kills him in a scene of drunken euphoria, it is a schizophrenic delirium, as Marlowe spends the metaphoric energy previously subtracted from apparent reality.

Mona Mars ("Silver-Wig") is the ostensible object of Marlowe's frenzy, as indicated by his overdetermination of her least expression. "Then she laughed. It was almost a racking laugh. It shook her as the wind shakes a tree. I thought there was puzzlement in it, not exactly surprise, but as if a new idea had been added to something already known and it didn't fit" (183). Each detail about her is this intense, yet Marlowe cannot possess this ideal woman, because Chandler identifies her with the girl of "cornflower-blue eyes" in his earlier poetry. Only with this in mind can we understand the kiss Marlowe bestows on Mona: " 'There's no hurry. All this was arranged in advance, rehearsed to the last detail, timed to the split second. Just like a radio program. No hurry at all. Kiss me, Silver-Wig.' Her face under my mouth was like ice. She put her hands up and took hold of my head and kissed me hard on the lips. Her lips were like ice, too" (185). Then Mona distracts Canino so that Marlowe can ambush him: "I shot him four times, the Colt straining against my ribs. The gun jumped out of his hand as if it had been kicked. He reached both his hands for his stomach. I could hear them smack hard against his body. He fell like that, straight forward, holding himself together with his broad hands" (189).

The celibate machine now consummated, Marlowe possesses another man's wife and must estrange the supposed object of his lust: "I had killed a man at Realito and was on my way over to Wilde's house with Eddie Mars' wife, who had seen me do it" (193). Mars reclaims his wife with "an abrupt smile," leaving Marlowe with the "cold, angry voice" of the law (194). He cannot bring home a "foreign whore"; in fact, the law is his true Penelope, the consolation of disillusionment in popular culture, yet so repressive that it sets the sailor in search of the sea again.

Farewell, My Lovely

Farewell, My Lovely seems at first a picaresque novel, a series of adventures among minorities, drunks, and fakes, told by a marginally employed detective determined to wrest from them a meaning he calls Velma Valento. Velma turns out to have little to do with this milieu but everything to do with economic mobility. Such a theme could not arise, however, without these portraits of the have-nots balanced by Marlowe's visits to the duplicitous haves. As in *The Big Sleep*, ideological figuration in *Farewell* arises from contrasted public and private worlds. But another, more profound level of ideology is created by the dramatic contrast of *Farewell*'s apparent and revealed plots, its narratives of improvement and alienation.

In the apparent story Marlowe witnesses the murder of a black bar owner by giant Moose Malloy, who is searching for his old flame Velma. Then Marlowe is gofer for gold-bricking Lieutenant Nulty, to whom he suggests the crime's solution after interviewing a hotel clerk, a widow, and the widow's neighbor: the way to find Malloy is to find Velma. A second apparent story begins when Marlowe is hired by effete Lindsay Marriott to deliver eight thousand dollars in ransom for a stolen jade necklace. Marriott is murdered, and Marlowe is blackjacked and then rescued by Anne Riordan, "the kind of girl Marlowe would have married had he been the marrying kind" (Raymond Chandler quoted in Durham 39). Efficient Lieutenant Randall gets this case; efficient Anne Riordan investigates, learning that a Mrs. Grayle owns the necklace and taking Marlowe to her. Marlowe's liaison with her is interrupted when "psychic consultant" Jules Amthor has him blackjacked, drugged, and confined in a Bay City hospital. There he spots Malloy, escapes, and follows him to Laird Brunette's gambling ship. The two apparent plots unite when Marlowe invites Mrs. Grayle (actually Velma) and Moose to his room. Velma kills Moose and flees to the East, where she eventually commits suicide.

The revealed plot is astonishing, for all the crime results from Velma's economic rise to become Mrs. Grayle, though she is treated benignly throughout the narrative. But she believes in the great American economic myth, so she takes the fall that Chandler took, showing the indissolubility of origins. She must cover up her profession, her real name, and her payoffs to Marriott and the widow Florian. Velma's husband even sells his radio station in Beverly Hills to hide her past. In real life, of course, the Lloyds paid off Chandler, who lost his profession and fled. Like Cora in *Postman*, Velma figures the price of economic power.

A girl who started in the gutter became the wife of a multi-millionaire. On the way up a shabby old woman recognized her—probably heard her singing at the radio station and recognized the voice and went to see—and this old woman had to be kept quiet. But she was cheap, therefore she only knew a little. But the man who dealt with her and made her monthly payments and owned a trust deed on her home and could throw her into the gutter any time she got funny—that man knew it all. He was expensive. But that didn't matter either, as long as nobody else knew. But some day a tough guy named Moose Malloy was going to get out of jail and start finding things out about his former sweetie. (Chandler, *Farewell* 239)

You become alienated from yourself by succeeding, says Chandler. Indeed Marriott, Malloy, and Marlowe are three faces of Raymond Chandler, all insisting that no wealth is immaculate. Yet what could be more American than to rise from "the gutter" to wealth? Why should a taxi dancer worry who "knew it all" or would "start finding things out"? In the Hollywood of Chandler's era, moguls married starlets quite ad hoc, with both parties becoming the more celebrated. But if this is historic fact, so is the instability of such unions. Loyalty, that demon of Chandler's youth and philanderings, was always purchased at the price of truth and always led to the necessity of greater and greater debt. Being thrown into the gutter at any time was the ultimate horror viewed through the Dickensian sensibility that Chandler never lost. But he loved those characters who reassembled themselves, however crudely, after the fall.

The force that seeks to reveal Velma Valento is too primitive to be called Marlowe, so it is named Moose Malloy—the embodiment of a naive belief, an idealism, a "love" so sentimental that Chandler cannot allow it on stage often. "The Great Bend bank job. Solo. Ain't that something?" Malloy asks Marlowe, underlining his origin in an era when crime, like the rest of life, was romantic (10). Like Rusty Regan, he is a lost brother whom Marlowe must find.

Marlowe has been on a "wandering husband" job, seeking a Greek barber in the Central District's growing black ghetto, when he sees Moose Malloy "looking up at the dusty windows with a sort of ecstatic fixity of expression, like a hunky immigrant catching his first sight of the Statue of Liberty" (1). This trope does not mean "impressed" or "rhapsodic." Malloy is fixated by an *image* of love as a hunky immigrant is hypnotized by the image of the Statue of Liberty. In an era of threatening immigration to the United States, irony springs from the several meanings of *hunky:* coming from Hungary; to be unformed, as a large piece, a chunk; and to agree, as in "That's hunky-dory with me." Choose any, Malloy stands in relation to his love at Florian's as an immigrant stands in relation to the "promise" of American life—headed for disillusionment. If his stance on the street recalls Gatsby's gesture toward the green light from his lawn, it may not be accidental that Malloy meets a similar end. Gatsby flaunted his yellow suit, and Malloy is dressed "about as inconspicuously as a tarantula on a slice of angel food" (1). This image recalls Dickens's *Great Expectations:* like Miss Havesham, from whose wedding cake a spider emerges, Moose will have his dreams dashed. Chandler knew the gulf between the immigrant's dream and experience. Velma will figure economic mobility, and Moose, a character from the naive, purely material world of Hammett's *Red Harvest,* must die. It is no accident that the figure of social mobility kills him, or that Marlowe arranges it.

IDEOLOGICAL FIGURES

As Marlowe searches for Velma, he perceives society to be hidden in "smoke," Chandler's figure for social change. Smoke smudges Marlowe's ability to read the class, race, and economic affinities of blacks, homosexuals, Chinese, Japanese, and Mexicans who were initially so accepted by genteel Arroyo culture. *Farewell* begins on one of "the blocks that are not yet all Negro" in the Central District, with Malloy smoking and telling Marlowe that Florian's is now run by "dinges" and "smokes," who move by as "soundless as shadows on grass" (1). After Malloy murders the black bar owner, Marlowe visits Lieutenant Nulty, who smokes and speaks of "dinges" and "shines" (28). When Marlowe takes work from Lindsay Marriott, they smoke, and Marlowe accompanies Marriott to his death in fog. The detective is saved by Anne Riordan, whose words hang in the air "like smoke in a closed room" (61), and then smokes with Lieutenant Randall and finds Marriott's marijuana cigarettes in an "imitation tortoise-shell frame [case from] Hooey Phooey Sing—Long Sing Tung, that kind of place, where a nice-mannered Jap hisses at you" (85). Later, at the Grayles' estate, Marlowe notices "a Jap gardener . . . pulling a piece of weed out of the vast velvet expanse and sneering at it the way Jap gardeners do" (102).[10]

Let us jump to the novel's final scene, a moment of clarity, with Marlowe "on the steps of City Hall. It was a cool day and very clear. You could see a long way—but not as far as Velma had gone" (249). In retrospect, we see too, that the resolution of the Velma-Moose conflict is the vanquishing of smoke, of minorities. Moose has actually been a figure for their raw muscle, their function as "labor" in an economic hierarchy. Moose is a critique of the Arroyo, a demonstration of the ill-starred credulity of those who take constitutional idealism too literally.

Many ideological figures from *The Big Sleep* persist in *Farewell*, such as the "pooling" of money and oil development: Anne Riordan owns "lots at Del Rey" that turn out to be oil lots, for which her father is "taken to the cleaners," reminding us of Ben Getzoff. But the novel is structured ideologically as five trips from the Basin west to Bay City and back: to Marriott's house, to Mrs. Grayle's house, to Amthor's aerie, to the Bay City police station, and to Venice Beach and the gambling ship *Montecito*. Considerable action may intervene, but Marlowe always returns to his apartment or to a police station in the Basin.

The model of Burt Ramsey and insubordination as a test of merit fade as Marlowe becomes self-sufficient. He remarks on the incompetence of the insubordinate Lieutenant Nulty (*null*-ty), who is assigned to Moose's crime, and he admires Lieutenant Randall, who investigates the machinations in Bay City. In *The Big Sleep* Chandler linked the Sternwood wealth to colonial forebears with "hot hard coal-black eyes" (2), entrepreneurial qualities and *la ancienne noblesse*. Now Chandler, weaned from the Lloyds' stipend, would live on the cuff of poverty until the 1950s. He had begun to suspect the American promise of social mobility, of class transformation. We have origins, and their immutability is a persistent Chandlerian theme.

That Los Angeles was to be a *white* middle-class utopia was widely understood. Starr points out that the oligarchy considered Los Angeles the latest and most promising English-speaking city on the planet and placed special emphasis on its Anglo-American heritage (*Inventing* 89–91). But economic contraction after 1929 changed the flow of migrants from easterners and upper midwesterners to Dust Bowl Okies, Mexicans, blacks, and Filipinos. Philadelphia gangsters liked sunshine as much as Chicago dentists and New England architects, so whites began to abandon the city center and to head for hills on the Basin's periphery. Beginning with *Farewell*, Chandler's fiction simmers with migrant-native tension, which he plotted geopolitically.

No trope better indicates the threats of the new migration or is so misunderstood as Marlowe's remark to Lindsay Marriott as they drive the latter's Rolls-Royce in those hills to an assignation with blackmailers: "This car sticks out like spats at an Iowa picnic" (*Farewell* 50). The car has just been described as "a huge black battleship of a car with chromium trimmings, a coyote tail tied to the Winged Victory on the radiator cap and engraved initials where the emblem should be." It is clearly a Rolls-Royce. Why stress again in a trope the car's blackness and rarity? That depends on the presuppositions we have about "Iowa picnic." In 1930s Los Angeles, "Iowa picnic" meant the annual gathering of the Iowa Society on Iowa Day, January 18. Held at Bixby Park in Long Beach, these "picnics" attracted as many as 150,000 transplanted Iowans. In 1927 Bruce Bliven picnicked with 125,000 former Iowans and wrote in *New Republic*:

It is the fashion to blame these Middle Westerners for all that is wrong with California civilization, but this indictment is a little too easy to be wholly true. It is a fact that the latter-day pioneer is usually an earnest church-goer, an aggressive Puritan, who believes there's enough sex in real life without bringing it into plays and books. But his aggressive good citizenship is also responsible for much genuinely admirable social legislation, of the sort which has made California one of the world's leaders in this respect. The retired farmer has a passion for education, which has given Los Angeles an amazing system of public schools. . . . As a taxpayer, he cheerfully maintains a fine series of municipal institutions. He is not afraid of city-owned waterworks, or of such "socialistic" enterprises as municipal summer camps in the mountains. ("Los Angeles" 198–99)

The former Iowans were provincial but politically active; they picnicked by home counties and wore "Hog and Hominy" buttons, and politicians came to court their votes. They were elderly (like Chandler's nosy

Mrs. Morrison, who came from Mason City in 1921) and had moved to Los Angeles to retire or because of illness. Adamantly middle-class, afraid of eastern political corruption, they had formed the backbone of the Good Government movement. Hamlin Garland attended one Iowa Society picnic and found the members "incredibly unaesthetic and yet they were worthy, fine serious folk who do not believe in drinking, smoking or philandering" (in Starr, *Material Dreams* 132). Louis Adamic was less kind: "One cannot get away from The Folks in Los Angeles. They are everywhere and their influence is felt in well-nigh every phase of city life. They are simple, credulous souls; their bodies are afflicted with all sorts of aches and pains, real and imaginary; they are unimaginative and their cultural horizons are sadly limited—and as such they are perfect soil to sprout and nourish all kinds of medical, religious and cultural quackery (in Starr, *Material Dreams* 132).

The only person who might wear spats to an Iowa picnic would be a politician come to court votes or an outsider unfamiliar with the Folks' immediate adoption of California's light clothing. The Iowa picnic grounds in Long Beach were close to the oil fields, and the Iowans were familiar with frauds like Julian, who had fleeced them twice. For Chandler, they formed the perfect counterpoint to the Julians and Bermans. Remember Hammett's "somebody in spats"? Spats had typified the dress of city slickers and dandies, types vilified by popular culture. In the 1920s speculators and New York mayor Jimmy Walker wore spats, part of the "sheik and sheba" slickness. In 1940, however, almost everyone had turned against such ostentation.

Marlowe utters this trope in Purrissima Canyon, where Marriott and his car stand out in the brush, a kind of frontier on which the young "sheik" proposes to meet those updated Indians, the gangsters, just like a dandy politician stands out at a gathering of old, practically attired voters. Marriott (and the politician) have style, but the Iowans (and criminals) are economically focused and inclined to ambush. It is also important that they are driving "down a broad avenue lined with unfinished electroliers and weed-grown sidewalks. Some realtor's dream had turned into a hangover there" (50). This abandoned subdivision epitomizes Chandler's view of the migration on which Los Angeles depended for growth. The metaphor is also personal, because Chandler, an older immigrant, sensed the foreignness of the Rolls-Royce and the phony decadence of its American owner in front of the Iowans. Indeed, Marriott turns out to be no match for the economic juggernaut that is Velma Valento.[11]

Some of the Folks, the Anne Riordans and Bernie Ohlses, were gradually coming to represent the good, the law, in Chandler's Los Angeles. Confirming them was a populist technology—a physical sign of the Folks' will to resist political corruption—symbolized by such projects as Boulder Dam (completed as Hoover Dam in 1936). The highest dam in existence, the most expensive public works project of the Depression, it nourished the Folks from a ten-trillion-gallon reservoir. The dam appears in several of Marlowe's metaphors (110, 144), an identification with technology that indicates the path of film noir.

The distinction between the smooth and the rough pioneered by Hammett continued to be a useful tool for Chandler. When Lieutenant Randall and Marlowe trade the following repartee, Marlowe's wisecrack about smooth shiny girls stands in high relief, saying something about the cultural value of smoothness.

"I like smooth shiny girls, hard-boiled and loaded with sin."
"They take you to the cleaners," Randall said indifferently.
"Sure. Where else have I ever been?" (166–67)

The rough was old-fashioned by 1940. Moose Malloy's superannuation is given tactile edge by his "shaggy borsalino hat, a rough grey sports coat with white golf balls on it for buttons, a brown shirt, a yellow tie, pleated gray flannel slacks and alligator shoes with white explosions on the toes" (1). His clothes are loud and physically rough, a sensation acute to Chandler because of his chronic eczema.[12] He even changed the buttons on the coat of Moose's model, Steve Skalla (smooth as "billiard balls") from "Killer in the Rain," into *dimpled* golf balls on Malloy's coat (Chandler, *Killer in the Rain* 128).

For Chandler smoothness was not problematic; you simply distrust it. It takes many forms. Marlowe parodies the "smooth" behavior of film stars: "I leaned against the door frame and put a cigarette in my mouth and tried to jerk it up far enough to hit my nose with it. This is harder than it looks" (*Farewell* 96). Chandler never denies the attraction of the smooth but teaches us to suspect it too. He uses it as a tool to sketch his villains: Jules Amthor's "face was as smooth as an angel's wing" (126); Dr. Sonderborg's hair was "so smooth that it appeared to be painted on" (149); Laird Brunette had a "soft, catlike smile" (225); the water-taxi thug had "a smoothly husky voice" (207).

Mrs. Grayle is thus no paradox to Marlowe. On first sight he describes her as "a blonde to make a bishop kick a hole in a stained-glass window. . . . Whatever you needed, wherever you happened to be—she had it" (78). She "had a nice way of talking, cool, half-cynical, and yet not hard-boiled. She rounded her words well" (108). Yet in this first encounter, her smile, which Marlowe can "feel in [his] hip pocket," is an accoutrement that she can put "back on her face" (105). Such smoothness indicates a Streamform succubus, but "physics" will undermine her.

In contrast Anne Riordan is a combination of Hammett's Effie Perrine and Chandler's girl with the "cornflower-blue eyes." Her attractiveness is explained via art deco values of the late 1930s: she has "a neat chin" and is "pretty, but not so pretty that you would have to wear brass knuckles every time you took [her] out." Minor dents distinguish her from Streamform Velma: "Her nose was small and inquisitive, her upper lip a shade too long and her mouth more than a shade too wide" (73–74). These specifics leave no room for equivocation: Anne is internally and externally consistent. The contrast between Velma and Anne develops the dialectic of smooth and rough sufficiently by the time of Randall's talk with Marlowe for him to pose the question of genuine interest. When Marlowe says he prefers the Streamform, he is ironic, and the ideologization is very compressed.

Unpacking the trope requires attention to *hard-boiled*, with its presupposition of cooking an egg, irreducibly female and symbolically potent. Other presuppositions invoke texture and uniform consistency, a homology of surface and content. In this sense, *hard-boiled* is the opposite of *sap* in Hammett and Cain. As the Lynds attested in *Middletown*, vernacular use of *hard-boiled* often meant the economics of social Darwinism, as when companies sloughed off older employees (32). To be hard-boiled is to eliminate the soft, the old, the fat, the feminine, and the emotional. By contrast, *soft-boiled* was a term of approbation.

The destruction of the female implicit in the trope is hardly less astonishing when we consider that what one "loads" on a hard-boiled egg is
salt. The woman as smooth and shiny as a peeled egg, cooked hard and
loaded with salt, becomes like a man, but she is consumed by him. She is
no longer soft, sweet, or ovarian: the male cannot penetrate or impregnate
or, as seems to have been a greater fear, become lost in her. She assents
to her metaphoric consumption and destruction. She adopts a stylization
that the emergent consumerism holds desirable, yet which is inauthentic.
This double bind in which ideology places woman is secured by Randall's
"They take you to the cleaners," with its allusion to the Keyes scandal.
Randall and Marlowe agree that the woman-made-man who attracts them
is a great danger. But the soft, the sappy, the emotional—these consume
men too, rather than, as Lévi-Strauss might say, being made fit for consumption by hard-boiling. How appropriate that Marlowe breakfasts, just
before Anne Riordan arrives, on two *soft*-boiled eggs.

Chandler seems to have enjoyed the crossings made by such commonplaces. *Hard-boiled* and the egg were, for him, related to *wisecrack*, with its
roots in divination and fortune-telling. *Cracking wise* acquired the meaning of "sharp remark" or fractured surface. Hence in "hard-boiled" repartee, the perfect wisecrack shatters the smooth facade, revealing the soft
insides of its target. When Marlowe's barbs reveal Velma, "suddenly, without any real change in her, she ceased to be beautiful. She looked merely
like a woman who would have been dangerous a hundred years ago" (238).

THE MEANING OF BAY CITY

Chandler's selection of Bay City (Santa Monica) to embody
inauthenticity overlooks the obvious choice of Hollywood. He treated the
film industry benignly until the late 1940s. The Anglo-American oligarchy
promoted it for its public relations and tourism value but snubbed the nouveau riche owners socially. Not yet writing for the studios, Chandler used
movies and their stars as metonymic markers for smoothness. His references to Rudolph Valentino, Carole Lombard, and John Barrymore attest
to now-lost presuppositions of immediate and telling power. Only after the
sale of film rights to *Farewell* in 1941 launched his screenwriting career

did Chandler seem to have pondered Hollywood. He did not attack it until *The Little Sister* (1949). Marlowe always has his office in Hollywood, and Chandler at his most negative was only skeptical about film.

Instead Chandler set up a straw figure in *Farewell*—vaudeville, an archaic entertainment form that he stigmatized by associating it with the Florians. Velma starts in vaudeville and goes on to radio. Looking at photos of vaudevillians, Marlowe thinks,

> Not many of them would ever get west of Main Street. You would find them in tanktown vaudeville acts, cleaned up, or down in the cheap burlesque houses, as dirty as the law allowed and once in a while just enough dirtier for a raid and a noisy police court trial, and then back in their shows again, grinning, sadistically filthy and as rank as the smell of stale sweat. The women had good legs and displayed their inside curves more than Will Hays would have liked. But their faces were as threadbare as a bookkeeper's office coat. Blondes, brunettes, large cowlike eyes with a peasant dullness in them. Small sharp eyes with urchin greed in them. (25)

From "get west of Main Street" through the Dickensian bookkeeper's office coat and the urchin greed, the idea is that Florian's acts were eastern imports, subnormal peasants, disapproved of by that good Republican and Methodist from Indiana, the Reverend William Harrison Hays. But while tweaking Hays's prurience by casting him as a benign disapprover of the acts, Chandler reverses the geopolitical facts. The call to clean up a licentious, scandal-ridden industry perceived as dominated by "outsiders" came from the American heartland. Hollywood responded only when profits were threatened. Will Hays had nothing to do with vaudeville, but he was no benign influence on film, where the Hays Commission exercised draconian authority. In fact, Los Angeles's vaudeville and burlesque houses were on Main Street, not Central Avenue, and they had been the object of a well-publicized crusade by radio evangelist Bob Shuler in the late 1920s. Shuler, who owned radio station KGEF, attacked "the lewd, vile and debasing performances" and may have been the model for Mr. Grayle (Starr, *Material Dreams* 136–39). "West of Main Street" is where this novel takes place, and the economic geography is consistent with the politics of the Folks.

Understanding this depends on comprehending "Bay City," a phrase used in Los Angeles in the 1920s and 1930s to designate San Francisco. Hardly a day passed without the *Los Angeles Times* printing headlines about Bay City, which in the critical areas of railroad and water development had surpassed Los Angeles. Politically, San Francisco was anathema. It was run by the Southern Pacific Railroad's Political Bureau for a period, and then by hand-picked bosses from 1902 onwards. The S&P political machine brought its "corruption" to Los Angeles around 1900, in a ten-year battle to build a privately owned port and railhead at Santa Monica. Thus there was reason for Los Angeleans to think of Santa Monica—with its links to the S&P—as San Francisco South.

Chandler's own associations with San Francisco, after his discharge from the Canadian army, were negative. He had worked for an English bank and had developed a distaste for "the kind of English who don't live in England, don't want to live in England, but bloody well want to wave their Chinese affectations of manner and accent in front of your nose as if it was some kind of rare incense" (MacShane, *Life* 31). Santa Monica was home to the largest English expatriate colony in southern California, offering a beautiful beach, hillside views, and abundant, reasonably priced housing. Chandler lived there with his mother until her death in 1924 while supporting Cissy in Redondo Beach. His own north-south travel may have suggested the motif of confinement versus eroticism that typifies the geography of the novel.

Santa Monica had some of the raffish aspects of all boardwalk communities, principally in its Ocean Park addition, but it was never the center of police corruption that Chandler depicts. The cause célèbre in his day was the battle of 1938 between gangster Tony Cornero and the state over whether Santa Monica's waterfront was a "bay" or a "bight." Cornero anchored his gambling ship, the *Monte Carlo* (called the *Montecito* in the novel), just outside the three-mile limit of state jurisdiction, if the limit was measured parallel to the indented coastline (making the latter a bight). But his freedom on the high seas was null if his ship lay within three

Three miles off Santa Monica, L.A. gangster Tony Cornero anchored two gambling boats, the *Monte Carlo* and, his pride, the *Rex*, here shown as police raided it in August 1939. Chandler made Santa Monica into "Bay City," the *Monte Carlo* into the "*Montecito*" for *Farewell, My Lovely*. (Daily News Photographic Morgue, Department of Special Collections, University Research Library, UCLA)

miles of a line drawn across the mouth of a bay. A half dozen expert witnesses testified that Santa Monica Bay was indeed a bight. Cornero lost in trial but won his appeal in 1939. Finally the state supreme court restored Santa Monica to "Bay City" status, and Cornero became the model for Laird Brunette.[13] "Alas, the gambling ships are no more," wrote Chandler (MacShane, *Selected Letters* 31).

The scenes Chandler set in Bay City stress confinement or hidden corruption, from the Grayles' mansion (the most realistic) to city hall and Chief Wax's office.

> Aster Drive had a long smooth curve there and the houses on the inland side were just nice houses, but on the canyon side they were great silent estates, with twelve foot walls and wrought-iron gates and ornamental hedges; and inside, if you could get inside, a special brand of sunshine, very quiet, put up in noise-proof containers just for the upper classes. . . .
>
> The cracked walk and the front steps led to open double doors in

which a knot of obvious city hall fixers hung around waiting for something to happen so they could make something else out of it. They all had the well-fed stomachs, the careful eyes, the nice clothes and the reach-me-down manners. They gave me about four inches to get in.

Inside was a long dark hallway that had been mopped the day McKinley was inaugurated. A wooden sign pointed out the police department Information Desk. A uniformed man dozed behind a pint-sized PBX set into the end of a scarred wooden counter. A plainclothesman with his coat off and his hog's leg looking like a fire plug against his ribs took one eye off his evening paper, bonged a spittoon ten feet away from him, yawned, and said the Chief's office was upstairs at the back. (*Farewell*, 101, 185)

The sense Chandler creates of Bay City as a focus of hypocrisy and corruption is also created by three other settings, establishing a scale. The psychic Amthor's house is in Stillwood Heights (Brentwood Heights), a bit inland from Lindsay Marriott's home in Montemar Vista (Pacific Palisades): both are north of Bay City. In contrast, Anne Riordan's house is in Bay City but south, on the grid of numbered streets nearer Los Angeles: she is affected by· corruption but far enough south in the Basin to be Folks. Laird Brunette's gambling ship *Montecito* lies west of Bay City but is named for an exclusive community farther north up the coast.

Marlowe embarks for the *Montecito* not from Bay City, but from the "waterfront hotels" and carnivalesque atmosphere on "the alley they called the Speedway" (201). This is south in Venice Beach. There Marlowe meets Red Norgaard, whose "violet eyes" and "skin soft as silk" led Gershon Legman to highlight the homosexual motifs in the violent boarding of the ship (209). The attainable Red is south of the available Anne, who is south of the unattainable Mrs. Grayle. This north-south axis of money/confinement versus marginality/sexuality draws and repels Marlowe repeatedly from his office and apartment, which are east and inland, so that his travel as a whole describes a triangle. What could this mean?

On one hand Chandler constructs out of personal experience and prejudice a topography of desire, one that incidentally dichotomizes two longstanding promises imputed to American experience in the West: sexual

One of Raymond Chandler's rare publicity photos. First published in his forties, older than other *noir* writers, Chandler tried to hide his age from readers.

freedom and social status. The resulting schizophrenia makes this axis the site for the frenzy Chandler is about to create. But Chandler also exploits the geography of a popular sales pitch among the Folks for real estate. There were many theories about the direction in which Los Angeles would grow, whether it was better to be close to the mountains or the sea, to have flat or sloping land, and the prospects of finding oil or for planting orange trees. By 1939 the appreciation in real estate values had been westward: Hollywood, Beverly Hills, and Bel-Air. This led speculators and the public to believe in a "development fan" west of downtown. Everyone saw, however, that mountains and ocean would limit the fan and result in a "funnel." As real estate ads for Huntington (Pacific) Palisades explained:

> Figures show one mile Westward and 100,000 increase in population every five years up to 1920. Since then, the expansion has been at the rate of 1 mile Westward and 100,000 increase in population per year. Each 100,000 increase in population has advanced the city one mile Westward. *And a million more people are coming!* Prior to 1920 the advance radiated Westward . . . it was fan-shaped. Today the fan is reversed . . . it becomes a funnel. The mountains and the ocean form the sides and Huntington Palisades the tip . . . the objective to which all westward progress converges. (*Los Angeles Times*, Dec. 13, 1928: 12)

The vector of development was Wilshire Boulevard, following the path of Pleistocene dinosaurs to the La Brea tar pits. In 1921 A. W. Ross had created a shopping district in the bean fields along Wilshire, and in 1924 it was renamed the Miracle Mile.

Chandler shared the concern of those who wondered what debouched at the end of the fan-funnel. His novel oscillates westward: Huntington Palisades, Santa Monica, Venice, and the *Montecito* are westerly and increasingly southern destinations. That Henry Edwards Huntington, co-owner of the Southern Pacific, should be defeated in his port project only to return as a real estate developer struck many Los Angeleans as diabolical. Chandler saw English expatriates he detested, Tony Cornero and his gambling boats, and an S&P campaign to create a Bay City South.[14]

Against Bay City Chandler has no real counterfigure, as he had in *The Big Sleep* (Wilde's house). The old genteel neighborhoods had been overwhelmed by the Central District. The Arroyo culture was decaying, and its patriarchal law was being questioned. So Chandler adopted the geopolitics of flight. "The schizo knows how to leave," Deleuze and Guattari remark (131). "I grunted and kept on driving," says Marlowe (*Farewell* 50).

Marlowe finds his values at the margin, in Venice Beach and on the voyage to the gambling ship. Like the Fulwider Building, Venice Beach is for Marlowe a site of tawdry sexual potential: "The reflection of a red neon light glared on the ceiling. When it made the whole room red it would be dark enough to go out. Outside cars honked along the alley they called the Speedway. Feet slithered on the sidewalks below my window. There was a murmur and mutter of coming and going in the air. The air that seeped in through the rusted screens smelled of stale frying fat. Far off a voice of the kind that could be heard far off was shouting: 'Get hungry, folks. Get hungry. Nice hot doggies here. Get hungry'" (201). Sexuality is the constant "smell" of Venice Beach. Marlowe will soon approach this vendor "tickling wienies," only to discover that the man believes he wants a woman: "You look like dick to me," the man says. As in the Fulwider Building, mechanical aspects of Venice Beach are emphasized: the building had its elevator; the boardwalk has electric sidewalk cars that zip pleasure-seekers along the beachfront. Marlowe takes one to "the end of the line," for transport is a key feature of the "machine" that induces frenzy. In both novels Marlowe must transfer to a potentially limitless mode—the car in *The Big Sleep*, the boat in *Farewell*—to complete his frenzy. More clearly than the building, the boardwalk represents a "mechanical" heterosexuality against which secret pleasures of solitary men take on meaning. The norm that Marlowe observes here is "sailors with girls" and "spooning couples" who "chew each other's faces" (202, 207, 206).

Heterosexuality is devalued by such details and the very tawdriness of Venice Beach. It is "grimed," "dusty," and "greasy." It smells of "hot fat and cold sweat," and its "sidewalks swarmed with fat stomachs," "sallow, sunken cheeks," and "wrinkled suits." Details about the frying fat smell are repeated, contrasting with the "smell of the ocean and the suddenly clear line of the shore and the creaming fall of the waves into the pebbled spume" (212).

Marlowe seeks the sexual equivalent of this clean and elemental sea smell. So his first encounter is not a fried food vendor but the hot dog man: "I had to wait sometime to get him alone. . . . I didn't know why I bothered with him. He just had that kind of face" (203). Marlowe throws money at the man, treating him like a hustler, then visits a restaurant where "a male cutie with henna'd hair drooped at a bungalow grand piano and tickled the keys lasciviously and sang Stairway to the Stars in a voice with half the steps missing" (204). Marlowe "gobbles" a martini and flees again to the waterfront. The tough water-taxi man and Marlowe stand apart from the couples in the boat, as Marlowe describes the allure of the ocean at night in figurative language ("sinister smoothness, like a cobra dancing"). His goal is the "scummed and rusted" *Montecito*, on whose landing stage an attractive man ("a smoothly husky voice, a hard Harry straining himself through a silk handkerchief") refuses him entry (207). Marlowe watches his "silent, sleek smile . . . and hunger[s]" (208). Chandler underlines desire searching for its appropriate object, which is the man Marlowe runs into when he returns, Red Norgaard, "a big redheaded roughneck in dirty sneakers and tarry pants and what was left of a torn blue sailor's jersey and a streak of black down the side of his face" (208). Like the *Montecito*, Red is "rusty" and befouled but almost allegorically attractive: "He had the eyes you never see, that you only read about. Violet eyes. Almost purple. Eyes like a girl, a lovely girl. His skin was as soft as silk. Lightly reddened, but it would never tan. It was too delicate. He was bigger than Hemingway and younger, by many years. He was not as big as Moose Malloy, but he looked very fast on his feet. His hair was of the shade of red that glints with gold. But except for his eyes he had a plain farmer face, with no stagy kind of handsomeness" (209). Norgaard keeps Marlowe "angled into a corner" and volunteers his price: fifty dollars to go out to the *Montecito*. But Marlowe retreats into the mechanized setting of a bingo parlor. There in the anonymity of the purely statistical, they make a deal.

Marlowe's voyage on water with Red splits off in schizoid fashion a realm of pure emotional and sensory intensities, which Chandler emphasizes at the outset: "Beyond the electroliers, beyond the beat and toot of the small sidewalk cars, beyond the smell of hot fat and popcorn and the shrill children and the barkers in the peep shows, beyond everything but the smell of the ocean and the suddenly clear line of the shore and the creaming fall of the waves into the pebbled spume. I walked almost alone now. The noises died behind me, the hot dishonest light became a fumbling glare. Then the lightless finger of a black pier jutted seaward into the dark. This would be the one" (212). In place of land's commercialization, the trip emphasizes intensities, confession, and power relationships. Marlowe uncharacteristically blurts out everything about his case, which Red analyzes in calm, prescient fashion: those back on land—Sonderborg, Amthor, Marriott, Chief Wax, Brunette, Malloy—are criminals, and "all rackets tie together these days" (215).

Norgaard is kind, understanding, and deft: "What he said had wisps of fog clinging to it" (213–14); "Red leaned close to me and his breath tickled my ear" (217); "He put my hands on the wheel, turned it just as he wanted it, set the throttle, and told me to hold the boat just as she was" (218). Is it surprising that Red, from eye color to coolness, recalls Mona Mars in *The Big Sleep?* "The wet air was as cold as the ashes of love," notes Marlowe (217). Red is an incarnation of the girl with the "cornflower-blue eyes" that Chandler evoked when he was "thrown in the gutter."

This image makes frenzy inevitable when Marlowe and Red arrive at the *Montecito.* But just here Chandler brackets with personal experience a narrative tending to homosexuality or a masturbatory solitude: he recovered from his firing alone, survived Vimy Ridge alone. Red is there to lead Marlowe to his frenzy; he scales the vessel's side and leads Marlowe across a catwalk to the boiler room, where he punches a "short dirty wop" (219). As they part, Marlowe remarks, "Either I do it alone or I don't do it" (220).

Marlowe's actions now repeat those of Red kinesthetically. He scales the phallic ventilator shaft, described in great detail. Topside, he captures the "youngish," yellow-eyed, gentle Brunette and evades more threatened beatings. The pivot of the celibate machine occurs when Marlowe gives Brunette his card, with an unrevealed five-word message to Malloy. It might be "I know where Velma is," but Chandler won't tell. Like the list of borrowers in *The Big Sleep,* the card is an "inner script" of the sort that Lacan discerned in Poe's "Purloined Letter." But whereas Poe's letter revealed the name-of-the-father, it seems clear that Marlowe's solves no genetic mystery but authorizes his own pleasure. Poe's letter was stolen; Marlowe is the author of words that bring Malloy to him. In fact, as D. A. Miller has written of *David Copperfield,* this novel's trajectory "provides . . . subjectivity with a secret refuge, a free, liberalizing space . . . a critical space in which he takes his distance from the world's carceral oppressions" (215).[15] Knowing "where" Velma is, Marlowe must know "who" and "what" Velma is, so he could even have written to Malloy, "I know what you want." But the point is that Marlowe knows what *he* wants, and he authorizes it.

Leaving the gambling ship, Marlowe heads for his apartment, where he calls Mrs. Grayle and invites her over for their long-delayed, much discussed tryst. Waiting in his pajamas in bed for her, Marlowe dreams about his adventures on the *Montecito* in vivid imagery. When he wakes, Malloy is watching. He received the note. He could be Marlowe's object of desire. But the fabula intercedes. Marlowe does not want to possess his long-lost brother but to watch his death, which he has arranged by his call to Mrs. Grayle.

Marlowe repeatedly reassures Malloy that he will not deceive him. "When do we do what you said on the card?" asks Malloy. "Where do we go?" (235). On cue, Velma knocks at the door, and Malloy hides in the closet. Still in bed, Marlowe invites her in: she pretends to be repelled by the obviousness of his seduction, but soon she is seated beside him on the couch with a drink in hand, saying, "Sit close to me" (237).

"Let's talk a little first," replies Marlowe. "About murder" (237). The set piece that Marlowe then delivers functions as partial denouement, but it also "cracks" Mrs. Grayle to reveal Velma Valento, the murderer of the homosexual Lindsay Marriott, who functioned as the prodigal brother in the original story. Velma's response is to pull a gun, but it is Marlowe's frisson to have another man, the unequivocally male Moose, die his death, so Malloy emerges from the closet. Velma shoots him "five times in the stomach. The bullets made no more sound than fingers going into a glove" (240). They "fit," a rare instance of appropriate sheathing in Chandler's work, especially since Malloy has been characterized by his "big hairy paws."

Marlowe lets Velma escape. He goes back to the bed, where, after calling an ambulance and the police, he watches his brother die: "Malloy was on his knees beside the bed now, trying to get up, a great wad of bedclothes in one hand. His face poured sweat. His eyelids flickered slowly and the lobes of his ears were dark" (241). These clinical details seem a bit understated for a celibate machine, but immediately in the next scene Anne

Riordan pipes up, "You ought to have given a dinner party" (242). Frye has taught us that concluding feasts are the hallmarks of social equilibrium restored. Anne is society's "appropriate other" for Marlowe, though not his own choice. They drink, banter, and recount the ways in which life has improved since Malloy's death: Chief Wax has been fired; Red got his police job back. But social reintegration has its dark side. Neither reconciliatory feasts nor comedy according to Frye preclude paying the costs. Velma takes up the prodigal's mantle now. She has provided herself an escape route from Los Angeles, a "little hideout where she could change her clothes and appearance" (242). The imputation of an ongoing double life to Velma and the imagery it is couched in are striking, for a double life on the margin of the sea is exactly what Marlowe has had.

The fabula requires that Velma be returned to her origins. That is why, in a striking coda, Lieutenant Randall tells Marlowe that Velma has been discovered singing in a Baltimore nightclub. Marijuana smoke wafted from her dressing room, and the ambience seems to indicate black musicians, perhaps jazz clubs. Velma was a "torcher who could sing as if she meant it." Figuratively, though, she has returned to the smoke and fog of the Central District. Discovered by a detective, Velma shoots him and then commits suicide, which puzzles Lieutenant Randall. He figures that her money and connections could have gotten her off if she had stood trial in Los Angeles. Marlowe thinks she ended her life in the East to avoid embarrassing Mr. Grayle. He imputes a scrap of sentimentality to her, a desire to "give a break to the only man who had ever really given her one. . . . An old man who had loved not wisely, but too well" (249).

But Mr. Grayle is no Othello, himself a prodigal of notable initial success. He is rather another declining father, an enfeebled General Sternwood, almost a joke, about to be retired by society's organization man, Lieutenant Randall. The Othello here, as the trope about the tarantula revealed, was Malloy. And this is actually Desdemona's story, told by a conniving Iago-like detective named Marlowe. Why else would the novel end thus: "It was a cool day and very clear. You could see a long way—but not as far as Velma had gone" (249). If the prodigal knows how to leave, the schizoid knows how to keep on going.

Landscape in the Los Angeles novel is always weighted with symbolic meaning. The fact that the writers, as outsiders, were playing the region contrapuntally against a home territory accounts to a large extent for the symbolic quality it acquired in fiction. The landscape offered itself readily to a vision of being cut off from a familiar sense of space.
—David Fine, *Los Angeles in Fiction*

From Roman Noir
to Film Noir

The debt of film noir to the novels of Hammett, Cain, and Chandler may by now seem clear, but it is challenged by film scholars. Film is visual, a highly technical medium whose optical qualities create its effect as much as its narrative does, they say. These effects set film noir apart, they contend, either as a style or a genre, from any literary origin.[1] This style-versus-genre debate, like the one over the term *film noir*, is tangled and can only be touched on here. Lost in the debate is the fact that film noir derives from the same techno-economic matrix that produced the roman noir, as a comparison of their narrative uses of setting reveals. Technological and economic imperatives simply cloak themselves better in film, while literature's anxiety about such influences makes them palpable. In this comparison, we will see that film noir is even more metonymic, its voice-over and flashbacks the logical step beyond Chandler's schizophrenia.

Let's begin with an admission: literary investigators seldom notice that the American roman noir is set mostly in California, principally Los Angeles, or remark that its authors were outsiders. This odd conjunction goes completely unexamined in films derived from the novels, because film criticism contends that setting is just not as important as lighting, tracking shots, or mise-en-scène. In American literary scholarship, however, setting has been the meat of the canonical stew, and cooks from Perry Miller through Leo Marx and Alfred Kazin have corrected the ideological seasoning according to the era. Native sons or daughters extolling the virtues or the complexity or, more recently, the limitations of a rural landscape have been the stock of a scholarship showing that beneath such bucolic or positivist surfaces, difficult negotiations with progress were taking place. That California, conceived by the reading (and viewing) public as among the world's beautiful places, should be selected by outsiders as the locus of "alienation" and "depravity"—this would have seemed a disparity to the cooks that required explanation. Landscape and region, they held, were significant in the American ideological complex, especially in its favored narratives about progress, technology, success, and integrity. Might not film noir be an example of the effects technology induces into narratives about social and economic change? Is it not probable that the technique of film noir continues a trend established by the technique of the roman noir, expanding upon the "invisibility" that technology creates for itself?

The narrative debt was originally clear. When French critic Jean-Pierre Chartier wrote "Les américains aussi font les film noirs" in La Revue du Cinéma in 1946, World War II had prevented his countrymen from seeing The Maltese Falcon, Double Indemnity, and other such films. Chartier found these films as dark as Pepe le Moko (1937) and Quai des brumes (1938). In coining the term film noir, he brought readers up to date on American tough-guy trends, which since the 1920s had attracted the French, especially writers (Camus was an early fan of Hammett). The comparison implied by aussi in Chartier's title appears to be "American roman noir," for as Alain Silver and Elizabeth Ward point out, "the majority of the *serie noir* [detective novels published in France] were translations of . . . such authors as Hammett, Chandler, James M. Cain and Horace McCoy" (1). So the source of American film noir was clear to Chartier. He didn't imply that the American films derived from French films, yet this is the faux pas attributed to him by scholars dating the coinage to moviemaker Nino Frank before 1946. Such quibbling led to radical disavowals of the form's parentage, as in Silver and Ward's comment that "the narrative of these noir films possessed an economy of expression and a graphic impact substantially different from the hard-boiled novels or the pulp stories of the *Black Mask* magazine" (1).

The source of film noir still seemed obvious to French critics Raymond Borde and Etienne Chaumeton in their pioneering 1956 genealogy of the genre. The "immediate source," they wrote, "is clearly the American or English detective thriller novel. . . . Hammett, Chandler, Cain, W. R. Burnett." These two said film noir was "a total submission by the cinema to literature" (quoted in Telotte 5). Indeed, in Silver and Ward's 1980 reference volume, of the thirty-six examples of film noir listed for the 1940–45 period, twenty-seven are based on published works, seven on unpublished works. Only two are original film scripts (see Telotte 6). Yet the authors write that "*noir* films have no precise antecedents either in terms of a well-defined literary genre or a period in American history." They propose an immaculate conception: that film noir is a "self-contained reflection of American cultural preoccupations" and "the unique example of a wholly American film style" with "no express chain of causality leading up to it" (Silver and Ward 1, 3).

Even David Bordwell, in otherwise magisterial scholarship, deprecates the literary sources of film noir: "We inherit a category constructed *ex post facto* out of a perceived resemblance between continental crime melodramas and a few Hollywood productions" (Bordwell, Staiger, and Thompson 243). But Bordwell then goes on to enumerate the "particular patterns of nonconformity within Hollywood" that make these noir films similar as narratives: they all assault the classic Hollywood construction of character through psychological causality, offering unstable heroes concerned with internal conflicts; they challenge the predominance of heterosexual romance, with the hero often finding that a woman bars him from success; they attack motivated happy endings; and their innovative visual techniques constitute a criticism of the classic "neutral and invisible" style (76). Bordwell implicitly acknowledges more literary debt than do most commentators, beginning with Paul Schrader, who see film noir as only a "style" (Schrader in Denby 278–90).[2] Bordwell prefers to consider it a genre, but rather than cite narrative sources, he posits a rebellion against Hollywood's "classic construction," which is conventionally narrative, that somehow avoids narrativity, as though no repertoire of narrative events and techniques had ever created "unstable heroes" before.

Most debate about the canonicity of film noir depends on retrospects about style, rather than on genealogies of plot, character, or other features. Beguiling techniques in *The Maltese Falcon* (1941) seem to lead to *The Big Sleep* (1946) and thence to *Chinatown* (1980). Thus discussion about film noir has become a debate about whether it was a genre or a style and has implicitly privileged technique over other narrative aspects.

There is a broad clue to the distinctness of film noir in Bordwell's argument about "classic" film, for in it the "causes" of character are external, usually deriving from events and other characters. The noir protagonist is, in fact, conceived by both the genre and the style camps to be preconditioned by setting; hence they give importance to establishing shots of cityscapes, the use of shadow, high- and low-angle shots, and the "alienating" effect of character position in the mise-en-scène. They agree that depiction of such "internalized" characters lends itself to energetic camera work. Hence they emphasize technique, which supposedly conveys "internal conflict" in and of itself, without narrativity or ideology. Silver and Ward offer an example of such assumptions:

> Fritz Lang, in discussing the camera movement in *The Blue Gardenia*, asserted that the film's fluid tracking shots, which relentlessly pursue his guilt-ridden heroine, could not have been executed without the compact crab dolly. The detailed exterior night work in *Kiss Me Deadly*, repeatedly framing its protagonists against drab structures and flashing street lights, is a conspicuous example of expressive implementation of higher speed lenses and film stock. Hand held camera work in that same film, or ten years earlier in the fight sequences of *Body and Soul*, under-

scores at yet another level that sense of instability so central to the noir vision. (3)

This seems to give technology its due, but it ignores such fundamentally narrative meanings as "guilt-ridden." The heroine is not guilt-ridden because of tracking shots any more than Stephen Daedalus has an Oedipus complex because of interior monologues. But if new technology creates new means of stylistic expression, a new arena for technique, which then create a new kind of character in film noir, isn't a relation between the technology and the character likely? Doesn't technological determinism rear its head? Could there be a link between the explosion in the means of making films and the nature of the films made? Could film noir be an example of the effects technology induces into narratives about social and economic change? Doesn't a sequence of film techniques create a figurative meaning?

The figuration of setting in film noir is unapparent. Silver and Ward describe the typical locale as "contemporaneous, usually urban, and almost always American in setting. The few exceptions involve either urban men in a rural locale or Americans abroad. There is a narrative assumption that only natural forces are at play; extraordinary occurrences are either logically elucidated or left unexplained—no metaphysical values are adopted" (3). Let us ask how contemporary, urban American settings lead to a "narrative assumption" of rational explicability—and how this judgment squares with the equally common one that characters in noir sense a determinism at work.

While no deity reigns, there are certainly metaphysical values present in film noir's settings. Rather than a neutralized setting, place and nature are always rationally explicable because they are managed by technology. We can see this clearly by contrasting noir settings to those of films made before 1930, the era of DeMille and Griffith. Hollywood then shared the older American practice of surveying the place where it found itself and liberating its subject from the pressures of time and locale. Whether the narrative was set in Babylon or at Bull Run, the "world elsewhere" created by technique and style in film, as Richard Poirier has noted of the novel, concerned the "creation of America out of a continental vastness" (4). Even the most naive moviegoer knew this "world elsewhere" was Los

Angeles. In the work of Sennett, Chaplin, Keaton, and Harold Lloyd, the viewer saw the wide, clean streets of Los Angeles, pleasant suburban bungalows, palm trees, and distant mountains. There were no clouds, no dark alleys, no claustrophobic rooms; nature was benign, and the light was special. In fact, bright light illuminated every corner. The harried Los Angeles life of Lloyd in *Safety Last* (1923) must have appeared idyllic to audiences in Iowa. The setting in a Keystone chase or even in Chaplin's most polemical films was potentially liberating. This tradition of "idyllic, pastoral treatment," as Louis Giannetti has pointed out, extends from the hundreds of films made by the influential D. W. Griffith virtually unbroken through his disciples John Ford and Frank Capra (Giannetti, *Masters* 74).

The revision of this setting in literature owes, as Poirier notes, to naturalism. In popular literature, it owes to Hammett, Cain, McCoy, Chandler, and others, who rendered a new socioeconomic California in which no expansion of self was possible. This did not have any substantial basis in reality; they were consciously involved in closing off, by technique, outlets to a world elsewhere. Scholarship by Starr and other historians of California shows that between 1900 and 1950 there was abundant, reasonably priced housing, relatively honest government, and little crime.[3] As David Fine notes, the figure of California as noir that these authors created was "contrapuntal," a reaction especially against two fatigued metaphors observed by Starr. The romantic metaphor, exemplified by Helen Hunt Jackson's *Ramona* (1884), was rooted in the Spanish-American pioneer era and influenced D. W. Griffith and his generation, as is evident in the "Mediterranean" and "Babylonian" premises of many of their films. This was followed by the "Progressive" view of Charles Arthur Loomis, Arroyo culture, and the Good Government movement, typified by Mary Austin's novels. Cain and McCoy then, notes Fine, focus on the finiteness of "the man-made landscape—the roadside motor court, the dance hall at the edge of the ocean, the car on the Coast Highway—as images of deception, metaphors for betrayed hope" (18).

These authors and the directors who filmed their work moved to California in midlife with high expectations, just as Iowans had a decade earlier, and they lived a good life. Twenty years before they would have labored for a penny a word in Greenwich Village's dime novel ghetto, but they now lived opulently. So what exactly was betrayed? When Cain reported on "Paradise" for *American Mercury* in 1933, he rhapsodized about California's cleanliness, quality of education, roads, and recreation, and "unfailing friendliness and courtesy" (266–80). There was no alienation in his initial, reportorial account.

When Cain and McCoy went on to portray what the reading public conceived to be a Valhalla of "sunshine and oranges" as the locus of deceit, murder, and treachery, they inverted, for a national audience, long-standing American themes of westward movement, progress, and self-improvement. Setting, especially nature, had played a part in such themes as the raw material, the stuff out of which protagonists created (or, tragically, did not create) themselves. Whether they mechanically subdued it or spiritually revered it, the heroes and heroines had significant relations to setting. Such a tradition is evident among California writers as late as Steinbeck, a native son, who focused on technology's impact on landscape even in the 1960s.

The inversion of this theme by outsiders appears due to their perception that California lacked something, something their places of origin had, namely conflict and technology. This lack was usually identified as an "industrial base," evidence that *things being made* sustained the good life. As Poirier remarks, these writers "ask us to believe that the strange environments they create are a consequence, not of their distaste for social, economic and biologic realities, but of the fact that these aren't more abundant in American life" (9). They cry "More reality!" Perhaps this explains why Hammett, in *Red Harvest*, opened a narrative that figures California politics and wealth in front of "smelters whose brick stacks stuck up tall against a gloomy mountain" (4). Cain wrote explicitly in "Paradise" that he missed the conflict of eastern labor disputes: Californians, he said, "suffer from the cruel feebleness of the play which the economy of the region compels them to take part in" (275). There was no "voltage" (a telling metaphor), wrote Cain, without economic conflict, which he associated with heavy industry. Similar critiques are offered by other writers and directors involved in film noir, all discomfited by the "vacuity" or "phoniness" of the first postindustrial U.S. economy.

The narrative emplotment of this anxiety was less a rebellion against material satiety, as most critics have assumed, than an instance of American perceptive habits in the throes of synecdochical withdrawal. The absence of a visibly mechanized economy must mean something—that the apparently polite Californian had been forced by the environment to internalize economic conflict. The representation of this internalization, after modernism, was to be accomplished through technique. It is in this sense that Fine's remark about the California novel's being "cut off from a familiar sense of space" is so valuable (18). Outsiders were specially equipped to suggest the contrapuntal home territory, in literature or film, by defamiliarizing the California setting through technique. The absent, mechanized economy could be immanentized, represented by technique.

The early narratives of Dashiell Hammett exemplify the way things were before the paradigm shifted, when setting was still an explicit topic. As a boy Hammett read "trash, mysteries" and esteemed the hunting stories of his maternal grandfather, as well as "stories about the West" heard "down at the railroad yard" (Johnson 39). His writing through *Red Harvest* employs the conventions of such sources: lone cowboys, rival gangs, trackers, gold miners, and dance hall whores drift down from the Sierra to San Francisco. The Continental Op depends on his tracking talent ("The Scorched Face"), shoots it out in an arroyo ("The Golden Horseshoe"), and fights off outlaw gangs ("The Gutting of Couffignal," "The Big Knockover"). In *Red Harvest* he is a just gunslinger who cleans up a corrupt town.

In *The Maltese Falcon* Hammett gave few descriptions of his setting, and many of those still derive from the Western. Most action takes place in the confined spaces of apartments, a new form of residence only notable, among California cities before 1930, in peninsular San Francisco. But that turns out to be one reason why *The Maltese Falcon* made such a good film noir: interiors. Lack of a world elsewhere, of sunshine, can be emphasized. There are few guns or cars in the novel, but many telephone calls, newspapers, and doorways, though none egress on a world of natural space. Their number was to grow in the film, as John Huston perceived the potential of what Silver and Ward gingerly term "certain relationships between elements of style—not icons—and narrative events or character sentiments" (5). This is the threshold of an insight: style can render character motivation figuratively. All of the clues necessary to this realization are, in fact, present in Hammett's famous objective style—in the passage about Spade's cigarette rolling, for instance.

Cain and Chandler continued this transformation of the world elsewhere into technique, but in opposed ways. Cain aligned California with national ideas about prodigality, using a metonymic, minimalist style. In contrast, Chandler attempted a prodigal style, universalizing local geographic figures about internalization and alienation. His embellishments actually aim to overturn the received impression of his setting, but they culminate in the "celibate machine."

Examples will make this clearer. Cain opens *Postman* with this celebrated passage: "They threw me off the hay truck about noon. I had swung on the night before, down at the border, and as soon as I got up there under the canvas, I went to sleep. I needed plenty of that, after three weeks in Tia Juana" (1). A national audience in the 1930s could not fail to perceive Cain's narrator as one of the drifters who roamed the nation seeking work. But Cain initially didn't know California well, so he chose settings already familiar to a national audience: the roadside restaurant and gas station, ·Spanish-style houses, "exotic" Mexico, and orange groves. His is an *already read* setting. His mountains and beaches are elements of a known pattern; his California is a metonymic reduction.

Chandler did not know national taste as Cain did, but he knew California. In the first sentence of his first novel he attempted to make a minor aberration in local climate into a synecdoche: "It was about eleven o'clock in the morning, mid October, with the sun not shining and a look of hard wet rain in the clearness of the foothills" (*Big Sleep* 1). The unseasonable rain, recalling but overturning Austin's *Land of Little Rain* (1903), refutes preconceptions about the land of sunshine. Chandler attempts to expand this aberration by tropes, allusions, and romantic embellishment, but his counterfigures are lost today. We don't grasp the "organic" bizarreness of unseasonal rain in Los Angeles. No film version of *Postman* or *The Big Sleep* uses setting for such pointedly figurative purposes. But while the counterpoint between California and an "other, previous" landscape—for Cain, the coalfields of West Virginia; for Chandler, the England of his youth—was lost, the projection of a world elsewhere by technique was not.

After the introduction of sound and the Mazda tests in 1928 that standardized film stock, lighting, and makeup, "character" became a site of burgeoning technological opportunity. When Chandler became a screenwriter, he noted that "the most important part is what is left out, because the camera and the actors can do it better and quicker" (MacShane, *Selected Letters* 298). Much of the diegesis in written characterization could be assumed by technique, for every shot had psychological implications. David Bordwell, Bill Nichols, and Barry Salt, among others, have argued variously that a progression of film techniques creates imaginative relations that suggest meaning: that a series of such figures creates a way of seeing things, an ideological position (see Bordwell, Staiger, and Thompson 234; Nichols, *Ideology* 112–34; and Salt 343–54). The qualities that Hammett had suggested in Spade by his cigarette rolling could be appropriated by film technicians. *Homo faber* became the cameraman, rather than the character, who would no longer understand, representationally or figuratively, the forces that made him.

Film scholarship, however, has been chary of cataloging a grammar of such techniques.[4] It exhibits a disingenuous refusal to recognize how audiences create narrative causality with even the barest hints, and it ignores, as Paul Kerr and James Damico point out, the advent of film noir at a time of massive economic and technical change in the means of production (Kerr in Denby 134–49; Damico 48–57).[5] The law of technology—Eliminate steps!—had already dislocated the perceptive habits of audiences from synecdoche to metonymy in other fields: a sequence of shots could become a metonymic reduction of motivation or character as well as of an event.

The advent of sound led the way. As sound became a competitive necessity, production shifted to sets and studio lots. There noise could be controlled, making purposeful sound as important a production value as light. The advance of film into musicals, into stories of hard-working chorus girls and ambitious young tenors, was not coincidental. It exploited the medium's new resources. Heroes and heroines who broke into song without provocation, ignoring psychological motivation, hardly stand apart from "production values." They are technologically blessed: they have diegetic power, as well as mimetic skill, will and opportunity. In the romantic comedies of the 1930s, as Elizabeth Kendall has argued (34), techno-economic opportunity even helps to create an emerging feminist heroine. The conventions and figures of sound grew out of its technology. As Salt shows, a single microphone connected to a camera in a blimp gave poor cognitive cues to viewers, and it was replaced by the boom mike and then by multipoint recording, which opened up a world of dialogue (256–81). But early cutting techniques resulted in silent spots or muddy overlays, until the adoption of synchronized sound on film in 1928–30. The sound overlap solved this problem with one or two frames of sound playing over the new scene and creating a sensation of seamless temporal unity. But shots had to be planned for these "dialogue cutting points": Whose words would cover what visual? This cutting point was a physical elision of reality, an opportunity to make metaphors, metonymies, and other figures, and the dictum that "sound leads" was broadly adopted by 1930. Bordwell writes that by 1930 "for every cut from point to point there must be an auditory shift as well. 'I can give you a closeup of sound, just as I can give you a closeup of a person' [said an engineer]. In the late 1920s, there was considerable controversy about whether it was more 'natural' for a close-up's volume to be louder than the volume for a long shot, but by the early 1930s, it was evident that volume should be in rough proportion to shot scale" (Bordwell, Staiger, and Thompson 302). Soon repartee appeared in film. Also in evidence were off-frame sound effects that prefigured the visual cut to another scene. As sound editing became more sophisticated, sound was conceived to have depth, and "virtual soundscapes" created another new diegetic quality—suspense through sound.

Such proportion and suspense are figurative, as artificial as Renaissance "laws" of visual perspective. But as it evolved, sound created a similar virtual reality: it was fast, smooth, and clear. It was instantly intelligible, patterned yet always new and bright. The film industry now calls this "production value." It was exactly what the emerging techno-economic climate required.

A glance at the troubles of sound's pioneer, Warner Brothers, a maker of movies for the working classes, suggests how economic factors may have contributed to film noir's figurative habits. Warner, as John Baxter writes, was "a desperate company that, casting around for some gimmick to boost sales, hit on the idea of putting more money and work into the then primitive sound cinema concept. The successful premiere in 1926 of *Don Juan*, with its synchronized sound effects and music, not to mention a film introduction spoken by Will Hays . . . encouraged Warners to produce *The Better 'Ole* and *When a Man Loves* (1926), both with synchronized music. . . . In 1927 it released *The Jazz Singer*" (50–51).

The capital investment required by sound was enormous and probably could only have been amassed in the giddy stock market of the late 1920s. Simply to enter this new technology, Warner had to issue four million dollars in debentures, buy Vitagraph, build a new film processing lab and a new studio, buy two radio stations (for publicity), expand foreign operations, and agree to buy twenty-four hundred sound systems by 1931 from Western Electric, which levied an 8 percent royalty fee on Warner's gross revenues for the period. Having mortgaged the future, Warner posted a one-million-dollar loss in March 1926. According to J. Douglas Gomery, "By the time Warner's brought out *The Jazz Singer* on October 6, 1927, it had invested $5 million in sound, including $500,000 in its first release. Quarterly losses declined from the $300,000 range to the $100,000 level and in 1928 Warner's made $2 million. In 1929 Warner's profits were an astonishing $14 million, more than double those of any other film company" (in Balio 209; see also 199–202).

The big studios, which had planned to wait for a mature technology, were forced to adopt Western Electric's Movietone system in February 1928. By autumn of the following year, "the dominance of the talkies was virtually complete, with only small towns and rural areas still showing silent pictures. A myriad of technical problems were solved: studios were sound-proofed, armies of technicians were hired to service the delicate equipment, and theaters were wired. Scriptwriters were replaced by playwrights skilled in writing dialogue. Actors without stage experience took voice lessons, and those unable to correct foreign accents, faulty diction, or unpleasant voices soon found themselves unemployed" (Gomery in Balio, 193). This was probably the most rapid change in narrative technique in history. By 1930, 80 percent of the nation's theaters were wired for talkies, a figure that rose to 98 percent by 1932. From a $5-million company, Warner grew in five years to a $230-million giant. Sound forced mergers among competing studios and created enormous economic and technological momentum, resulting in five companies (Warner, Loew's, Paramount, RKO, and Fox) that produced 50 percent of American films, 75 percent of all class A features. They received 70 percent of all box office receipts.

The borrowing that funded this growth pushed studios to the edge during the Depression, but moviegoers' enthusiasm for sound staved off collapse. In 1931 and 1932 all five posted losses, ranging from Fox's three million dollars to Paramount's twenty-one million. In 1933 Paramount went into bankruptcy, RKO went into receivership, and Fox was reorganized. Only Warner and Loew's made a modest profit. Tino Balio describes the situation:

Admission prices were slashed, audiences shrank—average weekly attendance dropped from an estimated eighty million in 1929 to sixty million in 1932 and 1933—production costs more than doubled because of sound, and revenues from foreign markets dwindled, but these factors in themselves did not cause the collapse. . . . the common stock value of these majors was reduced from a 1930 high of $960 million to $140 million in 1934. Theater after theater went dark. Paramount found it cheaper to close many of its unprofitable smaller houses than to pay overhead costs. The company also shut down its Long Island studio and laid off almost five thousand employees who had been earning between $35 and $50 a week. The number of unemployed and underpaid extras in Hollywood became a national scandal. Wages for those lucky enough to find work dropped from $3 a day to $1.25. (215–16)

Independent studios produced more films too and promoted them with games such as Bingo, Banko, and Screeno and, above all, with the double feature. Until the Depression, a single feature and short subjects prevailed, but in 1931 eighteen hundred theaters adopted the new format; by 1947 two-thirds of all theaters did so. As with other commodities in the Depression, increasing production of films failed to stop losses. The double feature "put a heavy burden upon production facilities," and "in the long run it did not affect attendance figures," writes Balio. "Few exhibitors could afford to pay the rentals of two quality pictures on a single bill. . . . Hollywood, in turn, lowered its production budgets and geared itself for the most part to quantity rather than quality" (220). Paul Kerr has shown that the second feature was not only a box office rival but also a production challenge to the A feature film: "To take two examples: Val Lewton's films at RKO had tight, twenty-one day schedules whilst Edgar G. Ulmer's at PRC were often brought in after only six days and nights. (To achieve this remarkable shooting speed night work was almost inevitable and Ulmer's unit used to mount as many as eighty different camera set-ups a day.) Props, sets and costumes were kept to a minimum, except on those occasions when they could be borrowed from more expensive productions, as Lewton borrowed a staircase from *The Magnificent Ambersons* for his first feature" (222). Bordwell has also noted that the Depression forced filmmakers to cut set construction and to reuse scenery when possible. Subsequent "wartime limits on set construction and the 'realism' of combat documentaries" even made location shooting desirable again and cheaper, now that sound problems were solved (Bordwell, Staiger, and Thompson 77).

The way to disguise reused sets and props was to shoot them differently. B directors, one cameraman told Kerr, "pick new angles and redress the foreground . . . [and] agree to shoot at night" (223). Light was expensive: the less used the better. Studio streets plunged into shadow not only were not recognized as the settings of feature films, but they also did not need to be detailed. Expensive three-point lighting gave way to "high key" (main and a small amount of fill) or single-source illumination. Directors avoided spectacular action sequences: "You can't shoot a first-rate crime wave on short dough, so you borrow or buy about twenty pieces of thrilling moments from twenty forgotten pictures," said cameraman Nick Grinde (46–47). Crowd scenes were avoided or borrowed, and casts were kept to a minimum, which reduced the number of titles. Technicians avoided the union ban on overtime by working straight time on contract for the tightly scheduled B units. Unclear scripts and poorly motivated characters were simply shot and later edited into coherence. Plot complexity, Kerr argues, actually increased.

In 1943 the government reduced the studios' raw film stock by 25 percent, with B films absorbing the brunt of the shortage. Again they turned economic necessity into stylistic virtue. The B film shrank from eighty minutes to sixty minutes. Average shot length, as Salt has shown, decreased, imparting a sense of action (256–81).[6] Shorter shots allowed even more film to be recycled, and exhibitors got to show these shorter films an extra two or three times per week. "Such economies as B units practised," concludes Kerr, "were not related to fixed assets like rents and salaries but to variable costs like sets, scripts, footage, casual labor and, crucially, power" (229).

The trend toward deep focus, a convention of film noir, began when 20th Century–Fox instituted a policy of shooting all films on interior sets at $f3.5$ to take advantage of a new standard film. Fox films from 1938 on have greater depth of field and sharper focus, features copied by other studios. Fox cameraman Gregg Toland, often cited as the pioneer of depth shooting (in *Citizen Kane*), developed the potential of deep focus, but the technique was based on technology adopted to save money (Salt 256–81). Deep focus required wider-angle lenses, incompatible with older cameras, especially those in soundproof blimps (Salt 259). In 1939 Fox introduced a camera with built-in soundproofing that accepted wide lenses, weighed only eighty pounds and had two thousand-foot film magazines. This led eventually to handheld shooting and the "subjective camera" of *Murder, My Sweet* (1944), *The Lady in the Lake* (1946), and *Dark Passage* (1947) (Salt 260). The repertoire of shots expanded when cranes built for filming musicals were borrowed by B units. Soon Bell and Howell began to manufacture small, highly maneuverable dollies, which had been handcrafted for earlier movies like *The Front Page* (1931).

Not only techno-economic factors but also the gangster movies of 1928–34 are slighted in most accounts of film noir's origins. They pioneered many techniques identified with film noir, and their narratives were often based on a story of two brothers or friends, usually members of a neighborhood gang from which one emerged to rise in crime. The conventional, stay-at-home brother foiled the criminal, as in *The Public Enemy* (1931). Crime was often figured as a new organization in an increasingly bureaucratic society. These films already showed a shift in film's underlying paradigm about technology. One has only to remember films of the 1920s—Keaton's *Our Hospitality* (1923) or *The Navigator* (1924), for example—to realize the extent to which technology as the butt of popular humor was replaced by technological positivism. This shift is already evident in *Little Caesar*, Warner's success of 1930 that spawned more than fifty imitations in three years. None shows the trend in relations between film and technology as well as Warner's follow-up, *The Public Enemy*, directed by William Wellman and starring James Cagney.

The Public Enemy opens with a high-angle shot of downtown Chicago in 1909. Antlike people thread a maze of daily existence, the quality of which is suggested by a subsequent high-angle shot of the stockyards. This is the sort of crowd scene that was recycled from older films. Then beer, the evil soporific that makes this life bearable, rolls out of a brewery on wagons and fills the sloshing pails of workmen. The Dreiserian crudeness of this 1909 Chicago is intended; in fact, it evokes D. W. Griffith's moralizing and his temperance melodramas. The opening montage also bears a message: by zooming back from these details to another long shot, the camera not only establishes the setting but also cues the viewer to three-dimensional space, centers attention, delays some information (suspense), and provides a parallel for future reverse zoom and tracking shots. Andrew Sarris saw early that Wellman's "images tend to recede from the foreground to the background," giving a sense of depth (Salt 252). This is a film figure set up by the opening montage. Wellman used few close-ups and many medium and long shots in this film. But few of his shots were stationary, as his camera zoomed, tracked, and panned. His technique also provides the audience with a diegetic résumé of recent American history. As film time passes, the number of sets increases, and the number of exterior shots decreases: technological progress becomes an implied actor in the narrative.

The second segment of *The Public Enemy* is set in 1917. It opens with a dolly shot, giving the impression that Cagney's good brother, Mike Powers, and his fiancée have established a channel of personal vision and calm planning on the eye level of the viewer. Life has become more rational than it was on the anthill. The third segment, set in 1920, opens with a long shot of a theater exterior that is apparently a set, on which the pandemonium that supposedly attended the beginning of Prohibition is organized by a sequence of mini-narratives in the repetitive rhythm of establishing, medium, and close shots. Each three-shot "story" makes the same figurative point: that old temperance melodrama about life deteriorating was silly. Technique clarifies history, and oddly enough, as technology increases, life gets better—and misfits like Cagney are eventually eliminated.

The Public Enemy returns to exterior locations only once more, to introduce Jean Harlow, who plays Cleopatra to Cagney's Caesar. Unlike other exterior scenes, this one is strikingly unglamorous. A modern Standard Oil station appears in the background, apparently on a Los Angeles street. The camera angle foreshortens Harlow, the light is hard and flat, and the sidewalk setting suggests she is a streetwalker. By contrast, in later nightclub scenes the set design, props, lower camera angles, and three-point lighting emphasize Harlow's sensual allure.

Sets replace exteriors completely late in The Public Enemy. Both the depiction of a Prohibition bombing and the sniper execution of Matt Doyle clearly occur on studio back lots. The second event demonstrates the additional artistry available to the director who controls every production element. Wellman used the camera point of view, the framing device of the window, and deep focus—three techniques specifically associated by scholars with film noir—to put his audience in the shoes of the assassins, suggesting viewer complicity in Prohibition and also the thrill of illicit violence.

The Public Enemy reaches its climax when Cagney, in a studio rainstorm notable for its torrential volume, the water's failure to puddle, and the equidistant raindrops, arrives at his rivals' hideout to kill them. By mixing the rain noise, the gunplay, and Cagney's voice, by employing dramatic lighting, and by using doors, windows, and the camera aperture as framing devices, Wellman created a soundscape and sense of spatial depth far superior to reality. His city street is particularly superior to the antlike reality in the opening scene, of which viewers may be reminded by tracking shots that suggest the parallel. This subsumption of setting to technique becomes more conscious in film noir in the 1940s.

During the rest of the Depression, the genre developed sporadically. Aside from Scarface (1932) and The Glass Key (1935), based on a Hammett novel, most of the films adapted from novels relied on the lighter English detective tradition. But the style of the earlier gangster movies, in which technology figured history, was not forgotten. Moviemakers clung to the new technology and hemorrhaged money, but their anxiety infiltrated the narratives they produced. The musicals that endorsed sound repeated insistently the economic conventions of Algerism, and concluded happily. So did many of the gangster films, as David Cook and Jon Tuska have pointed out. This accorded with the movie moguls' visions of their own success. But in the mid-1930s, when attendance plummeted, the gulf between the consumer and this narrative of improvement became evident. The decline in the economy affected patrons, and these narratives had to be redressed.

Sex was the first, tentative answer. Figuring to build on permissive attitudes in the 1920s, producers "began to introduce salacious subject matter into their pictures in an attempt to attract patrons," writes Balio (221). By 1934 protests against sexual content from religious groups forced the Hays Commission to rewrite the Production Code of 1930. A new Production Code Administration was created under Joseph Breen, whose department scrutinized all *scripts* for sex. By 1937 nearly 98 percent of all films exhibited had PCA approval. This did not mean that sexuality disappeared from films but that it ceased to be textual—part of dialogue. Salacious events had to be figured in icons, symbols, gestures, stage business, costuming, lighting, expression, and intonation. The manipulation of cigarettes and lighters, telephones and guns, doors and windows, soon developed the desired diegetic overtones for an audience accustomed to what Bordwell has termed "generic motivation" (Bordwell, Staiger, and Thompson 20). While economically unconscious, this response is today recognizable as a major mediation by which film noir developed. It introduced a double discourse, linking Chandler's schizophrenia to noir's voice-over. As Bordwell notes in regard to lighting, the figurative power of technique could be understood quite apart from representation: "After the mid-1920s, lighting was coded generically as well. Comedy was lit 'high-key' (that is, with a high ratio of key plus fill light to fill light alone), while horror and crime films were lit 'low-key.' The latter practice was considered more 'realistic,' since one could justify harsh low-key lighting as coming from visible sources in the scene (e.g., a lamp or candle). By means of this generic association with 'realism,' filmmakers began to apply low-key lighting to other genres" (Bordwell, Staiger, and Thompson 20).

Figures of sexuality, from proffered cigarettes to come-hither smiles, turned out to have the same transferability as lighting, plus an enticing ambiguity, dovetailing perfectly with the "assault on psychological causality." This allowed a narrative level to the sexual politics so long buried in the fabula. The tale of two brothers could focus, as Egyptian papyri had, on the younger brother and the older brother's wife. In fact, James Damico has described film noir just this way:

> Either because he is fated to do so by chance, or because he has been hired for a job specifically associated with her, a man whose experience of life has left him sanguine and often bitter meets a not-innocent woman of similar outlook to whom he is sexually and fatally attracted. Through this attraction, either because the woman induces him to it or because it is the natural result of their relationship, the man comes to cheat, attempt to murder, or actually murder a second man to whom the woman is unhappily or unwillingly attached (generally he is her husband or lover), an act which often leads to the woman's betrayal of the protagonist, but which in any event brings out the sometimes metaphoric, but usually literal destruction of the woman, the man to whom she is attached, and frequently the protagonist himself. (54)

Damico notes this pattern in a dozen of the canonical noir films made between 1941 and 1949, such as *Double Indemnity, The Postman Always Rings Twice, The Blue Dahlia, Murder, My Sweet,* and *The Maltese Falcon.*

Compared with the parable of the prodigal son, Damico's version of the fabula may seem unbalanced, narrating only the prodigal's adventures in a far country. In the parable, remember, alienation is embedded within a greater narrative of improvement. And the brief period of films castigating gangsters in the late 1930s (*Bullets or Ballets,* 1936) did reintroduce the function of the elder brother briefly and boringly. But with new techniques, the destruction of the prodigal and his female counterpart could be caused by an actantial force representing improvement, without the narrative of improvement's being told. The latter could be immanentized, transubstantiated into a diegetic voice. This immanent improvement is sometimes overt, a technological representation of society (the insurance offices that open *Double Indemnity*), but it is often manifest only in the death of the prodigal, the sign of the elder brother, by which we know the fabula's implied third point of view and actant.

The ways in which such narratives can be delivered through technique is the subject of recent scholarship by J. P. Telotte, Sarah Kozloff, and others.[7] Telotte approaches a description of the narrative devices of film noir as actantial when he writes that the "retrospective approach . . . retained for the screen versions of the novels" produces a sense that the protagonist is "violated" by a kind of diegetic narrative presence. This arises from the mix of classic third person, voice-over and flash-back, subjective camera, and documentary style. The mix of these narrative voices in a classic like *Double Indemnity*, Frank Krutnik observes, can produce an "intermittent" third-person actor whose "voice-over does not have the same authoritative hold in the channeling of the discourse of Truth" that the novel's simple first-person narrator did (in Telotte 22). Telotte adds, "The Cain novel had established the potential for this focus, although it subordinates a concern with discourse to the threatening power of desire itself. What inspires the film's voice-over narration and its added complications, though, is the novel's structure as a written statement, a notarized confession of murder by its protagonist" (45). In other words, film can make manifest technically the diegetic quality of confession that Foucault described.

Kozloff argues not only that voice-over is *not* the "voice" of the protagonist but also that it creates something other than the counterpoint to image that has long been presumed. Rather, voice-over is an example of the "double time demand" of film described by Seymour Chatman. Since film contains an overabundance of visual detail, we do not know what to absorb unless some aspect of the narrative calls it to our attention. Devices like voice-over tell us what details matter and how to connect them in patterns, how to figure the visual surfeit. Kozloff points out that such a film noir staple as the dark rainy street can suggest culture and romance if overlaid with a graceful calligraphic title reading "Vienna, About 1900" (73).

A film like *Double Indemnity*, with its voice-over, third-person "actual" voice, third-person "confessional" voice, and visually objective modes, is for Kozloff like a series of embedded narrators who progressively focalize a narrative in symphony with the repertoire of the camera. This gives rise to a more sophisticated kind of understanding, as Kozloff details in an account of *Mildred Pierce*:

> Mildred's narrating voice remarks, "At first it bothered Monte [her lover] to take money from me, then it became a habit with him." The shot accompanying this statement does not show Monte taking a check from her; instead, we see a sheaf of bills from fancy men's clothing stores. The unspoken implication is that these are Monte's bills, that this is what he's spending her hard-earned money on. The combination of picture and narration forcefully reveals Monte's profligacy without stating it explicitly on either track: it quietly leads the viewer to make the connection himself or herself. (106)

In this example, voice-over clearly impels a metonymic reduction, making bills stand in a part-to-part relation to profligacy. More forcefully and concisely than if Monte had been seen at his haberdashers, such a figure elides setting and substitutes technique for motivation. This is immanent focalization.

Feminist critiques of this focalization are partially responsible for unmasking it.[8] Janey Place noted that

> the femme fatale ultimately loses physical movement, influence over camera movement, and is often actually or symbolically imprisoned behind visual bars (*The Maltese Falcon*), sometimes happy in the protection of a lover (*The Big Sleep*), often dead (*Murder, My Sweet, Out of the Past, Gun Crazy, Kiss Me Deadly*), sometimes symbolically rendered impotent (*Sunset Boulevard*). The ideological operation of the myth (the absolute necessity of controlling the strong, sexual woman) is thus achieved by first demonstrating her dangerous power and its frightening results, then destroying it. (in Kaplan 45)

Obvious but unmentioned is that such control is achieved by technique, the more invisibly the more powerfully. But this analysis presumes that women are the subject of the fabula of deterioration, when they are usually secondary, the object or helper or opponent of a male actor enacting a more comprehensive narrative that can readily have other objects, such as money, murder, or power. To understand film noir as concerning only the control of strong, sexual women is to underestimate its ambition and to accept the self-cloaking operations of technological ideology. Salacious content, or sexuality, as Telotte and Kozloff show, has to be specified out of the visual plenitude. Rather than what is specified, we must attend to what specifies.

The immanent focalization of technique in film noir becomes clearer in the 1940s. Although the mid-1930s was a period of prodigious production of the American roman noir, Hollywood did not revive its interest until 1941. Then it returned to filming on location, with new technological options that could remake setting. *High Sierra*, directed by Raoul Walsh in 1941, is a stunning example of this change. W. R. Burnett (author of *Little Caesar*) teamed with John Huston to write the script. The Sierra Nevada appear, rugged and untamable, under the opening credits. Then a montage of increasingly tighter shots shows the power of nature's opponent, mankind, as figured by government, prison, and a governor's pardon. Accompanied by music rather than voice-over, this diegetic frame prepares us for Roy Earle (Humphrey Bogart), who, on his release from prison, goes to commune with a bucolic version of nature in the local park. Then he begins a trip to California, and a new narrative about nature takes shape. Stopping at the old family farm in Indiana, he finds that the catfish no longer bite at the fishing hole and the farmers are hayseeds. But since the yokels recognize his face (apparently they're newspaper readers), this "old nature" becomes a threat to Earle, and he flees. The landscape changes from lush Indiana to Mojave Desert, emphasizing nature's harshness. The rest of America is elided. Unconventional in film noir, the bright, flat light of desert recalls earlier U.S. history—here perished the pioneers—as it did in *The Public Enemy*.

When Bogart arrives at the Sierra Nevada, however, even Walsh's best shots of the mountains seem bland, and we see that they were a specifically cinematic as well as a larger technological problem. The Sierra Nevada resisted the infusion of production values that could be added by technique on a set. This problem Walsh solved for most of the film by treating his landscape like an interior. The gangsters pass the time in the mountains inside cabins, and when Walsh uses locations, he treats them like complex interiors. The trees in his campground scenes would be obstacles, except that Walsh can use them, like the pillars in the lobby of a building, to enhance the film by flourishes such as reverse point of view, dollying, and deep focus. These trees are challenges to his technical mastery.

Only in the final scenes does Walsh use the dark palette typical of film noir. There his positivist rendering of technology becomes unmistakable. A montage of shots depicts the communications and police grid closing down on Bogie, whom we now understand to embody an archaic notion of nature's goodness and nobility, like the park that initially delighted him. Walsh worked hard to subsume the Sierra Nevada to technique in a celebrated car chase (a double 360-degree shot following Earle, then the police, as they drive up a hairpin curve in a mountain road), but the swirling dust only emphasizes his battle for control. When Bogie reaches the "Road Closed" sign and scrambles up the cliff with a machine gun, we understand that nature is no refuge. There are no Earle family farms; there is no world elsewhere. The technological matrix that traps Earle is constituted by police lines, the radio reporter, the searchlight, and the report of an airplane coming to bomb him. Earle may be living a romantic narrative of alienation, but the Folks in this film, who have turned out to see him die, live a narrative of technological improvement, against which Earle rebels. Nature is not only no sanctuary for Earle, but it can be reduced to rubble by a phone call from the Folks.

Walsh avoids the darkness of this implication by summoning nature's avatar, a Hawkeye figure—the man with "the queer-looking gun"—to wipe out the "injustice" that is Roy Earle. This reveals an astonishing aspect of *High Sierra*, for the film reprises much of James Fenimore Cooper's *The Pioneers* (1823) with respect to technology. Like the novel's Oliver Edwards, Roy Earle has been pardoned. Like Edwards, he meets an upright family (the Temples, the Goodhues). The patriarchs of both families suffer technological trouble: Edwards pulls Judge Temple's wagon off a cliff; Earle fixes Mr. Goodhue's car. Edwards falls in love with Elizabeth Temple, Earle with Velma Goodhue. As Judge Temple is frustrated by the ravages of progress on nature, so is Earle surprised by the decline of

Humphrey Bogart (Sam Spade) sends off Gladys George (Iva Archer) in John Huston's version of *The Maltese Falcon* (1941). Huston emphasized such icons of technology as the Golden Gate Bridge, not finished until six years after Hammett's novel. (©1941 Turner Entertainment Co. All rights reserved.)

his Indiana homestead. But Cooper salvaged from such forebodings the hope of a fair future by marrying Edwards into the Temple clan. His protagonist lives an overt narrative of improvement, symbolic of that expected for all American society. In *High Sierra*, a similar positivism operates, but by sleight of hand. The "bad" Earle (expert with a machine gun) is removed by marriage to his gun moll and by death, while the "good" in Earle is figured by his funding the medical procedure on Velma's clubfoot— an endorsement of technology for the Folks. The world elsewhere that Cooper suggested lay to the west now resides in technology's transforming possibilities, if it exists at all.

Such a perspective on *High Sierra* focuses the same issue in *The Maltese Falcon*, also filmed in 1941. Shot almost exclusively on sets, John Huston's first solo effort as director was a model of planning and economy. Recognizing that little needed to be done to Hammett's novel to turn it into a screenplay, Huston changed only the exterior scenes and added telephone calls and spinning tires as transitions between interior sets. Setting is minor. As Bruce Crowther notes, the novel could have taken place in any harbor city (28). But a technological conception of San Francisco *becomes* important in the film.

The film opens with a wide shot of the Golden Gate Bridge, which was not even a gleam in the collective eye of civil engineering when Hammett wrote his novel in 1928–29. A montage of San Francisco scenes follows, then the bridge again, and a reverse zoom that leaves us in the offices of Spade and Archer, who are thus connected to this icon of technology, which remains visible in their windows during most office scenes. Completed only four years before, the bridge celebrates a particular kind of technology, like Hoover Dam and the California Aqueduct, all massive and geographically transforming, located in California and viewed popularly as New Deal remedies for the Depression.

Following Brigid's visit to Spade's office, Huston created a celebrated noir sequence. A telephone rings in a darkened room, and Spade, answering but never visible, hears of his partner's death. The effect is of Spade voicing-over his own absence-as-presence, for the camera remains focused on the base of the phone, behind which a curtain blows languidly over a window opening on city lights and night sounds. No cigarette rolling here—Huston took Hammett's hint, making technique stand for character.

Spade takes a cab to Stockton and Bush streets, where Archer's body lies at the bottom of a slope. By alternating high-angle shots (down on Archer) with low-angle shots (Spade looking up to the place where Archer was shot), Huston establishes not only the urban equivalent of the Western's box canyon but also Archer as dead prodigal brother. On three sides buildings rise up, while the far end is enclosed by a hill, trees, and the lights of distant buildings. The setting is surprising, initially because of the trees and natural elements but also because of Spade's unease. (Hammett had ironically described detectives hunting futilely under a billboard at this scene.)

Huston shot most of the middle of the film on beautifully lighted sets that could have served any musical or Philo Vance detective film. The scenes between Bogart and Mary Astor employ conventional camera angles and three-point lighting. What is unusual is the number of telephone calls (a dozen) and the tightly framed shots of the phone itself. Telephones not only deliver more information than in the novel but also become transitions to cut from scene to scene: telephones are used figuratively, and we soon understand that they entail the plot.

Toward the film's end, Huston returns to exteriors, once to replicate the novel's wild goose chase to Burlingame, another time to depict fire-fighting equipment that saves the ship bearing the falcon. In the first scene, Spade walks down a deserted wooden sidewalk, past shuttered stores with archaic wares, giving an impression of time travel back in the economy. He ends up between buildings in a vacant lot with a small "For Sale" sign, a "box canyon" that pairs neatly with the earlier one. As in the first, Spade turns from the scene, and a taxi whisks him away. Nothing like this happens in the novel, in which Spade searches an empty house in Burlingame. In the second scene, the fire-fighting equipment, absent from the novel, presents us with production values, "nature" out of control, and apparently very effective technology.

In the film's final scenes at Spade's apartment, Huston laid great emphasis on the fabula of the prodigal son. Hammett had typed Gutman as Arbuckle by his abuse of an adolescent daughter. Huston eliminated the daughter and clarified Gutman as the symbolic father, forced by Spade to choose either Cairo or Wilmer as fall guy. Gutman tells Spade that he "feels toward Wilmer exactly as if he were my own son." Whereas Hammett elected Wilmer as the scapegoat because of his homosexuality (though Cairo is homosexual too), Huston specified the economic basis of the fabula by having Gutman say to Wilmer, "I couldn't be fonder of you if you were my own son. But if you lose a son it's possible to get another. There's only one Maltese falcon." Temporarily in the position of the elder son, Cairo rages at Gutman for being an "imbecile" and "incompetent" when the falcon turns out to be a fake. But no member of this prodigal family can finally command our sympathy. That must rest with Spade, who has acted as diegetic facilitator of their unmasking. He alone resists the allure of foreign travel and of a beautiful woman, to conserve society as it is.

The only problem with the novel as a movie script would seem to be the question of Spade's honesty with Brigid, hidden by the third-person "objective" point of view. As Robert Edenbaum pointed out, if Spade knows that Brigid killed Miles, then he strings her along immorally. He would be a vehicle of allegory, and Brigid would be truly the wronged party (Edenbaum in Madden, *Tough Guy Writers* 80–103). But Huston took much of Spade's "objective" complexity and transferred it by technique to the diegetic frame. Bordwell points out that Huston abandons Spade's point of view early by showing the death of Miles Archer but "declines to show the killer (we see only a gloved hand)" (Bordwell, Staiger, and Thompson 40). The "film," rather than Spade, knows whodunit, suggesting that whatever diegetic force affects him affects us as viewers too.

This diegetic sharing of hero and audience is balanced by misdirection in the film's clues. The opening titles that scroll over the falcon suggest that its value is established fact, but in the novel the tale of pedigree is delayed until late and never certain, coming from Gutman. The novel's statuette is unseen until it is finally unwrapped, and it dupes the crooks, not Spade. The film's statue, coming first, dupes us too. In this way Huston maintains Hammett's equivocation about the relation of sheathing to content, but without the "objective" point of view that made such focalization retrospective. The mystery of the novel concerns who Spade really is, but the mystery of the film is how the actors and audience could be duped into believing that this art moderne statue is "concealing" anything. The novel warns about the costs of being Spade, but the film presents his elder brother–ism as the only intelligent position.

Double Indemnity (1944) is regarded by many as film noir's masterpiece. As a conjunction of eccentric talents, it is probably unrivaled: James M. Cain's novel as scripted by Raymond Chandler, who said Cain was "every kind of writer I detest, a *faux naif*, a Proust in greasy overalls, a dirty little boy with a piece of chalk" (MacShane, *Selected Letters* 23), and directed by Billy Wilder (who called Chandler "a virtuoso alcoholic"). But Wilder's casting—he hounded Fred MacMurray, who had never played any but personable roles, until he consented to play Walter Huff—and his outsider's eye for the unique in California settings combined in a work of genius. It is at once a distinctly Los Angeles film and one that embraces technology's position in the fabula.

Only five minutes into the film does Wilder allow the sunny Hollywood hills of Cain's first page to appear. The Nirdlinger house is as Cain described it outside, but inside it is cool and gothic, rather than the tacky Tijuana decor that Cain satirized. The initial meeting between Huff and his femme fatale lasts much longer than in the novel, and when Mac-Murray departs he stops first at a drive-in, where he orders a beer, and then at a bowling alley, to "roll a few lines and calm my nerves." These scenes are not in the novel—Cain sent Huff to his office—but they are brilliant additions, expanding on a secondary theme in Cain, the extent to which marketing seems to have anticipated his protagonist's desires. For Wilder (and Chandler), the California landscape had become marketing, so Huff operates in a consumer setting that prefigures even his leisure.

Cain's idea of a good California setting was a nationally known oddity, such as a moonrise over the Pacific, but Wilder discarded such scenes, dispensing with nature altogether. He substituted a supermarket, where MacMurray and Barbara Stanwyck meet repeatedly to discuss their crime amid pyramids of cans and boxes of baby food. Murder, the film suggests, is a series of marketing decisions combined with lucky breaks, such as whether your product appears at eye level. A passing patron, in fact, complains to MacMurray about her difficulty in reaching baby food on a high shelf, as though he were a store employee.

Wilder also discarded Cain's ending (Huff and Phyllis commit suicide on a cruise ship) and made the technological theme overt: first he filmed MacMurray dying in the Folsom gas chamber, a set that cost Paramount $150,000 and took five days of shooting. Then he decided to make the same statement less emphatically: Huff completes his confessional Dictaphone roll just as his boss and pursuer, Keyes, walks in. Keyes allows Huff to flee, predicting that he "won't make it as far as the door," where indeed the salesman collapses. Wilder, following the predictive, statistical portrait of life in Cain's novel, simply technologized the novel's retributive elder brother.

Wilder allows no world elsewhere, only obedient techno-economic consumerism or technological death. All settings may be subsumed by technology, just as all directors control films by technique. We may optimize, but we may not escape. Most earlier film noir, whether *The Public Enemy*

Technology's control of Fred MacMurray (Walter Huff) and Barbara Stanwyck (Phyllis Nirdlinger) is emphasized throughout Billy Wilder's *Double Indemnity* (1944) by deep focus, single-source lighting, deep shadow, hallucinatory patterns, and mechanical icons. Here the two murderers arrange the evidence of her husband's "suicide." Copyright by Universal City Studios, Inc. Courtesy of MCA Publishing Rights, a Division of MCA Inc.

with its good brother or *High Sierra* with its lovable cripple and devoted dog, offered some way out of technological determinism. *Double Indemnity* does not. It is a pure endorsement of technology's momentum. Instead of man creating himself from or against a landscape, technology composes or reduces character on the field of its possibilities. In such a state, as Foucault noted, the internalization of surveillance is the foreseeable outcome.

Why did film noir arise? Film scholarship offers us simplified and confusing answers. After World War II "customers had a different attitude toward personal violence," writes Crowther, "a change engendered in part by the exposure of servicemen to fear, disablement and the bloody reality of sudden death" (157). It's also fashionable to point to the spread of communism and the backlash against it: "While McCarthy held his kangaroo courts in Washington, out in Hollywood others followed his example" (158). One critic even reads director Edward Dmytryk's *Farewell, My Lovely* in light of his *subsequent* involvement in the Hollywood Ten (Clark 55). Such explanations, as Janey Place and Lowell S. Peterson note wryly, exude a "claustrophobia, paranoia, despair and nihilism" more reminiscent of French existentialism in the mid-1950s than of events in the 1940s (Nichols, *Movies and Methods* 327).

But is the answer to abandon history, as Place and Peterson do, and view film noir as merely a "style," while alluding generally to "fear of the bomb" and "the repressive nuclear family"? The banality of such phrases aside, it is difficult to understand how film scholarship since Schrader could be so limited in its historic understanding. At least Schrader understood that historic judgments are figurative, that they consist of two parts. Though he elected "style" himself, his evaluation was comparative: "The acute downer which hit the U.S. after the Second World War was, in fact, a delayed reaction to the Thirties. All through the Depression, movies were needed to keep people's spirits up, and, for the most part, they did. The crime films of this period were Horatio Algerish and socially conscious. Toward the end of the Thirties a darker crime film began to appear . . . and, were it not for the War, *film noir* would have been at full steam by the early Forties" (in Denby 280). But after positing World War II as an interruption in an already pessimistic trend, Schrader goes on to cite it as the source of "sardonic" "bite" that leavens the "amelioristic cinema" built up (for propaganda purposes, he implies) during the war. There are clearly problems with such a reading, not the least of which is an implied model in which film responds primarily to film.[9] But Schrader's inclination was to compare periods; figuration of history can only happen after history, and its only material is previous history. Does film noir somehow compare World War II and the Depression? Or does it, like American roman noir, figure the Depression against the Roaring Twenties?

Paul Fussell's scholarship and Studs Terkel's oral histories permit us to understand something of public attitudes in these periods. The assumption about film noir, remember, is that external causality was out, and unstable, individualized protagonists with "internal conflicts" were in. But we learn from Fussell's book that the war reduced individuals to faceless anonymity. It "soon revealed itself as less a struggle of men with men than a contest in methods of mass production with which to debase the intrinsic value of martial daring," remarks Vera Britain (Fussell 67). The subjects of Randall Jarrell's wartime poems have no names: they are "just collective Objects, or Attitudes, or Killable puppets," writes James Dickey (in Lowell 44). "To recall the sights and sounds and smells of the war is to invoke the memory of crowds everywhere," writes Fussell. "The bus, indeed, can be thought of as the Second World War's emblematic vehicle" (69). This facelessness, he argues, created a hunger for "fiction, memoirs and plays [that] swarm with bizarre male individualists. They are doubly welcome as lost ideals in this drab culture of anonymity and uniformity" (70). Clearly the noir hero is not a mimetic reflection of the war years that deepened the trend toward anonymity of the Depression. But individualism had been a prominent feature of life in the 1920s.

The most prevalent kind of characterization in popular narrative during the war was typecasting, at the bottom of which was "the most despised of categories, the 4-F or physically unfit and thus defective, the more despicable the more invisible the defect" (Fussell 116). But Dick Powell, a well-known 4-F, was the *hero* of several canonical films noirs, in which he portrayed highly individualized and unconflicted detectives (such as Philip Marlowe in *Murder, My Sweet,* 1944). Other actors playing similar roles avoided the war entirely or performed only propaganda functions (Clark 49). German émigré directors like Fritz Lang, Joseph von Sternberg, and Billy Wilder not only avoided the war but grew rich making noir classics.

The war itself was boring, plotless, and random. Writes Fussell,

Waiting itself and nothing else becomes a large element in the atmosphere of wartime, for both soldiers and civilians. You are waiting for induction into the services, waiting for D-Day, for someone to come home on furlough, for a letter, for a promotion, for news, for a set of times, for the train, for things to get better, for your release from POW camp, for the end of the war, for your discharge. Attention—as always, but with a special wartime intensification—focuses not on the present but on some moment in the future. . . . If you were a civilian, daily life was boring. If you were a soldier, daily life was very boring. (75–76)

In film noir, of course, there is always mystery and tension. The present is all: characters act for immediate gratification, and something unexpected occurs. Not only is film noir dense with event, but it packs the story with information about times, places, and possible motives, with visual information in new and arresting styles, with the complexities of voice-over, multiple voices, and embedded voices. It redoubles the importance of information by suspending certainty.

"Sex seemed often in short supply," notes Fussell of the 1940s (105). The most explicit magazine was *Esquire* with its Vargas girls. Women's fashion had retreated from short skirts, sheathing, and form-fitting fabrics to become boxy and unsuggestive. In film noir sex is anything but scarce. Not only is it present in the icons and double discourse discussed earlier, but it is overt in Mae West, in the daring swimwear of John Garfield and Lana Turner in *Postman*. Sexual opportunity floods the screen, despite the Hays Commission.

Between 1930 and 1950 alcohol was an important part of American life, especially after the repeal of Prohibition in 1933. "By the time of the Second World War," Fussell writes, "the notion that everyone has a perfect, even a Constitutional, right to a binge was thoroughly established in the United States" (96). James Jones wrote that his unit in the Pacific "got blind asshole drunk every chance we got" (in Fussell 102). This response to life appears in Hammett and Chandler, but with some exceptions, it does not figure in film noir.[10] True, the Hays Commission forbade the positive portrayal of alcoholism, but films from *The Thin Man* to *From Here to Eternity* got around that.

A final disparity between film noir and reality is material deprivation. During and after the war, gas and food were rationed in the United States. New cars were unobtainable. Suits, shirts, skirts, and shoes were patched and reused. People learned to roll their own cigarettes from little bags of Bull Durham. But none of this privation appears in the world of film noir. Its protagonists have new cars and never wait in gas lines. Indeed, the Fred MacMurray character, in its darkest film, lives in a consumer cornucopia.

If film noir is not a reflection of society, then what is it? In some aspects it is the antithesis, excited rather than bored, acting rather than waiting, affluent instead of deprived, libidinous rather than celibate. But a number of elements do not invert. The rationalization of the workplace, the "legalization" of society, the growth of the media, public relations and propaganda functions, the jobs in statistics, insurance, and service industries— these aspects of film noir depict the emerging economy more accurately.

This mixture is clearly a reconciliation of two forces. But the period from the 1929 stock market crash to 1945 can provide only one term, because those years were similarly dark. How did film noir attract viewers who recently "needed [films] to keep their spirits up"? The comparative period must be further in the past: the depiction of individualism, of sexual freedom and material excess, can only draw on a collective consciousness of the 1920s, retrospectively interpreted as a decade of indulgence. This understanding existed in the 1930s. But newer, straitening elements, such as the increasingly legalistic aspects of life, urbanization and technology, statistics, the annual model change, the mutual suspicion of the Depression, had never been figured into the narrative. To see them, writers and directors held them up against the 1920s for contrast; hence flashback and voice-over in film noir played a special role as focalizing devices. The technologization of perception—the metonymic revolution—increasingly relegated organic understanding and synecdochical storytelling to the category of the "old-fashioned." The new meanings of the 1930s had to take form metonymically, as technique and its qualities rather than as events or persons. The tale of excess that film noir tells, still the historiography of the elder brother, is sometimes about a prodigal, but it is always about prodigality's danger.

Notes

Introduction: 1927

1 See also Nye 287–335; Frost 141.
2 *White collar* and *working class* are the Lynds' terms.

I The Prodigal's Tale

1 The terms *fabula, focalization,* and *actant* are drawn from narrative theory. I have tried to keep jargon to a minimum and to provide in-text definitions. More elaboration can be found in Mieke Bal's *Narratology.* On *fabula,* see 11–24.

2 Bal explains *focalization* (100–102): "Point of view" and "perspective" do not distinguish between those who see and those who speak. The term's origin in photography (focus, focal plane, focal lens, focal length) emphasizes the aspects of narrative it seeks to isolate. Focalization becomes an issue in the sections of the father and elder son because it shifts from external to character-bound. See Bal 111–14. Much narrative privilege is created by the latter, which expresses the imperceptible as opposed to the merely perceptible. The elder brother's charge of libertinism is the only character-bound imperceptible knowledge in the parable, which gives it special status. In contrast, imperceptible knowledge associated with the prodigal and the father comes from the narrator by external focalization.

3 For exegesis cognizant of literary theory, see Stephen D. Moore, *Literary Criticism and the Gospels,* and John R. Donahue, S.J., *The Gospel in Parable.* A good summary of literary approaches to the parable is Leland Ryken's *The New Testament in Literary Criticism.* Yukihiro Takemoto has written on medieval prodigal son plays in *Language and Culture* (18: 1–13; 17: 1–18). Darryl Tippens examined Shakespeare's use in *Explorations in Renaissance Culture* (14, 57–77). Robert W. Baldwin has written "A Bibliography of the Prodigal Son Theme in Art and Literature," and David Wyatt discussed the prodigal's self-discovery as a paradigm for American writers in *Prodigal Sons.* Jill Robbins's *Prodigal Son / Elder Brother* uses the parable as an interpretive matrix for Augustine, Petrarch, Kafka, and Levinas.

4 According to Propp (*Theory and History of Folklore*), as well as Scholes and Kellogg, there is a difference between the unquestioned authority of the ancient storyteller, who embodies tradition, and the investigatory Greek *histor*, who "examines the past with an eye toward separating out actuality from myth. . . . The histor can present conflicting versions in his search for the truth of fact" (Scholes and Kellogg 242–43). Scholes and Kellogg's example is Thucydides, who makes "history rather than mimesis" dominant. Space precludes an explanation of the ways in which Breech's concept of narrators runs afoul of this distinction, especially as it overlooks the possession of imperceptible knowledge.

5 Tom Thumb is Bal's example (4–7). My use of these terms follows her definitions. An exception will be the later use of *function*, which owes to A.-J. Greimas's suggestion that actors (characters) attain their *actantial* quality due to the function of the events with which they are associated.

6 The actant is that group, or member of a group, of actors who share a characteristic related to the teleology of the fabula as a whole. What is their intention? To what do they aspire? What do they want? The verb that relates them to this object, or to other actants, reveals what in narratology is called the function of the actant. See Bal 25–30, and Greimas, "Les actants."

7 Patte's four models are narrative sequences and actantial roles, Lévi-Strauss's structuralism, the semiotic square of Greimas, and the relation of these three to "elementary structures." This analysis in *Semiology and Parables*, from a 1974 seminar in France with Greimas's associates (published in *Semeia* and *Soundings*), is richly suggestive and full of productive leads.

8 The fabula of villainy puts Patte in the position in his fourth analysis of positing the elder son's "rebellion" as parallel to the prodigal's and of arguing that it is embedded within the father's narrative; hence, he ends where so many others began, with the alternate title of "The Loving Father."

9 Peter Gay suggests that Freud scanted sibling rivalry because it struck too close to home: "Only seventeen months separated him from his younger sibling Julius, whose arrival he had greeted with rage and with death wishes" (506–7).

   Alan Sheridan, Lacan's translator, observes: "Freud, says Lacan, was led irresistibly 'to link the appearance of the signifier of the Father, as the author of the Law, to death, even to the murder of the Father,' thus showing that although this murder is the fruitful moment of the debt through which the subject binds himself for life to the Law, the symbolic Father, in so far as he signifies this Law, is certainly the dead Father" (Lacan 281–82). This is a useful key for a Lacanian reading of the fabula.

10 Bettelheim's analysis (90–93) may be better than those of Jeremias and others because it is broader, but it is still limited by the view of all narrative as intrinsically ameliorative and psychologically proscriptive.

11 My thanks to Eldon Epp, who guided me to the Michigan Collection, inventory no. 283 (second or third century A.D.) unpublished, and the Longus papyrus, B.G.U. II, 846 (second century A.D.), found in *Michigan Papyri* 37, and Deissmann 153.

12 The debt this study owes to the "cultural materialism" of Marvin Harris, with its foci of control of the material environment and control of reproduction, will be obvious to readers of *The Rise of Anthropological Theory*, *Cannibals and Kings*, and Harris's other works. Given his profound skepticism of Lévi-Strauss and structuralism, however, Harris should not be construed as endorsing the kinds of semiotic or narratological analyses employed here.

13 The "figurative exaggeration" is synecdoche, introduced in the next chapter. In this view, the parable itself might be a reading of history, per Hayden White. As opposed to metonymy (in White's scheme), synecdochical readings seize upon intrinsic (as opposed to extrinsic) characteristics and integrate the two terms based upon perceived qualitative similarities, rather than part-for-part replacement. "Synecdoche," White writes, "suggests a . . . combination of physical and spiritual qualities, which is qualitative in nature" (36). Thus all "far countries" in which the prodigal might waste his patrimony are synecdochically afflicted by famine. Synecdoche has the advantage of being rhetorically integrative and related (in White's borrowing from Frye) to "comic" emplotment, which is conservative in its "mode of ideological emplotment." Such a way of reading the past accords with the savings function that closes what I take to be a patriarchal and materially conservative fabula. Terms and concepts appear throughout this study that owe to White's *Metahistory*. His synopsis of the political implications of rhetorical figures such as metonymy and synecdoche (1–42) is especially germane.

14 See Bal 26–27, for details on function. It is the teleological relation between the actor and his goal; it is the verb that relates them, what the actor wants and desires.

15 This is a good gloss by a late mercantile thinker on the integrative obligations of capital. What is the elder son saving for? Savings implies a goal, an object of desire, as opposed to mere hoarding. Part of the father's lesson is

that the elder son has not yet articulated the object of his desire. If he is to become the giver, however, the elder son must understand his power over the prodigal as this object.

16   Some recent studies that explore the economic functions in literature (not necessarily treating gender) are Donald N. McCloskey, *The Rhetoric of Economics* and *If You're So Smart*; Walter Benn Michaels, *The Gold Standard and the Logic of Naturalism*; Michael T. Gilmore, *American Romanticism and the Marketplace*; Leonard N. Neufeldt, *The Economist*; and David S. Reynolds, *Beneath the American Renaissance* (see especially chapters 6 and 7, on the sensational press and erotic imagination). Teresa de Laurentis's *Technologies of Gender* is excellent on film and gender. My own inspiration came from Dennis Porter's *Pursuit of Crime*.

17   The use of "Sacco and Vanzetti" to identify a narrative, rather than the individuals, is intended to specify the figurative functions of narrative, not to be disrespectful.

18   Details on the trial come from the narrative and transcript in Weeks. Arrested on a streetcar, in a police trap laid for another anarchist, Sacco and Vanzetti were prodigiously armed. Sacco carried a .32-caliber pistol with nine rounds and twenty-three shells in his pocket. Ballistics tests matched this gun to a slug found in one victim's body. Vanzetti carried a fully loaded .38 revolver, likely belonging to the same victim, and four shotgun shells. Police found the weapons when Sacco twice moved to pull his gun. At the police station, the men lied about the guns, their citizenship, their whereabouts the day of the crime, and their reason for being on the streetcar.

A Sacco and Vanzetti Defense Fund, with funds from the ACLU, hired Fred H. Moore, the California lawyer who had defended IWW members in the Lawrence strike of 1912. Eugene Lyons was hired to publicize the case in England and America. The emphasis on public relations was strikingly modern: Lyons began telegraphing stories to radical papers in France, Italy, Spain, and South and Central America. Soon there were marches in Lisbon, Rome, and Paris; in Paris bombs killed twenty people. Sympathizers in South American capitals announced boycotts of American goods, and newspapers from Puerto Rico to Algeria protested. Money flowed in—$360,000 by 1925—as American intellectuals from Upton Sinclair to Eugene Debs and Helen Gurley Flynn took up the cause.

19   Madeiros made up new details about weapons, transportation, and times that conflicted with physical evidence and chronology that everyone agreed

upon. There is also evidence that he was bribed by members of the Sacco
and Vanzetti Defense Fund. See Montgomery.

20   Frankfurter's tactic was to attribute the prosecution's strategy to the judge:
"By 'consciousness of guilt' Judge Thayer meant that the conduct of Sacco
and Vanzetti after April 15 was the conduct of murderers" (35). How could
this be, asked Frankfurter, when neither man went into hiding, assumed
another name, or was found to possess or to have spent any of the payroll?
Thayer could only mean this, wrote Frankfurter, in the terms of a preexist-
ing narrative: "To exculpate themselves of the crime of murder, they had to
disclose elaborately their crime of radicalism" (77). The judge was removed
from his role as "father" and recharacterized as a vindictive villain. Frankfurter asked intellectuals to identify with the prodigal—to find themselves
charged with cultural dissent.

21   Montgomery provides these titles and authors (62) but omits the visual representations of the trial by painter Ben Shahn, which are in Martin H. Bush's
Ben Shahn. John Dos Passos's *Facing the Chair* is now available in a reprint
edition.

22   Film scholars point out that the film had been a Broadway play first and was
not the first true sound recording or Jolson's first screen appearance. Besides,
Fox Movietone newsreels had presented Lindbergh, Coolidge, and Musso-
lini giving speeches four months earlier. There would be a "100% talkie,"
Lights of New York, in 1928. All of this misses the larger narrative point.

2 Metonymic Sources

1   David Hounshell, Kenneth E. Bailes, Daniel J. Keyless, and John M. Staudenmaier are other contributors to the momentum model of technological
history. My account relies on Staudenmaier (11). Like literary formalism, the
previous "internalist" histories had roots in a disciplinary scientism whose
practitioners, at the turn of the century, preferred to study objects in isolation. Later, writes Staudenmaier, scholars in economics, sociology, and
political science began to include technology in their analyses and to write
nonhistorical, cross-disciplinary accounts: the names Marcuse, Habermas,
and Ellul indicate practitioners but also the deterministic assumptions that
became problematic. In the 1930s and 1940s, Mumford and Usher anticipated a synthetic view that would be known as contextualist in the studies
of Louis Hunter and Lynn White Jr. White thought of the internal design

of technologies as interacting with economic, political, and cultural factors. But while amplifying the fields that impacted on technological success or failure, contextual histories still found their paradigms in the principles of technology. These assumptions imply that the relation of society to technology is adaptation, a "cultural lag," to use William Fielding Ogburn's phrase. Technology drives society—only one way. Hence histories of technology tended to become success stories, the narratives of evolutionary, positivist, or moral accomplishment, sometimes allied with political or social reform (as in Edward Bellamy's 1888 *Looking Backward*). As Howard Mumford Jones noted, there is a paucity of "failure studies." Technological narratives end up justifying the triumph of the West over other cultures, while maintaining that technology is nonideological. Among the growing number of studies of technology's impact on American literature are Cecilia Tichi, *Shifting Gears*, and Lisa M. Steinman, *Made in America*.

2   Carroll Pursell has analyzed the most sustained governmental attempt to "foresee and control long-term effects of technological change on American society" germane to this study, that of the Roosevelt "Brain Trust" in the 1930s, and concluded that the technological good and bad were so "closely mixed" in real life as to form a political zero-sum game (Staudenmaier 157).

3   The cultural values of mobility and travel are explored in such studies as Cynthia Golumb Dettelbach, "In the Driver's Seat"; Karal Ann Marling, *The Colossus of Roads*; and William W. Stowe, *Americans Abroad*.

4   When Ford directors decided to give a 10 percent bonus to employees of more than three years service, only 640 qualified out of a workforce of 15,000. Needing dedicated workers to make the moving assembly line functional, Ford dramatically doubled the prevailing $2.50-a-day wage, earning publicity for the company and hero status for himself. "The basic psychology of the plan, however," writes Hounshell, was that "now the company could ask its workers to become for eight hours a day a part of the production machine" (258–59).

Innovations then occurred so quickly that no detailed record could be kept. The most important were on the engine line, which required the moving assembly of subsystems, including the transmission. In the first effort, an engine fell on and seriously injured a worker, threatening to halt the experiment, but within four months, the entire engine was assembled on an integrated assembly line, reducing the man-minutes of work involved from 594 to 226.

5   The object of physical mobility had shifted from production (pioneers suf-

fered when they journeyed to more productive situations) to mass consumption (consumers rewarded themselves with travel as a result of work). While the common denominator of upward mobility remained, travel was increasingly associated with ease and cultured consumption, beginning with the travel literature of the Genteel Age.

6   Ford, according to Hounshell (276), continued to frame his car bodies in wood until 1925 (though the chassis was steel) and had problems stamping and welding even a gas tank for his Model A. He insisted that inconvenient features of the Model T—the gas tank was at first under the seat, then under the engine cowl—were functionally efficient, contributing to a lower selling price. "The Ford car is a tried and true product that requires no tinkering," he asserted. He despised advertising: "I sometimes wonder if we have not lost our buying sense and fallen entirely under the spell of salesmanship. The American of a generation ago was a shrewd buyer. He knew values in the terms of utility and dollars. But nowadays the American people seem to listen and be sold; that is, they do not buy. They are sold; things are pushed on them." This attitude went hand in hand with Ford's refusal to consider installment buying until the enormous success of the Chevy, which could be purchased through the General Motors Acceptance Corporation, forced him to set up credit operations for the Model A in 1928 (Hounshell 277).

7   The "dynamo" that so inspired Henry Adams at the 1900 Paris Exhibition led to an era in which the forces of propulsion were arranged off-line to maximize the use of momentum and to minimize torque and vibration. Eugene O'Neill's play Dynamo (1929) depicted the worship of electricity replacing belief in God: "The center must be the Great Mother of Eternal Life, Electricity, and Dynamo is her Divine Image on earth!" Poet MacKnight Black, after his job at Ford's advertising agency and a trip to the River Rouge plant, adopted the Corliss engine as his central metaphor in Machinery (1929).

8   Plastics also spurred new techniques of formation, the most important being molding, which allowed the joining of concave and convex features (gloves), the even filling of tiny extrusions (combs), and seamless spheres (buoys, floats, balls). Injection, heat, and pressure were the component forces of molding, but in such diminished magnitude that the resulting object seemed formed by magic. Plastic lent itself immediately to figurative speech (the unabridged Random House Dictionary lists fourteen metaphoric uses). What is called rubber is actually a kind of plastic that supplanted the vulcanized organic compound, beginning in 1930 with Thiokol. Oliver 597–601.

9   See Encyclopaedia Britannica (1958) 21: 896.

10 See particularly the chapter on Pound, in which Kenner stresses the "encasement of machines" and streamlining (41–42).

11 The statistics in this section are from Fearon, *Slump* 123–45; Lester V. Chandler 53–55; and Fearon, *Slump* 81.

12 As Fearon explains, one school of economists, including Galbraith, assigns blame to overproduction of luxury goods, while another, which includes Lester V. Chandler, argues for other factors. See Fearon, *Slump* 32.

13 Only Frank Capra flirted with the embezzlement plot, in *It's a Wonderful Life* (1946).

14 Urban ethnic tension was, in a sense, facilitated by an investment in suburban housing between 1921 and 1929 that Lester V. Chandler estimates at thirty-five billion dollars (16). This created a white-collar suburbia and removed the traditional bearers of norms from the urban setting.

15 Manufacturers of quality furniture had used credit plans in the nineteenth century, but their customers tended to pay when it was convenient. An attempt to schedule payments failed when fly-by-night operators fleeced customers with bad furniture. Popular prejudice kept installment credit from increasing until the auto came along. *Encyclopaedia Britannica* (1958) 12: 431–33.

16 As Lester V. Chandler has shown, unemployment was unevenly distributed according to age, race, geographic location, and industry. The most recent edition of the U.S. Department of Commerce's *Historical Statistics of the United States*, on which most scholars rely, revises upward the figures of previous editions. Fearon (*Slump* 138, 206) points out that the numbers for the civilian labor force are lower—if you accept the theory that workers on federal emergency relief projects were "employed." They are higher if you accept the argument that the official figures understate the case by ignoring part-time work, among other factors. See Fearon, *War* 207–8, for a brief account of the controversy.

17 Ferebee's concise history supplies much of the data on design in this section.

18 Sinel's claim is disputed by Loewy, Geddes, and design historians and seems more a matter of nomenclature than practice.

19 The momentum of "planned consumption" was such that Geddes, like many intellectuals of the twenties, endorsed Soviet planning: "One of the greatest experiments the world has ever known is now in progress in Soviet Russia," he wrote in *Horizons*. "Here is a government that is trying to run its affairs like a business. They are treating each separate undertaking, industry, art,

or whatever it is, as though each were a subsidiary of the holding company"
(289). Two years earlier, *Fortune* celebrated Geddes for "demonstrating that
poetic qualities and scientific values may be combined for mutual benefit"
(57). In 1935 Geddes took his vision to a popular audience when he produced the Broadway play *Dead End* (a Bogart film gris of 1937), in which an
architect tries to "rationalize" New York's slums.

20 This powerful economic moment, when the consumer's momentum surpassed the designer's, cowed even Loewy, as he eventually conceded: "I
believe one should design for the advantage of the largest mass of people,
first and always. That takes care of ideologies and sociologies" (279).

3 Dashiell Hammett, Copywriter

1 Johnson provides details unavailable to earlier biographers, such as Layman *(Shadow Man)* and Nolan *(Casebook and Life)*. The works of Johnson
and Layman show the memoirs of Lillian Hellman to be questionable in
chronology and details.

2 Starr explains the series of arrests of Arbuckle that led up to Zukor's decision, including bribes to police of over one hundred thousand dollars
(Inventing 325).

3 Starr notes tellingly that "admiration turned to resentment as the rags-to-
riches story reversed itself" *(Inventing* 327).

4 Hammett, flush with Hollywood money, would later behave much like
Arbuckle, wasting thousands on parties, prostitutes, and Prohibition liquor
during the Depression. But he would justify his behavior by his willingness
to fall, his adoption of communism. For the California artiste, this crisis had
been anticipated by Jack London in the sections of *Martin Eden* (1909) that
"explain" London's new wealth. During the Depression, Hammett found
the same contradictory embrace of Nietzsche and Marx that London had
found. If he became rich, it was because of his superhuman talent. But if he
sold out, if he failed in ruthlessness, then he owed the "people of the abyss"
(London's term), the melodrama of disaccumulation or of prison, especially
if, as Hammett believed, he would die shortly anyway. Beneath this theatri-
cality, of course, lay a political unconsciousness that was profoundly split
about the trade-offs between economic mobility and stability of personality.

5 Jeannette Rankin was elected to Congress in 1916.

6 This is not the fashionable view of Hammett's politics, which remains

colored by his later Communist sympathies, as well as the interpretations of *New Masses* and mid-1930s socialists: to wit, *Red Harvest* is a Marxist critique of political corruption. The latter is "imaginative . . . but misguided," writes Richard Layman: "There are no masses of politically dispossessed people," and IWW leader Bill Quint is a "hollow idealist" (*Shadow Man* 96). The latest attempt to find "praxis" in *Red Harvest* is Carl Freedman and Christopher Kendrick's "Forms of Labor in Dashiell Hammett's *Red Harvest*." They dissect "four forms of labor" against a tableau of "ownership of means of production," though they present no evidence that Hammett intended this or had read Marx then. Some idea of their reasoning may be had by their notion that the runs in Dinah Brand's stockings suggest "an abstract form of surplus energy" (213). Such interesting observations as "Hammett at one point seems to draw a parallel between fascist Italy and gangster-dominated Personville" (213) go unsupported. In their view, the Op is a "dialogic dialectician" (214).

7   Film had its own internal competition, with genres almost from its birth appealing to dissimilar publics. Producers of spectacles, such as D. W. Griffith and Cecil B. DeMille, looked backward to the Broadway play and forward to the cinema epic. The detective novel could not compete with these forms but adjusted to its resources. While the epic cinema might diminish the popularity of hardback detective Philo Vance, whose tales featured recherché dialogue and a tableau of the social classes (and thus made better sound film than fiction), it did not dare approach the overt violence in a Carol John Daly novel.

8   California produced the term *gold-digger* around 1830 and gave it a negative inflection. See *Random House Dictionary.*

9   "The Sign of Four" concerns the usurped patrimony of Miss Mary Morstam. Hammett took the love interest of Mary and Dr. Watson and transferred it to the detective, making Mary one of the crooks. But he retained Doyle's three prodigals: Sholto (Cairo), Tonga (Wilmer), and Small (the "large" Gutman). Like the falcon, the treasure chest that Watson and Holmes recover is empty, but this enables Watson to continue his courtship, since Mary remains at his socioeconomic level. The provision of an "appropriate other" that closes both stories is made ironic in *The Maltese Falcon* by the fragmentation of "woman" into three roles. Doyle's "revealed story" concerns the perfidy of foreigners, but Hammett's concerns "meiosis": telling less than the full truth, at both the interpersonal and stylistic levels.

10   There were earlier male-female detective pairs in the pulp mags, as William
     F. Nolan points out in *The Black Mask Boys*.

11   In Dreiser's work, however, momentous chance events draw out the inner
     man, revealing him as distinctly Frank Cowperwood or Clyde Griffiths:
     chance elicits a dormant predetermined personality that does not then change
     again. Edenbaum's subsequent turn to the *context* of the Flitcraft parable
     is necessary exactly because Spade's view is not naturalistic but an ironic
     comprehension of naturalism. If allegory dominated, neither Brigid nor the
     reader could leave the scene uncomprehending of the parable's meaning.

12   Hammett's discovery of the compatibility between romantic emplotment
     and a mechanistic (instrumental) prefigurative mode suggests much about
     his adoption of communism. As White notes, the thinking of Marx grew
     from similar dispositions, though in the great romantic drama of man's re-
     demption Marx used tragic emplotments for such figures as the proletarian
     hero. But Marx based his analysis of the "elementary units" of the "wealth
     of societies in which the capitalist method of production prevails" on the
     distinction between the content and the phenomenal form of commodities.
     Use value is the familiar way of referring to Marx's notion of "content," while
     exchange value describes its often, or usually, unequal commercial form.
     Like the objective world of Spade, "the world of things, in Marx's view, is a
     world of isolated individualities," writes White (329). Behind it one finds the
     mechanistic principles of exchange that reveal the economic base.

4 James M. Cain, Journalist

1   Hoopes provides some trial details, but most included here owe to the *New
    York Times* of May 3–10, 1927.

2   The competing figures were conspiracy (Snyder was innocent and framed by
    a mysterious man in western New York State, possibly with Gray's aid), ad-
    vanced by Snyder's attorneys, and "Annabel Lee" (Ruth was driven to murder
    by Albert's infatuation with a deceased fiancée, whose picture he hung in
    their house).

3   Hoopes and the *Times* say Snyder was the first woman electrocuted, but
    Kobler says she was the third.

4   Hoopes refers to "Goebel's" lion farm in his biography, which is the name
    Cain used in *Postman*, but the Gay Lion Farm, twelve miles northeast of

Los Angeles, in Cain's neighborhood, and the novel's setting, was far more famous, for it supplied film animals, including the MGM lion. See Henstell 85–86.

5 *Ideologeme* means a character, conflict, or plot that carries a predetermined ideological outcome with it. It has been used variously by Bahktin, Kristeva, Jameson, and a number of semioticians and sociocritics. See Marling, "Formal Ideologeme."

6 A good explanation of A. J. Greimas's techniques is offered by Ronald Schliefer in his introduction to Greimas's *Sémiotique narrative et textuelle.* Rather than binary opposition, Greimas's values "exist on the paradigmatic as opposed to the syntagmatic axis. Isotopies are the elements of Greimas's semiotic square; isomorphism guarantees their possible homologation" (xxx).

7 The only interior scene after this is the attempted blackmail of the couple by Kennedy, an old-style melodrama that Cora handles with businesslike aplomb even as Frank indulges in his usual brutality.

8 Hemingway had recently used the same plot to rid Lieutenant Henry of his child and Catherine Barkley in *A Farewell to Arms* (1929), as Judith Fetterley has pointed out in *The Resisting Reader.*

9 In this sense, we can actually see the beginning of this erotics in the uses section of Mather's sermon on Hannah Dustin: "The Use which you are to make of [it]," advised Mather, "is to Humble your selves before the Lord exceedingly" (Slotkin 113). But he added that the victims are neither morally worse than others for having undergone captivity nor better for having escaped: they had been "under the hand" of God. Mather counseled against the hermeneutics of identification and pointed out the authority resident in a discourse of commodified desire.

5 Raymond Chandler, Oil Executive

1 Details on Julian come from Henstell 35–43, and Woehlke. Harry Haldeman, head of the Better America Foundation, was the grandfather of H. R. Haldeman, Nixon's aide.

2 See the *Los Angeles Times*, Nov. 1, 1928: 1; Nov. 2, 1928: 1; and Nov. 4, 1928: 1, 15.

3 Developers had already carved Beverly Hills, Windsor Square, and Hancock Park out of the once-vast hacienda. The core would eventually become Hancock Park, site of the Los Angeles County Art Museum.

4 Julian's story had several subsequent chapters, including fabulous silver and lead mine promotions in Nevada, a putative strike in Oklahoma with a new oil syndicate in 1929, and a denouement in 1934 in China, where he staged a banquet for friends at the Shanghai Astor House, during which he excused himself, went to his room, and committed suicide. He had no money to pay for the meal. See Henstell 41–43.

5 It could be objected that the novel is cobbled together from "Killer in the Rain" and "The Curtain," as Philip Durham has shown. Thus the introduction of law at the end of the first source story is only opportune. But Marlowe could just as well hand his case and suspect to officers Ohls or Cronjagger, and the reconciliation scene with Wilde makes an awkward transition to the second half. Rather, the central position of the law points to the vindication of insubordination, for Marlowe has returned to his true father, an idealized patriarch (Lloyd), who contrasts with the initial and concluding presences of the actual patriarch, General Sternwood. The rhythm of narrative events and geographic or spatial relations is actually governed from this center, the fulcrum of an apparently awkward joining of two magazine stories.

6 The door that has "come out of a church" seems to allude to Henry's separation of England from the Roman Catholic Church in Shakespeare's play, as well as to the question of succession (marriage to Anne Boleyn and birth of the future queen Elizabeth).

7 In 1962 Max Black proposed in *Models and Metaphors* that metaphor consists of a focus—the unknown term—and a frame—the remainder of the sentence (40–44). Black's ideas have since been attacked, but the overthrow of I. A. Richards's model of tenor and vehicle opened up inquiry. In Black's model, the focus (tenor) of a metaphor was invested with the "system of associated commonplaces" of the frame (vehicle). The commonplaces about any subject were known, said Black, by experts as well as laymen, for everyone knew "what the man on the street thinks about the matter." When we say "man is a wolf," we do not mean that he is like the animal; rather we wish to invoke a system of commonplaces that we share about the frame of "wolf." Black's "system of associated commonplaces" calls attention to the task of "unpacking" metaphors to examine the commonplaces they invoke.

8 In 1973 Dorothy Mack advanced Black's insights in her article "Metaphorical Ambiguities" (75–85). Following structural linguistics, Mack argued that metaphors are the "comparison-conjoining of an Assertion with a Presupposition." She argued that there were two types of metaphor, differing in their

"predicate" parts (Black's "frame"): one refers to a presupposition and appropriates that meaning for the metaphor's subject, while the other, lacking a
presupposition, makes the predicate part of the subject. The first she called
agent promotion ("personification" in an older parlance), the second, predicate incorporation ("objectification"). In the phrase "the chair laughed,"
agent promotion presupposes that laughing is a human quality—the chair
becomes animate. This is a kind of synecdoche. But in predicate incorporation, the word *laugh* has no presupposition and becomes an objective quality
of the chair, a species of metonymy. That both types of metaphor are potentially ideological becomes clearer as Mack explains how their construction
consists of asserting, presupposing, conjoining, comparing, deleting, and
reinterpreting. Mack writes that "this basic procedure may then be part of a
pre-coded language process using cultural associations and formulas occur-
ring in a particular genre and mode," so that "even metaphors which appear
to be direct statements function very much like weak commands, suggestions
to see or feel in a certain way" (84).

9   Eugene Holland (296) gives this genealogy and uses this phrase in reviewing
Deleuze and Guattari. The path to my analysis here begins with William W.
Stowe's contribution to Most and Stowe (366–88). For example, Stowe writes
of Marlowe's first encounter with Malloy that the latter "mutely asks, Who
am I? and Marlowe replies, You are a symbol of the dangerous American
combination of ignorance and innocence" (376). Marlowe, I believe, is also
both, in the consumer era.

10   The list of instances in which ethnicity and uncertainty are conjoined with
smoke is extensive. Helen Grayle chain-smokes, brushing her clouds away.
Second Planting, the Indian who drives Marlowe to see cultist Amthor,
smells and is compared to a horse, a chimpanzee, and an old woman.
Amthor's wife speaks with a heavy foreign accent. Amthor has Marlowe
beaten up and sent to a private asylum where "the smoke hung straight up in
the air, in thin lines, straight up and down like a curtain of small clear beads"
(*Farewell* 139). Marlowe escapes, and Randall comes to visit, "the veil of his
smoke almost a solid thing to one side of him" (164). The asylum scene not
only emphasizes smoke as a uniting/dividing motif but also ties it to Malloy,
for Marlowe remarks that the smoke "was a grey web woven by a thousand
spiders" (140). Malloy's objective correlative, as it were, is the spider, from
the tarantula on page 1 to the black widows that precede Marlowe's discovery
of dead Jesse Florian, whom Malloy has murdered.

11   The economic level works through what Mack calls agent promotion. Its form is "A is to B as C is to D." But B is implied, C is not current, and D is lost. The ideological operators are *and* and *equals:* (car *and* B) *equals* (spats *and* Iowa picnic). This is a narrow set of truth conditions.

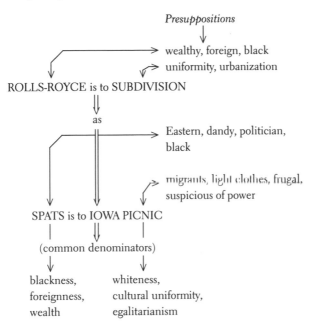

Presuppositions

wealthy, foreign, black
uniformity, urbanization

ROLLS-ROYCE is to SUBDIVISION

as

Eastern, dandy, politician, black

migrants, light clothes, frugal, suspicious of power

SPATS is to IOWA PICNIC

(common denominators)

blackness, foreignness, wealth

whiteness, cultural uniformity, egalitarianism

12   On Chandler's eczema, see MacShane, *Selected Letters* 14, 191, 199, 283, 358.

13   Earl Kynette, a notorious "bad cop" in Los Angeles, may have suggested Brunette's name. Santa Monica did boast an extraordinary development of expensive beachfront homes that practically walled off Los Angeleans from the ocean, but if Chandler's grudge against Santa Monica was personal, its exact nature has not yet been revealed. In letters, however, he repeatedly calls Santa Monica "Bay City" (e.g., MacShane, *Selected Letters* 31).

14   The fan-funnel may have seemed the epitome of commercialization to Chandler because of Earle C. Anthony, a local Packard auto dealer who made possession of a shiny black Packard sedan into a brand-name ritual for Los Angeles consumers. He built a series of identical twenty-four-hour gas stations, created a Packard club, and, like Mr. Grayle, pioneered a radio station (KFI), which broadcast "music for the road" and auto commercials

and hyped the real estate market (Starr, *Material Dreams* 80, 130). He was just the sort that Chandler detested, and he was an apostle of the fan-funnel.

15 Miller's analysis is apt to Chandler because it treats two of the latter's favorite authors, Wilkie Collins and Charles Dickens. The analysis of the way in which disciplinary structures and spaces are created in *Bleak House* and *David Copperfield* could be applied to Chandler also.

6 From Roman Noir to Film Noir

1 For an overview, see Bordwell, Staiger, and Thompson 74–77; Crowther 7–39; Paul Schrader in Denby 278–90; Tuska 149–99; and Silver and Ward 3–9. The third edition of Silver and Ward was not available when this study was written.

2 Schrader contended that noir was not exactly a genre, but a specific, unwieldy period. "It harks back to many previous periods: Warner's Thirties gangster films, the French. . . . Film noir can stretch at its outer limits from *The Maltese Falcon* (1941) to *Touch of Evil* (1958)." Schrader thought that noir was defined by tone rather than genre (Denby 279).

3 See Starr, *Inventing, Material Dreams*, and *Americans*; and McWilliams.

4 We read, for example, that "there is nothing intrinsic in side-light or a moving camera that connotes such qualities as alienation, obsession, or paranoia in the manner that a tied-down pistol may imply a gunfight [e.g. an icon]" (Silver and Ward 3). The disingenuity is that it recognizes synecdoche (the pistol), but not that metonymy results from eliding the old sequence of event → icon (figure) → style. What was an icon, after all, but an event associated with an object by a recognizable technique? It could be reduced to event → (technique) → style.

5 A new book by William Luhr, *Raymond Chandler and Film*, promises to address these issues in Chandler better.

6 Salt has also shown how the studios leapt at opportunities to reduce their huge electrical consumption. New higher-speed films introduced by Agfa and Kodak in 1938 reduced the light required by half. The films were not used to increase depth of field, however, but to reduce light and heat on the set. Studios commonly overexposed the film, then underdeveloped it to produce a flatter, lower-contrast print with more gray tones.

7 In *Voices in the Dark*, Telotte writes that "what makes the *noir* voice so distinctive is that the patterns of violation it speaks of also appear to be the pat-

terns of our cultural and human order. That identity, of course, forestalls any easy or conventional imaginary resolution" (1). It seems clear that this violation is a diegetic force that interrupts a visual filmic silence. Telotte writes that its "narrative voice" makes noir different and allows it an "ambiguous posture on the borders of genre" (2). He poses the issue as a rhetorical question: "Is noir, then, simply a cycle of films that flourished in the backwash of World War II and the early cold war days, borrowing its markings from a variety of established genres; or is it a genre in its own right, simply appearing, disappearing and then reappearing, in keeping with the usual principles of audience popularity and *need?*" (3). There seems no mistaking Telotte's inclination, especially when he cites art deco repeatedly for its dominance in design, including that of theaters.

Sarah Kozloff, in *Invisible Storytellers*, applies narrative theory, Labov's *Language in the Inner City*, the semiotics of Pierce, Eco, and Barthes, and Gennette's taxonomy of narrators. She finds layers of embedded narrators who focalize a written narrative, for her analogous to the possible points of view of the camera (e.g., synonymous with the main character, a reaction shot of him, a perfect impartial observer). She identifies irony as the chief mode of voice-over narration (102). The information conveyed in the voice-over can parallel or counterpoint the image or, to use Kozloff's terms, be complementary or disparate, which allows more shadings and is less binary. An example she cites is Wilder's *The Apartment* (1960), which opens with a voice-over by a narrator who quotes statistics and works for Consolidated Life of New York (104–5). Long shots of cityscapes then change to medium shots of large, organized office interiors, then to a close-up of Jack Lemmon as C. C. Baxter: "Most people call me 'Bud.' "

8   See Christine Gedhill in Kaplan 6–21; and Silvia Harvey in Kaplan 22–34. Gedhill contends that film noir's voices tend to be male. Harvey has argued that the genre not only lacks depictions of families or of women in families but also focuses on femmes fatales at a moment when women were increasingly employed in the labor force.

9   Schrader wants to have the war both ways: it peeks through pessimism of the thirties, and it peeks through official optimism of the forties. In such an explanation, "war" is actually the figure rather than one of the terms; it relates the 1930s to the 1940s synecdochically. This tendency in Schrader's thought is also apparent in his cybernetic notion of film's adaptations and in his tropes, from "Horatio Alger" to "full steam," which express more techno-

logical positivism than he dares admit. His notion that films such as *Scarface* or *The Public Enemy* were "Horatio Algerish" will strike anyone who has actually read Alger as bizarre, for he never rewards crime or evil.

10 The obvious exception is Wilder's *Lost Weekend* (1945). Drinking does figure in some noir films, but while it was a major social fact, and significant in Hammett, Cain, and Chandler, film noir made it secondary. If film noir "reflects" reality, why did it discard such a powerful tool?

Works Cited

"Advertiser and Artist: A Portrait of Bel Geddes." *Fortune*, July 30, 1930: 57.

Agee, James. *Let Us Now Praise Famous Men*. Boston: Houghton, 1989.

Allen, Frederick Lewis. *Only Yesterday*. New York: Harper, 1964.

Americana Yearbook. Danbury, Conn.: Grolier, 1928.

Avrich, Paul. *Sacco and Vanzetti: The Anarchist Background*. Princeton, N.J.: Princeton UP, 1991.

Bal, Mieke. *Narratology: Introduction to the Theory of Narrative*. Trans. Christine van Boheemen. Toronto: U of Toronto P, 1985.

Baldwin, Robert W. "A Bibliography of the Prodigal Son Theme in Art and Literature." *Bulletin of Bibliography* 44 (Sept. 1987): 167–71.

Balio, Tino, ed. *The American Film Industry*. Madison: U of Wisconsin P, 1976.

Barthes, Roland. *The Fashion System*. New York: Farrar, 1983.

Bauer, S. F., L. Balter, and W. Hunt. "The Detective Film as Myth: The Maltese Falcon and Sam Spade." *American Imago* 35 (1978): 275–96.

Baxter, John. *Hollywood in the Thirties*. New York: Barnes and Co., 1968.

Beard, Charles A., and Mary R. Beard. *The Rise of American Civilization*. New York: Macmillan, 1930.

Bercovitch, Sacvan. *The Puritan Origins of the American Self*. New Haven, Conn.: Yale UP, 1975.

Bettelheim, Bruno. *The Uses of Enchantment*. New York: Vintage, 1977.

Black, Max. *Models and Metaphors*. Ithaca, N.Y.: Cornell UP, 1962.

Bliven, Bruce. "Flapper Jane." *New Republic*, Sept. 9, 1925: 67.

———. "Los Angeles." *New Republic*, July 13, 1927: 198–99.

Boorstin, Daniel J. *The Image*. New York: Atheneum, 1978.

Bordwell, David. *Narration in the Fiction Film*. Madison: U of Wisconsin P, 1985.

Bordwell, David, Janet Staiger, and Kristin Thompson. *The Classical Hollywood Cinema*. New York: Columbia UP, 1985.

Breech, James. *The Silence of Jesus: The Authentic Voice of the Historical Man*. Philadelphia: Fortress, 1983.

Burke, Edmund. *Burke's Politics: Selected Writings and Speeches of Edmund Burke on Reform, Revolution, and War*. Ed. Ross J. S. Hoffman and Paul Levack. New York: Knopf, 1949.

Bush, Martin H. *Ben Shahn: The Passion of Sacco and Vanzetti*. Syracuse, N.Y.: Syracuse UP, 1968.

Cain, James M. *The Baby in the Icebox*. London: Penguin, 1981.

———. *Double Indemnity*. New York: Random, 1978.

———. *Mildred Pierce*. New York: Random, 1989.

———. "Paradise." *American Mercury* 28.111 (Mar. 1933): 266–80.

———. *The Postman Always Rings Twice*. New York: Random, 1978.

Chandler, Lester V. *America's Greatest Depression, 1929–1941*. New York: Harper, 1970.

Chandler, Raymond. *The Big Sleep*. New York: Random, 1976.

———. *Farewell, My Lovely*. New York: Random, 1976.

———. *The High Window*. New York: Random, 1976.

———. *Killer in the Rain*. New York: Random, 1976.

———. *The Simple Art of Murder*. New York: Random, 1980.

Clark, Al. *Raymond Chandler in Hollywood*. New York: Proteus, 1982.

Cleveland, Reginald McIntosh. "How Many Automobiles Can America Buy?" *World's Work* 27 (1914): 679–89.

Clifton, N. Roy. *The Figure in Film*. Newark: U of Delaware P, 1983.

Cook, David A. *A History of Narrative Film*. New York: Norton, 1981.

Cowley, Malcolm. *Exile's Return*. New York: Viking, 1959.

Crèvecoeur, Hector St. Jean de. "Letters from an American Farmer." *The Norton Anthology of American Literature*. 3rd ed. Vol. 1. Ed. Nina Baym et al. New York: Norton, 1989. 262–75.

Crowther, Bruce. *Film Noir: Reflections in a Dark Mirror*. New York: Ungar, 1989.

Damico, James. "Film Noir: A Modest Proposal." *Film Reader* 3 (1978): 48–57.

Deissmann, Gustav Adolf. *Licht vom Osten*. Tübingen: Mohr, 1923.

de Laurentis, Teresa. *Technologies of Gender*. Bloomington: Indiana UP, 1987.

Deleuze, Gilles, and Félix Guattari. *Anti-Oedipus: Capitalism and Schizophrenia*. Minneapolis: U of Minnesota P, 1983.

Denby, David, ed. *Awake in the Dark*. New York: Random, 1977.

Dettelbach, Cynthia Golumb. "In the Driver's Seat: A Study of the Automobile in American Literature and Popular Culture." Diss. Case Western Reserve U, 1974.

Donahue, John R., S.J. *The Gospel in Parable*. Philadelphia: Fortress, 1988.

Dos Passos, John. *Facing the Chair: The Story of the Americanization of Two Foreign Born Workmen*. Reprint. New York: Da Capo, 1970.

Durham, Philip. *Down These Mean Streets a Man Must Go*. Chapel Hill: U of North Carolina P, 1963.

Erikson, Erik H. *A Way of Looking at Things*. Ed. Stephen Schlein. New York: Norton, 1987.

Esler, Philip Francis. *Community and Gospel in Luke-Acts*. Cambridge: Cambridge UP, 1987.

Faulkner, William. *The Sound and the Fury*. New York: Random, 1986.

Fearon, Peter. *The Origins and Nature of the Great Slump, 1929–1932*. Atlantic Highlands, N.J.: Humanities, 1979.

———. *War, Prosperity, and Depression: The United States' Economy, 1917–1940*. Lawrence: UP of Kansas, 1987.

Ferebee, Ann. *A History of Design from the Victorian Era to the Present*. New York: Van Nostrand Reinhold, 1980.

Fetterley, Judith. *The Resisting Reader*. Bloomington: Indiana UP, 1978.

Fine, David, ed. *Los Angeles in Fiction*. Albuquerque: U of New Mexico P, 1984.

Fitzgerald, F. Scott. *The Great Gatsby*. New York: Scribner's, 1953.

———. *The Last Tycoon*. New York: Scribner's, 1941.

Fitzmyer, Joseph A., ed. and trans. *The Gospel According to Luke (X–XXIV)*. Vol. 28a of *The Anchor Bible*. Garden City, N.Y.: Doubleday, 1985.

Foucault, Michel. *The History of Sexuality*. Vol. 1, *An Introduction*. Trans. Robert Hurley. New York: Random, 1980.

Frankfurter, Felix. *The Case of Sacco and Vanzetti*. New York: Grosset and Dunlap, 1927.

Franklin, Benjamin. *The Way to Wealth*. *The Norton Anthology of American Literature*. 3rd ed. Vol. 1. Ed. Nina Baym et al. New York: Norton, 1989. 159–65.

Freedman, Carl, and Christopher Kendrick. "Forms of Labor in Dashiell Hammett's *Red Harvest*." *PMLA* 106.2 (1991): 209–21.

Freud, Sigmund. *The Standard Edition of the Complete Works of Sigmund Freud*. Trans. and ed. James Strachey and Anna Freud. Vol. 22. London: Hogarth, 1964.

Frost, Robert. *The Poetry of Robert Frost*. New York: Holt, 1975.

Frye, Northrop. *Anatomy of Criticism*. Princeton, N.J.: Princeton UP, 1957.

———. *The Great Code*. New York: Harcourt, 1982.

Fussell, Paul. *Wartime: Understanding and Behavior in the Second World War*. New York: Oxford UP, 1989.

Galbraith, John Kenneth. *The Great Crash, 1929*. Boston: Houghton, 1954.

Garraty, John A. *The Great Depression*. New York: Harcourt, 1986.

Gay, Peter. *Freud: A Life for Our Time*. New York: Norton, 1988.

Geddes, Norman Bel. *Horizons*. Boston: Little, 1932.

Giannetti, Louis. *Masters of the American Cinema*. Englewood Cliffs, N.J.: Prentice, 1981.

——. *Understanding Movies*. Englewood Cliffs, N.J.: Prentice, 1976.

Gibson, Walker. *Tough, Sweet, and Stuffy*. Bloomington: Indiana UP, 1975.

Gilmore, Michael T. *American Romanticism and the Marketplace*. Chicago: U of Chicago P, 1985.

Girard, René. "Differentiation and Reciprocity in Lévi-Strauss and Contemporary Theory." *To Double Business Bound*. Baltimore: Johns Hopkins UP, 1978. 155–77.

Goldberg, Rube. *Rube Goldberg: A Retrospective*. Ed. Philip Garner. New York: Putnam, 1983.

Gregory, Sinda. *Private Investigations: The Novels of Dashiell Hammett*. Carbondale: Southern Illinois UP, 1985.

Greimas, A. J. "Les actants, les acteurs et les figures." *Sémiotique narrative et textuelle*. Ed. Claude Chabrol. Paris: Larousse, 1973. 161–76.

——. *Sémiotique: Dictionnaire raisonné de la théorie du langage*. Paris: Hachette, 1979.

——. *Structural Semantics: An Attempt at Method*. Trans. Daniele McDowell, Ronald Schleifer, and Alan Velie. Lincoln: U of Nebraska P, 1983.

Grinde, Nick. "Pictures for Peanuts." *Penguin Review of Film*. London: Scolar Press, 1977. 44–48.

Guetti, James. "Aggressive Reading: Detective Fiction and Realistic Narrative." *Raritan* 2.1 (Summer 1982): 128–38.

Hall, Mordaunt. "The Screen." Rev. of *The Jazz Singer*. *New York Times Film Reviews, 1913–1931*. New York: New York Times and Arno Press, 1970. 390–91.

Hammett, Dashiell. *The Big Knockover*. New York: Random, 1972.

——. *The Continental Op*. New York: Random, 1975.

——. *The Maltese Falcon*. New York: Random, 1984.

——. *Red Harvest*. New York: Random, 1972.

Harris, Marvin. *Cannibals and Kings: The Origins of Cultures*. New York: Random, 1977.

——. *Cultural Materialism*. New York: Random, 1980.

——. *The Rise of Anthropological Theory*. New York: Crowell, 1968.

Hemingway, Ernest. *In Our Time*. New York: Scribner's, 1970.

Henstell, Bruce. *Sunshine and Wealth: Los Angeles in the Twenties and Thirties.* San Francisco: Chronicle Books, 1984.

Herbst, Josephine. "Moralist's Progress." *Kenyon Review* 27 (Autumn 1965): 772–77.

Hirsch, Foster. *The Dark Side of the Screen.* New York: Da Capo, 1981.

Holland, Eugene K. "The Anti-Oedipus: Post-Modernism in Theory; or, The Post-Lacanian Historical Contextualization of Psychoanalysis." *Boundary* 2 (1986): 294–301.

Holme, Bryan. *Advertising: Reflections of a Century.* New York: Viking, 1982.

Hoopes, Roy. *Cain.* New York: Holt, 1982.

Horan, T. Owen. *Cleveland Plain Dealer,* Mar. 17, 1992: 4C.

Hounshell, David A. *From the American System to Mass Production, 1800–1932.* Baltimore: Johns Hopkins UP, 1984.

Humanities Research Center. U of Texas. Austin, Tex.

Issel, William, and Robert W. Cherny. *San Francisco, 1865–1932.* Berkeley: U of California P, 1986.

Jameson, Fredric. "On Raymond Chandler." *The Poetics of Murder: Detective Fiction and Literary Theory.* Ed. Glenn W. Most and William W. Stowe. New York: Harcourt, 1983. 153–71.

———. *The Political Unconscious.* Ithaca, N.Y.: Cornell UP, 1981.

Jeremias, Joachim. *The Parables of Jesus.* New York: Scribner's, 1963.

Johnson, Diane. *Dashiell Hammett: A Life.* New York: Random, 1983.

Kaplan, E. Ann, ed. *Women in Film Noir.* London: British Film Institute, 1978.

Kendall, Elizabeth. *The Runaway Bride: Hollywood Romantic Comedy of the 1930s.* New York: Anchor, 1991.

Kenner, Hugh. *The Mechanic Muse.* New York: Oxford UP, 1987.

Kenney, William P. "The Dashiell Hammett Tradition and the Modern American Detective Novel." Diss. U of Michigan, 1964.

Kerr, Paul. "Out of What Past? Notes on the B *Film Noir.*" *Film Comment* (Winter 1979–80): 220–30.

Knight, Stephen. *Form and Ideology in Crime Fiction.* Bloomington: Indiana UP, 1980.

Kobler, John, ed. *The Trial of Ruth Snyder and Judd Gray.* New York: Doubleday, Horan, 1938.

Kozloff, Sarah. *Invisible Storytellers: Voice-over Narration in American Fiction Film.* Berkeley: U of California P, 1988.

Lacan, Jacques. *The Four Fundamental Concepts of Psycho-Analysis.* Ed. Jacques-Alain Miller. Trans. Alan Sheridan. New York: Norton, 1978.

Layman, Richard. *Dashiell Hammett: A Bibliography.* Pittsburgh: U of Pittsburgh P, 1979.

————. *Shadow Man: The Life of Dashiell Hammett.* New York: Harcourt, 1981.

Lears, Jackson. *No Place of Grace: Anti-Modernism and the Transformation of American Culture, 1880–1920.* New York: Pantheon, 1983.

Legmon, Gershon. *Love and Death.* New York: Breaking Point, 1949.

Linnemann, Eta. *Gleichnisse Jesu, Einführung und Auslegung.* Translated as *Jesus of the Parables: Introduction and Exposition.* Trans. John Sturdy. New York: Harper, 1967.

Loewy, Raymond. *Never Leave Well Enough Alone.* New York: Simon, 1951.

Lowell, Robert, Peter Taylor, and Robert Penn Warren, eds. *Randall Jarrell, 1914–1965.* New York: Farrar, 1967.

Luhr, William. *Raymond Chandler and Film.* Gainesville: U Presses of Florida, 1993.

Lutz, Tom. *American Nervousness, 1903.* Ithaca, N.Y.: Cornell UP, 1991.

Lynd, Robert S., and Helen Merrell Lynd. *Middletown: A Study in Modern American Culture.* New York: Harcourt, 1929.

Lyons, Eugene. *The Life and Death of Sacco and Vanzetti.* New York: Da Capo, 1970.

McCloskey, Donald N. *If You're So Smart.* Berkeley: U of California P, 1990.

————. *The Rhetoric of Economics.* Madison: U of Wisconsin P, 1985.

Mack, Dorothy. "Metaphorical Ambiguities." *Meaning: A Common Ground of Linguistics and Literature.* Ed. Don L. F. Nilsen. Cedar Rapids: U of Northern Iowa, 1973. 75–85.

McQuade, Donald. "Intellectual Life and Public Discourse." *Columbia Literary History of the United States.* Gen. ed. Emory Elliott. New York: Columbia UP, 1988. 715–32.

MacShane, Frank. *The Life of Raymond Chandler.* New York: Dutton, 1976.

————, ed. *Selected Letters of Raymond Chandler.* New York: Columbia UP, 1981.

McWilliams, Carey. *Southern California: An Island on the Land.* Santa Barbara, Calif.: Peregrine Smith, 1973.

Madden, David. *James M. Cain.* Boston: Twayne, 1970.

————, ed. *Proletarian Writers of the Thirties.* Carbondale: Southern Illinois UP, 1979.

————, ed. *Tough Guy Writers of the Thirties*. Carbondale: Southern Illinois UP, 1977.

Malone, Michael P., and Richard B. Roeder. *Montana: A History of Two Centuries*. Seattle: U of Washington P, 1976.

Manchester, William. *Disturber of the Peace*. Amherst: U of Massachusetts P, 1986.

Marling, Karal Ann. *The Colossus of Roads*. Minneapolis: U of Minnesota P, 1984.

Marling, William H. *Dashiell Hammett*. Boston: Twayne, 1982.

————. "The Formal Ideologeme." *Semiotica* 98, nos. 3–4 (March 1994): 277–99.

————. *Raymond Chandler*. Boston: Twayne, 1986.

Mencken, H. L. *The American Language*. New York: Knopf, 1982.

————. *A Mencken Chrestothamy*. New York: Knopf, 1949.

Michaels, Walter Benn. *The Gold Standard and the Logic of Naturalism*. Berkeley: U of California P, 1987.

Michigan Papyri. Ann Arbor: U of Michigan P, 1933.

Miller, D. A. *The Novel and the Police*. Berkeley: U of California P, 1988.

Modleski, Tania. *Loving with a Vengeance*. New York: Methuen, 1984.

Monroe, Harriet. *The Difference and Other Poems, Including the Columbian Ode*. New York: Macmillan, 1925.

Montgomery, Robert. *Sacco-Vanzetti: The Murder and the Myth*. New York: Devin-Adair, 1960.

Moore, Stephen D. *Literary Criticism and the Gospels: The Theoretical Challenge*. New Haven, Conn.: Yale UP, 1989.

Most, Glenn W., and William W. Stowe, eds. *The Poetics of Murder: Detective Fiction and Literary Theory*. New York: Harcourt, 1983.

Neufeldt, Leonard N. *The Economist: Henry Thoreau and Enterprise*. New York: Oxford UP, 1988.

Nichols, Bill. *Ideology and the Image*. Bloomington: Indiana UP, 1981.

————, ed. *Movies and Methods: An Anthology*. Berkeley: U of California P, 1976.

Nolan, William F. *The Black Mask Boys*. New York: Morrow, 1985.

————. *Dashiell Hammett: A Casebook*. Santa Barbara, Calif.: McNally and Loftin, 1969.

————. *Hammett: A Life at the Edge*. New York: Congdon and Weed, 1983.

Nye, David E. *Electrifying America: Social Meanings of a New Technology*. Cambridge, Mass.: MIT P, 1990.

Oliver, John. *History of American Technology.* New York: Ronald, 1956.

Pabst, Charles. "Doctor's Warning to Flappers." *Literary Digest,* Oct. 30, 1926: 21–22.

Parrington, Vernon L. *Main Currents in American Thought.* 3 vols. New York: Harcourt, 1927–30.

Parrott, Ursula. *Ex-Wife.* New York: Penguin, 1989.

Partridge, Eric. *Name This Child.* New York: Oxford UP, 1938.

Patte, Daniel. "Structural Analysis of the Parable of the Prodigal Son: Towards a Method." *Semiology and Parables.* Pittsburgh: Pickwick, 1976. 83–146.

Pinkerton, Allan. *The Molly Maguires and the Detectives.* New York: Dillingham, 1905.

Poirier, Richard. *A World Elsewhere: The Place of Style in American Literature.* New York: Oxford UP, 1966.

Porter, Dennis. *The Pursuit of Crime.* New Haven, Conn.: Yale UP, 1981.

Propp, Vladimir Ikovlevich. *Morphology of the Folktale.* Trans. Laurence Scott. Austin: U of Texas P, 1968.

———. *Theory and History of Folklore.* Minneapolis: U of Minnesota P, 1984.

Rabinowitz, Peter J. "Rats Behind the Wainscoting: Politics, Convention and Chandler: *The Big Sleep.*" *Texas Studies in Language and Literature* 22.2 (1980): 224–45.

Random House Dictionary. 2nd ed. unabridged. New York: Random, 1987.

Reynolds, David S. *Beneath the American Renaissance.* New York: Knopf, 1988.

Robbins, Jill. *Prodigal Son / Elder Brother.* Chicago: U of Chicago P, 1991.

Ryken, Leland, ed. *The New Testament in Literary Criticism.* New York: Ungar, 1984.

Salt, Barry. *Film Style and Technology: History and Analysis.* London: Starword, 1983.

Scholes, Robert, and Robert Kellogg. *The Nature of Narrative.* New York: Oxford UP, 1966.

Schudson, Michael. *Advertising, The Uneasy Persuasion: Its Dubious Impact on American Society.* New York: Basic, 1984.

Shakespeare, William. *The Riverside Shakespeare.* Boston: Houghton, 1974.

Silver, Alain, and Elizabeth Ward. *Film Noir: An Encyclopedic Reference to the American Style.* London: Stecker, 1980.

Slide, Anthony. "The Jazz Singer." *Magill's Survey of Cinema.* Vol. 2. Englewood Cliffs, N.J.: Salem, 1980. 867–68.

Slotkin, Richard. *Regeneration Through Violence.* Middletown, Conn.: Wesleyan UP, 1973.

Smith, Charles W. F. *The Jesus of the Parables.* Philadelphia: Pilgrim, 1974.

Sparke, Penny. *An Introduction to Design and Culture in the Twentieth Century.* London: Allen, 1986.

Starr, Kevin. *Americans and the California Dream, 1850–1915.* New York: Oxford UP, 1973.

———. *Inventing the Dream.* New York: Oxford UP, 1985.

———. *Material Dreams: Southern California Through the 1920s.* New York: Oxford UP, 1990.

Staudenmaier, John M. *Technology's Storytellers: Reweaving the Human Fabric.* Cambridge, Mass.: MIT P, 1985.

Steinman, Lisa M. *Made in America: Science, Technology, and American Modernist Poets.* New Haven, Conn.: Yale UP, 1987.

Stowe, William W. *Going Abroad.* Princeton, N.J.: Princeton UP, 1994.

Swanberg, W. A. *Citizen Hearst.* New York: Scribner's, 1961.

Sward, Keith. *The Legend of Henry Ford.* New York: Atheneum, 1972.

Takemoto, Yukihiro. *Language and Culture.* Vols. 17–18. Sapporo, Japan: Lang and Co., 1988–89.

Teague, Walter Dorwin. *Design This Day: The Technique of Order in the Machine Age.* New York: Harcourt, 1940.

———. *Good Design Is Your Business.* Buffalo, N.Y.: Buffalo Fine Arts Gallery, 1947.

Telotte, J. P. *Voices in the Dark: The Narrative Patterns of Film Noir.* Champaign: U of Illinois P, 1989.

Terkel, Studs. *The Great War.* New York: Random, 1974.

———. *Hard Times.* New York: Random, 1970.

Tichi, Cecilia. *Shifting Gears: Technology, Literature, and Culture in Modernist American Literature.* Chapel Hill: U of North Carolina P, 1987.

Tippens, Darryl. *Explorations in Renaissance Culture.* Lafayette, La.: EIRC, 1988.

Tuska, Jon. *Dark Cinema: American Film Noir in Cultural Perspective.* Westport, Conn.: Greenwood, 1984.

Twain, Mark. *Selected Letters of Mark Twain.* Ed. Charles Neider. New York: Harper, 1982.

United States. Dept. of Commerce. Bureau of the Census. *Historical Statistics of the United States: Colonial Times to 1970.* Washington, D.C.: GPO, 1975.

Urdang, Lawrence. *The Timetables of American History.* New York: Simon, 1981.

Via, Dan Otto, Jr. *The Parables: Their Literary and Existential Dimension.* Philadelphia: Fortress, 1967.

Weeks, Robert P., ed. *Commonwealth vs. Sacco and Vanzetti*. Englewood Cliffs, N.J.: Prentice, 1964.

Wentworth, Harold, and Stuart Flexner. *Dictionary of American Slang*. New York: Crowell, 1967.

White, Hayden. *Metahistory: The Historic Imagination in Nineteenth Century Europe*. Baltimore: Johns Hopkins UP, 1973.

Whitman, Walt. *Song of Myself. The Norton Anthology of American Literature*. 3rd ed. Vol. 1. Ed. Nina Baym et al. New York: Norton, 1989. 855–948.

Wicke, Jennifer A. *Advertising Fictions: Literature, Advertisement, and Social Reading*. New York: Columbia UP, 1988.

Williams, William Carlos. *Collected Poems*. New York: New Directions, 1990.

Wilson, Edmund. *Commercials and Classics*. New York: Farrar, Straus, and Co., 1955.

Woehlke, W. V. *Sunset* 59 (Sept. 1927): 12–15; 59 (Oct. 1927): 16–19; 59 (Nov. 1927): 18–20.

Wolfe, Peter. *Beams Falling: The Art of Dashiell Hammett*. Bowling Green, Ohio: Popular, 1980.

———. *Something More Than Night: The Case of Raymond Chandler*. Bowling Green, Ohio: Popular, 1985.

Wyatt, David. *Prodigal Sons: A Study in Authorship and Authority*. Baltimore: Johns Hopkins UP, 1980.

Young, William. *Post-mortem: New Evidence in the Case of Sacco-Vanzetti*. Amherst: U of Massachusetts P, 1985.

Index